S NY 2650

AMG

TO JOHN LAMM (1944–2020): Writer, photographer, collaborator, friend extraordinaire

Quarto.com

First Published in 2025 by Motorbooks, an imprint of The Quarto Group,
100 Cummings Center, Suite 265-D, Beverly, MA 01915, USA.
T (978) 282-9590 F (978) 283-2742

EEA Representation, WTS Tax d.o.o.,
Žanova ulica 3, 4000 Kranj, Slovenia.
www.wts-tax.si

29 28 27 26 25   1 2 3 4 5

ISBN: 978-0-7603-9445-8

Digital edition published in 2025
eISBN: 978-0-7603-9446-5

Library of Congress Cataloging-in-Publication Data
Names: DeLorenzo, Matt, 1953- author
Title: Mercedes-AMG : race-bred performance / Matt DeLorenzo.
Description: Beverly, MA : Motorbooks, 2025. | Includes index. | Summary: "Mercedes-AMG covers the full history of these German powerhouse cars, from the early racing exploits of the 1960s to the iconic Hammer and Black Series cars to today's high-performance Mercedes-AMG models"-- Provided by publisher.
Identifiers: LCCN 2025010950 | ISBN 9780760394458 hardcover | ISBN 9780760394465 ebook
Subjects: LCSH: Mercedes automobiles--History
Classification: LCC TL215.M4 D45 2025 | DDC 629.222/09--dc23/eng/20250327
LC record available at https://lccn.loc.gov/2025010950

Design: Amy Sly, The Sly Studio
Page Layout: Emily Austin, The Sly Studio
Cover Image: Mercedes-AMG; Back flap: Mercedes-Benz Classic

Printed in Guangdong, China TT 062025

MERCEDES-AMG

Race-Bred Performance

Matt DeLorenzo

Foreword by Sam Posey

motorbooks

Content

Foreword by Sam Posey. . . . .

Introduction . . . .

CHAPTER 1: This Pig Can Fly . . . .

CHAPTER 2: Meeting of the Minds . . . .

CHAPTER 3: AMG Is Born . . . .

CHAPTER 4: One Man, One Engine . . . .

CHAPTER 5: From Burgstall to Affalterbach . . . .

CHAPTER 6: From Road Back to Track . . . .

CHAPTER 7: The Hammer Drops . . . .

CHAPTER 8: Official Business . . . .

CHAPTER 9: The Black Series . . . .

CHAPTER 10: Partners in Performance . . . .

CHAPTER 11: Dawn of a New Era: The Mercedes-AMG S

CHAPTER 12: Mercedes-AMG GT: Foundation for the Fut

CHAPTER 13: Going Beyond the End of the Road . . . .

CHAPTER 14: The AMG ONE Story . . . .

CHAPTER 15: AMG Today and Tomorrow. . . . .

About the Author. . . . .

Acknowledgments . . . .

Index . . . .

FOREWORD

BY SAM POSEY

I bought a 300 SL in 1958, the fourth year of the Gullwing's existence. The car was for sale for a modest $2,500 at a nearby dealership run by John Fitch, a hero of mine and a mentor who drove me around Lime Rock. My mother opposed my having the car because she didn't think the image was right for a young kid, but she too had fallen in love with it. I've had it ever since.

The allure of the car for me was a combination of its beauty and performance and what I knew of its racing heritage. In 1955, Mercedes won both the sports-car championship with the SLR and the World Championship with Manuel Fangio and Sterling Moss. These were mythic teams; closer to my reality was John Fitch, who'd just finished fifth at the Mille Miglia, winning the highly prestigious GT class. In owning the car, I felt some connection to that history.

Many years later, Mercedes offered me one of their SLS AMGs for a week. I eagerly accepted. We did a photo shoot with the car beside my old one and took it to Lime Rock to see what it could do. What it did was pound around for three hours at an average of 90 mph without any hint of overheating or brake fade. On the local roads, it was equally thrilling, the prodigious acceleration allowing for bursts of over 100 mph at the slightest excuse for a straightaway. I could feel the brilliance of the engineering at work, how AMG had created a car with all the modern amenities and safety features that still retained the magic of its racing heritage.

That magic is what a young Hans Werner Aufrecht must have felt when he first dreamed of joining Mercedes. By the time he did, the company's racing program had largely ceased. It would be up to Aufrecht and the talented engineer Erhard Melcher to strike out on their own and start a legacy of performance that would keep Mercedes relevant in the sport through fifty years of continual change. This book tells that story, one that I hope any fan of Mercedes will enjoy.

Sam Posey raced in Trans-Am, the Indy 500, at Le Mans, and in Formula 1 before embarking on a career as a racing analyst for ABC.

Richard Prince photo

INTRODUCTION

A simplistic take on what AMG means to Mercedes is typified by an on-air discussion I once heard between radio host Don Imus and his guest, former New York detective Bo Dietl. They talked about which Mercedes S-Class model to buy and Imus said, in effect, get the S65 AMG. His reasoning? It was the most expensive Mercedes you could buy. And in his mind, having the highest price tag meant it had to be the best one.

While there's no doubt that some people agree with that sentiment and buy a Mercedes-AMG for the prestige factor of a big sticker price, fortunately for enthusiasts, there's much more to the AMG story. There's far more value in the cars and the way that they are engineered, built, and enjoyed than money alone.

From mere trim levels to hypercars such as the AMG ONE, the brand has grown exponentially to include bespoke models like the AMG GT, a full line of AMG-tuned Mercedes vehicles, a wide-ranging motorsports effort focused on privateers, and even a relationship with the offshore power boatmaker Cigarette. There also are more than 600 AMG Performance Centers throughout the world and AMG Experiences that provide clients driving opportunities on everything from legendary racetracks to Arctic ice fields.

No doubt the scale and reach of Mercedes-AMG far outstrips even the most fevered dreams of the two modest engineers, Hans Werner Aufrecht and Erhard Melcher, who started the company in 1967 in Aufrecht's German hometown of Großaspach, the initials of each comprising the AMG moniker.

With AMG helping Mercedes gain notoriety on racing circuits by turning sedate Mercedes sedans into race winners, customers soon began requesting similar performance upgrades for their everyday drivers. Many of these early efforts led to the production of a seminal vehicle, such as the 1986 W124-based Hammer. It now has attained collectible status with one version recently changing hands for an astounding $750,000.

A corollary to the rising prices of these early vehicles made by an independent AMG is the opinion in some enthusiast circles about pre- and postacquisition AMG. The implication here is that some of the magic of the original independent company has been lost by the corporate takeover by Mercedes-Benz.

However, a closer look at what the company is today, especially considering its origins, reveals a very different picture. AMG was born out of Mercedes. That's where Aufrecht and Melcher came together as young engineers, though as we'll see, the relationship didn't necessarily start off on the right foot between the two and even their Mercedes employer. However, Aufrecht's and Melcher's single-minded pursuit of excellence in the racing and road cars they built perfectly aligns with Mercedes' culture. It was inevitable that AMG slowly would progress from tuner to trusted partner and finally to a pillar in the German automaker's brand structure. And the people there today are no less passionate about race-bred performance than the founders.

Aufrecht is quoted as saying that "you can't really improve a Mercedes, but you can make it different." The creativity, passion, and engineering genius of Aufrecht and Melcher opened new doors for Mercedes to offer the ultimate in performance to go along with its luxury tradition. While it's true that Mercedes's legendary motorsports history long predates AMG's efforts on behalf of the marque, its contribution goes far beyond the time-worn cliché of win on Sunday, sell on Monday.

What AMG has brought to Mercedes is to take the technology developed for the track and to translate it directly to improved performance and handling for the street. Until then, the only vehicle to reflect that ethos in Mercedes' modern history was the 300 SL Gullwing. While Mercedes-AMG's first effort at its own car in the 2010 SLS is a modern interpretation of that icon, the fact is that its strength lies in its ability to enhance performance levels of coupes, sedans, wagons, and SUVs across the Mercedes-Benz lineup.

AMG surprised enthusiasts in the early 1970s by turning staid Mercedes-Benz sedans into autobahn burners. It's this ability to infuse this time-honored luxury marque with spirited performance that has contributed immeasurably to Mercedes' reputation for building not just the most luxurious vehicles in the world, but also some of the fastest and best-handling models in existence.

The story of how this tiny company was able to grow and eventually add a new dimension to Mercedes-Benz is a remarkable testament to the genius of Hans Werner Aufrecht and Erhard Melcher.

AMG

1

THIS PIG CAN FLY

The 1971 European Touring Car 24 Hours of Spa-Francorchamps was shaping up to be an epic battle among the Ford Capri 2600 RS factory entries, Alpina and Schnitzer BMW 2800 CS coupes, and Steinmetz-prepared Opel Commodores. Throw in a pole-sitting, V-8-powered Chevrolet Camaro, and you have enough drama to hold 80,000 spectators in rapt attention.

If that wasn't enough, there was a wild card—a Mercedes-Benz 300 SEL prepared by AMG. This small tuner outfit from Burgstall, Germany, was founded four years earlier by engineers Hans Werner Aufrecht (the A) and Erhard Melcher (the M) with a backstory that started in Aufrecht's hometown of Großaspach (the G).

It seemed out of character for Mercedes, much revered in Germany for producing well-engineered high-quality luxury cars. Though admired, these cars weren't coveted by the go-fast set like the pumped-up performance cars, which included the aforementioned BMWs, Capris, and Commodores that would be racing around the bucolic Spa circuit for the next twenty-four hours.

But the big red 300 SEL was packing something relatively new for Mercedes in touring car racing: a large-displacement V-8 engine that had migrated from the even larger 600 limousine. Just a few years earlier, the W109 300 SEL replaced its top 3.0-liter inline-six (I6) with the M100 6.3-liter V-8 engine that produced 247 hp and 369 lb-ft of torque. Equipped with single-overhead cams and two valves per cylinder, the fuel-injected M100 turned the staid SEL into an autobahn cruiser capable of hitting 60 mph (97 kph) in fewer than 6.5 seconds and reaching a top speed of 137 mph (220 kph).

As impressive as those numbers were, no one expected to see a Goliath mixing it up with much smaller and nimbler Davids. Because it was so out of proportion to the other touring car entrants, this big AMG-prepped Mercedes was dubbed the "*Rote Sau*" by the press. That's "Red Sow" in German, and why it's commonly referred to as the Red Pig in English. It wouldn't be the last time that a journalist would come up with a catchy name for an AMG product. But Aufrecht came prepared for battle, taking full advantage of the touring car rules adopted a year earlier, which helped change the car's nickname from one of derision to the stuff of legend.

Competing in the over-2,000cc category, AMG capitalized on the opportunity to bore out the engine, which in this case had no upper limit because it was in the top class. So displacement was increased from 6.3 to 6.8 liters. While the engine and its components had to remain original equipment manufacturer (OEM), lightening and balancing of parts was allowed. AMG was also free to machine the heads and change the valves, guides, and seats.

The heads were ported and polished, then shaved to boost the compression ratio. The intake manifold was reworked to feature separate tracks for each bank of cylinders. Output increased to 428 hp and 448 lb-ft of torque, thanks to the wizardry of engine maestro Melcher.

Other changes included fitting the car with wider wheels and wheel flares. AMG obtained from its contacts within Mercedes the same 10-inch-wide (25-cm) front and 12-inch-wide (30-cm)

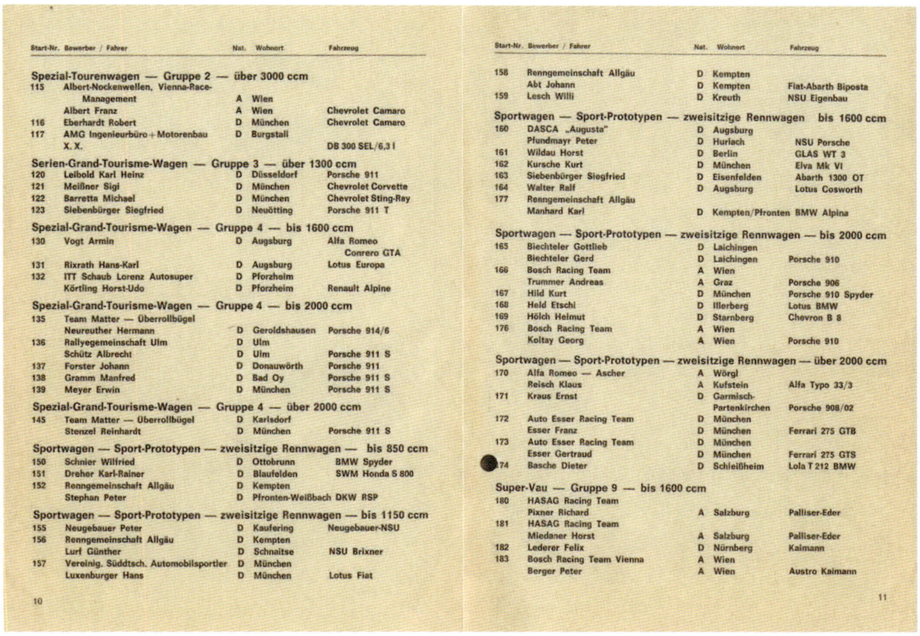

Start-Nr.	Bewerber / Fahrer	Nat.	Wohnort	Fahrzeug
	Spezial-Tourenwagen — Gruppe 2 — über 3000 ccm			
115	Albert-Nockenwellen, Vienna-Race-Management	A	Wien	
	Albert Franz	A	Wien	Chevrolet Camaro
116	Eberhardt Robert	D	München	Chevrolet Camaro
117	AMG Ingenieurbüro + Motorenbau	D	Burgstall	
	X. X.			DB 300 SEL/6,3 l
	Serien-Grand-Tourisme-Wagen — Gruppe 3 — über 1300 ccm			
120	Leibold Karl Heinz	D	Düsseldorf	Porsche 911
121	Meißner Sigi	D	München	Chevrolet Corvette
122	Barretta Michael	D	München	Chevrolet Sting-Ray
123	Siebenbürger Siegfried	D	Neuötting	Porsche 911 T
	Spezial-Grand-Tourisme-Wagen — Gruppe 4 — bis 1600 ccm			
130	Vogt Armin	D	Augsburg	Alfa Romeo Conrero GTA
131	Rixrath Hans-Karl	D	Augsburg	Lotus Europa
132	ITT Schaub Lorenz Autosuper	D	Pforzheim	
	Körtling Horst-Udo	D	Pforzheim	Renault Alpine
	Spezial-Grand-Tourisme-Wagen — Gruppe 4 — bis 2000 ccm			
135	Team Matter — Überrollbügel			
	Neureuther Hermann	D	Geroldshausen	Porsche 914/6
136	Rallyegemeinschaft Ulm	D	Ulm	
	Schütz Albrecht	D	Ulm	Porsche 911 S
137	Forster Johann	D	Donauwörth	Porsche 911
138	Gramm Manfred	D	Bad Oy	Porsche 911 S
139	Meyer Erwin	D	München	Porsche 911 S
	Spezial-Grand-Tourisme-Wagen — Gruppe 4 — über 2000 ccm			
145	Team Matter — Überrollbügel	D	Karlsdorf	
	Stenzel Reinhardt	D	München	Porsche 911 S
	Sportwagen — Sport-Prototypen — zweisitzige Rennwagen — bis 850 ccm			
150	Schnier Wilfried	D	Ottobrunn	BMW Spyder
151	Dreher Karl-Rainer	D	Blaufelden	SWM Honda S 800
152	Renngemeinschaft Allgäu	D	Kempten	
	Stephan Peter	D	Pfronten-Weißbach	DKW RSP
	Sportwagen — Sport-Prototypen — zweisitzige Rennwagen — bis 1150 ccm			
155	Neugebauer Peter	D	Kaufering	Neugebauer-NSU
156	Renngemeinschaft Allgäu	D	Kempten	
	Lurf Günther	D	Schnaitse	NSU Brixner
157	Vereinig. Süddtsch. Automobilsportler	D	München	
	Luxenburger Hans	D	München	Lotus Fiat

10

Start-Nr.	Bewerber / Fahrer	Nat.	Wohnort	Fahrzeug
158	Renngemeinschaft Allgäu	D	Kempten	
	Abt Johann	D	Kempten	Fiat-Abarth Biposta
159	Lesch Willi	D	Kreuth	NSU Eigenbau
	Sportwagen — Sport-Prototypen — zweisitzige Rennwagen bis 1600 ccm			
160	DASCA „Augusta"	D	Augsburg	
	Pfundmayr Peter	D	Hurlach	NSU Porsche
161	Wildau Horst	D	Berlin	GLAS WT 3
162	Kursche Kurt	D	München	Elva Mk VI
163	Siebenbürger Siegfried	D	Eisenfelden	Abarth 1300 OT
164	Walter Ralf	D	Augsburg	Lotus Cosworth
177	Renngemeinschaft Allgäu			
	Manhard Karl	D	Kempten/Pfronten	BMW Alpina
	Sportwagen — Sport-Prototypen — zweisitzige Rennwagen — bis 2000 ccm			
165	Biechteler Gottlieb	D	Laichingen	
	Biechteler Gerd	D	Laichingen	Porsche 910
166	Bosch Racing Team	A	Wien	
	Trummer Andreas	A	Graz	Porsche 906
167	Hild Kurt	D	München	Porsche 910 Spyder
168	Held Etschi	D	Illerberg	Lotus BMW
169	Hölch Helmut	D	Starnberg	Chevron B 8
176	Bosch Racing Team	A	Wien	
	Koltay Georg	A	Wien	Porsche 910
	Sportwagen — Sport-Prototypen — zweisitzige Rennwagen — über 2000 ccm			
170	Alfa Romeo — Ascher	A	Wörgl	
	Reisch Klaus	A	Kufstein	Alfa Typo 33/3
171	Kraus Ernst	D	Garmisch-Partenkirchen	Porsche 908/02
172	Auto Esser Racing Team	D	München	
	Esser Franz	D	München	Ferrari 275 GTB
173	Auto Esser Racing Team	D	München	
	Esser Gertraud	D	München	Ferrari 275 GTS
174	Basche Dieter	D	Schleißheim	Lola T 212 BMW
	Super-Vau — Gruppe 9 — bis 1600 ccm			
180	HASAG Racing Team			
	Pixner Richard	A	Salzburg	Palliser-Eder
181	HASAG Racing Team			
	Miedaner Horst	A	Salzburg	Palliser-Eder
182	Lederer Felix	D	Nürnberg	Kaimann
183	Bosch Racing Team Vienna	A	Wien	
	Berger Peter	A	Wien	Austro Kaimann

11

PREVIOUS The Red Pig surprised and delighted the crowd at Spa in the Summer of 1971 with its booming V-8.

TOP LEFT Hans Werner Aufrecht (left) and his brother Friedrich (right) stand with two others in front of the Red Pig built from a doctor's wrecked 300 SEL 6.3.

TOP RIGHT The program cover for the Salzburgring race where the Red Pig made its first start.

LEFT The entry list for the Salzburgring race shows the Red Pig assigned number 117.

rear magnesium five-spoke wheels that were used on the C-111 Wankel prototype. These five-spoke wheels would become a signature look for AMG-prepared cars.

According to Melcher, the donor car was a crashed 300 SEL 6.3 owned by a doctor. The reworked body was fitted with four weight-saving aluminum doors and plexiglass windows. The bumpers were removed, a roll cage welded inside, and an auxiliary 4-gallon (15-L) fuel tank installed in the trunk. The car retained its stock interior, including the rear bench seat, door panels, and dashboard, although the driver's side sported a Recaro racing seat with a four-point safety harness.

The four-speed automatic was altered to allow for sequential shifting, though later a ZF five-speed manual would supplant it. Stiffer air springs, Bilstein shocks, and larger roll bars tightened the suspension. Larger front discs and calipers were fitted, but braking still remained a weak point on the car, which tipped the scales at a hefty 3,597 pounds (1,632 kg)—portly, but still about 430 pounds (195 kg) less than a stock 300 SEL 6.3.

The Red Pig had two outings before the big twenty-four-hour race at Spa. Its debut came at the ADAC Bavaria race at the Salzburgring on June 19, 1971. According to *touringcarracing.net*, "Sometimes a race that seems to be less important has a surprise in store. What turned up was a big red Mercedes 300 SEL 6.3 that qualified second fastest in its race. The driver was someone called 'Enrico,' but his identity couldn't be made out."

It turns out "Enrico" was Erich Waxenberger, a development engineer who was nominally in charge of Mercedes' backdoor support of racing. The pseudonym was part of an effort to keep his participation secret from the higher-ups at the company. And while the factory wasn't quite on friendly terms with the upstarts from Burgstall, Enrico was there to keep tabs on the latest efforts by Aufrecht and Melcher.

The AMG entry appeared two years after a V-8 SEL had last been raced. In 1969 factory-prepared cars had won a six-hour event in Macau and had entered and qualified but were withdrawn from the twenty-four-hour race at Spa.

TOP ROW, LEFT The Red Pig is pushed off the starting grid, but rejoined the race to finish third. The driver, "Enrico," was Mercedes engineer Erich Waxenberger.

TOP ROW, RIGHT The second outing for the car at the Solitude race ends in disaster when Helmut Kelleners crashes out. Only three weeks remain before the Spa 24 Hours race in July.

BOTTOM ROW, LEFT Drivers Clemens Schickentanz (left) and Hans Heyer share a moment before the race.

BOTTOM ROW, RIGHT Thanks to the additional power of the now 6.8-liter V-8, the Red Pig pulls away earlier, with a Ford Capri in hot pursuit.

OPPOSITE, TOP While the Red Pig possessed tremendous straight-line speed, it also cornered well thanks the wider tires and beefed-up suspension. Braking, however, was another story.

OPPOSITE, BOTTOM LEFT Spa's hilly terrain and extended straightaways were ideally suited for the Red Pig's V-8, allowing Heyer and Schickenatz to run flat out for long stretches.

OPPOSITE, BOTTOM RIGHT The flared fenders and wider wheels addressed tire wear problems encountered by the factory team two years earlier. Here, Aufrecht wheels some spares to AMG's pit box.

The account continued, "The car was entered by AMG, the tuning company that specialized in Mercedes. It was rumored that Mercedes itself had a hand in it (I don't think they had, but they didn't stop it either). The engine was said to have 500 hp, but then it would have been much faster—more accurate would be something like a little over 350 hp. The earlier tire troubles were cured by wing [fender] extensions and fat wheels. It looks like the car didn't make the start, but it would turn up two weeks later in Hockenheim and in just over a month it would race at Spa. This was neither the first racing 6.3 nor the first AMG car. But this one looked more serious than ever before."

That second race at Hockenheim on July 4 was the ADAC Solitude Race. Helmut Kelleners crashed out. The driver reportedly returned to the pits, tossed the keys to Aufrecht, and said, "you won't be needing them." Three weeks of feverish work back at the old mill in Burgstall was required to make the nearly totaled car race ready.

At Spa, the Red Pig would be driven by Hans Heyer and Clemens Schickentanz, both of whom quickly realized how potent this new mount would be on the Belgian circuit. Schickentanz qualified fifth, gridding the car in the second row for the three-abreast start in a field of sixty cars.

On the pole was the Ivo Grauls/Peter Hoffmann Chevy Camaro. Next up was the BMW Alpina 2800 CS of Niki Lauda and Gerard Larrousse. The Ford factory team Capri 2600 RS of Dieter Glemser and Alex Soler-Roig was next followed by Schnitzer Racing's BMW 2800 CS manned by Kelleners and Rauno Aaltonen.

"Everyone was surprised," Schickentanz said in a press release, "No one expected, even insiders, that the car was so fast and so successful." Heyer added that "[w]e knew we could win, but the others didn't know it yet!" A big factor in their confidence was the length of the Spa circuit. At nearly 9 miles (14 km) long, the high-speed track featured many long straights ideal for full-throttle running.

"It was so fast, and it handled pretty great," Heyer recalled in an interview with *Hagerty Media*. "All the fast corners except Eau Rouge were flat [out], which was simply not possible with other cars of the time, and uphill it was amazing. To get around it that fast though, you needed a lot of courage, more than you normally needed at the time. But it was fun and manageable, and it would drift with all four wheels."

AMG AMG

FERODO
FERODO
MARTINI
FINA
AMG AMG

ABOVE Aufrecht keenly monitors the Red Pig's progress throughout the twenty-four-hour race. Heyer, right, waits for another turn behind the wheel.

OPPOSITE, TOP Hans Werner and Friedrich Aufrecht guide the Red Pig into the pit box while Schickenantz prepares to take over from Heyer.

OPPOSITE, MIDDLE While the Red Pig ran near the front in the closing stages of the race, the thirsty V-8 required additional pit stops that put it three laps down to the winning car. Still, second place and first in class caused a sensation.

OPPOSITE, BOTTOM For its outing in November at Hockenheim, the Red Pig sported a yellow paint scheme with a new sponsor, Hannen Alt Brewery.

The bravery required to make a fast lap had as much to do with the Red Pig's brakes as its 165-mph (266 kph) top speed. "It was an amazing car—enormous with huge speed," Heyer told *Hagerty*. "We had enormous speed compared to the Capris, but no brakes at all." Despite the modifications to the system, the brakes remained underpowered. "But on the old Spa course the brake discs had plenty of time to cool down," he explained, "and nobody could catch us on the long straights."

Even though it was stripped down and ready to race, the Red Pig still retained some trappings of its luxury car underpinnings and trim. It had power steering, the floors were carpeted, the stiffer air suspension still had some give to it, and the door panels and wood trim were left intact.

With its rumbling V-8 exhaust note, which competed with the three Camaros and sole Mustang in thrilling the crowd, the Red Pig also endeared itself to the fans with its sheer size. Heyer summed it up this way: "The outsider quickly became the absolute darling of the public."

Ford's Glemser had taken the early lead in the race, with the pole-sitting Camaro second and the Mercedes third. The V-8 cars, while fast, were also thirsty, having to pit more often for fuel than the V-6 Capri. Because of its weight, the Mercedes also saw significant tire wear compared to its smaller and lighter rivals.

As is the nature of a twenty-four-hour race, mechanical problems and retirements came in droves. Lauda's BMW had its gearbox give out after the first hour. The car retired after the transmission was replaced a second time. The Camaro suffered from overheating problems, while all the Opel Commodores suffered fuel pump issues. Even in the middle of summer, Belgian weather can turn. The race started with overcast skies, which turned into a thunderstorm in the middle of the night. The downpour caused an accident that unfortunately claimed the life of Raymond Mathay, who was driving a BMW 2800 CS for Ecurie Azur.

By daybreak, only twenty-three cars were running. By the end of the race, that number was down to eighteen. The Red Pig was running in second when the checkered flag fell on the Glemser/Soler-Riog Capri. That car completed 311 laps, three more than the Red Pig. The AMG Mercedes had a comfortable nineteen-lap margin on the third-place Autodelta Alfa Romeo 2000 GTA driven by Carlo Facetti and Toine Hezemans.

In bringing home the Red Pig in the runner-up position, Heyer and Schickentanz secured a class victory in the over 2,000cc category. In summing up the race, *Road & Track* had this to say about AMG's effort: "During the race, the big V-8 had an insatiable thirst for fuel, and its weight meant that it quickly wrecked its tires. However, the straight-line speed of the Red Pig more than made up for its inefficiencies . . . and after 24 hours, it ended up storming its way to an incredible second place behind a Ford Capri."

Even Germany's main newscast, *Tagesschau*, which means Day's Show or Review of the Day, reported on the Red Pig's class win. "It was certainly a sensation at the time," said Aufrecht. "For Spa was a dramatic kickoff and a huge success. All of a sudden, we were world famous."

Heyer's signature Tyrolean hat became equally famous. He remembers it automatically opening doors for him. "There were times when I did not need to show identification for anything," he recalled. "My hat was so well-known that I got in everywhere, even at Formula 1 events."

The Red Pig would make two more races that season, a twelve-hour event at Paul Ricard in France and the season finale at Hockenheim. The Paul Ricard race featured two heats. The Red Pig, again piloted by Heyer and Schickentanz, completed 264 laps before retiring with a broken rear suspension. A sister car with an AMG engine in silver livery fielded by Klaus Behrmann and co-driven by Jose Dolhem and Jean-Pierre Jabouille finished fifth. In the second heat, the Red Pig finished eleventh and the Behrmann car retired with oil pressure problems.

The November Hockenheim race saw the Red Pig painted yellow with sponsorship from Hannen Alt Brewery. Heyer piloted the car to twelfth overall and seventh in class. The season ended with the European Touring Car Championship eliminating displacements greater than 5.0 liters. AMG did take the car to the Le Mans qualifying races in March 1972, again in yellow, but did not enter the twenty-four-hour race the following June.

Midway through 1972, the ETCC lifted the 5.0-liter ban and AMG went to the Nürburgring for the twenty-four-hour race in June (the ban had still been in effect when entries were closed for the July Spa twenty-four-hour race). Heyer was joined by Thomas Betzler, and the car, again in red, qualified fourth and led a lap but retired to the pits to address overheating. Later in the race, the differential gave out forcing a withdrawal.

A non-points race at the Norisring in Nürnberg would be the last time the Red Pig would face competition. Heyer took it to a class

ABOVE When Mercedes took full control of AMG in 2005, it tried to find the Red Pig, but failed. The company's classic department then built a replica that debuted at that year's Geneva Motor Show.

victory to close out the car's short, but illustrious career. Unfortunately, like most race cars of the era, it had its own ignominious end.

In those early days, AMG was at best operating on a shoestring, as evidenced by the Red Pig owing its existence to a wrecked car rebuilt on the cheap. French aerospace firm Matra came calling, looking for a car that could accelerate to 200 kph (124 mph) in 1,000 meters for use in testing tires that would be used on fighter jets. At first AMG toyed with the idea of converting as existing Mercedes 600 Pullman for the task, but acquiring the car would cost too much. Besides, a stock model would be too heavy and not have the power required to hit the acceleration mark specified by Matra.

As a result, Aufrecht's eyes fell on the Red Pig. It was, after all, an old race car, and back in the day, there was nothing older than last year's entry. It was stretched like a Pullman, with a center door section added to accommodate the test tire and equipment. The Red Pig went to France where it retained the pace to match the takeoff and landing speeds of fighter jets. There, the car toiled in anonymity until it was scrapped in 1994.

The car's significance, however, resonates to this day. It is a testament to what two men, Hans Werner Aufrecht and Erhard Melcher, could accomplish since meeting less than a decade earlier as two young Mercedes-Benz engineers with a passion for performance.

Gone, But Not Forgotten

THE RED PIG MAY NO LONGER EXIST, but its memory lives on in a number of replicas built long after the original thrilled the spectators at Spa in 1971. Naturally, Mercedes-AMG's own classic center has built two, but there is a growing fleet of Red Pigs. Some being built commercially for customers, others the work of passionate enthusiasts from as far afield as South Africa.

After Mercedes fully acquired AMG in 2005, it discovered that the Red Pig no longer existed after conducting an extensive search for the car or what remained of it. As a result, it built a running replica that retained a standard 6.3-liter M100 V-8 instead of a bored-out 6.8-liter used in the race car, and then a second one primarily for display. The pair would soon be joined by others, mostly one-offs done by small shops and passionate enthusiasts with varying degrees of verisimilitude to the original.

In 2019 Mercedes restoration specialist Arthur Bechtel Classic Motors in the Stuttgart suburb of Böblingen built its first Red Pig replica for a South Korean customer. The conversion proved so popular that Bechtel continues to build about four to five per year, selling them for about $400,000 each. It takes about nine months for the conversion. A 2020 sale of one of them by RM Sotheby's in Paris netted over $520,000.

According to Bechtel's website, "This classic racing car (replica) is a firm component of the portfolio of our restoration. The base of a Mercedes-Benz 300 SEL (model series W109) is used, which we equip with all the technical as well as the visual features of the original 'Red Pig.' Provided with the racing touring car equipment from AMG, the installed V-8 engine and a displacement of 6,332 cc, the vehicle gives a real racing feeling."

continued

LEFT Mercedes-AMG has two replicas of the Red Pig. One is primarily used for drive events, the other for display.

RIGHT The engine in the replica is a stock 6.3-liter V-8 rather than the modified 6.8-liter M100 used in the original.

Bechtel retains the stock M100 6.3-liter engine, which makes 250 hp. Buyers can opt for either a six-speed Getrag manual transmission or the original four-speed automatic as well as specifying the original air-spring suspension or a sportier coil spring setup. The body panels include the flared wheel arches and period correct decals. The interior features black leather upholstery, modern sport bucket seats, a roll cage, and multipoint harnesses.

While customers can buy turnkey replicas either at auction or from restorers such as Bechtel, there are a number of individuals who have built their own. Grant Viljoen of Pretoria, South Africa, is one of them. He created the Rote Sau website, which not only chronicles his decade-long conversion of a 300 SEL into a Red Pig, but it also provides a full history of the original along with crowd-sourced never-seen-before photos of the car in action at Spa.

He told South Africa's *Car* magazine after the finished car's launch in 2021 that "[t]he idea to build a race replica of the Red Pig came about after I had raced a Fintail-era Mercedes-Benz 230 S in the Historics series at Zwartkops [Raceway] for a few years. I developed a real affinity for oddball Mercedes-Benz racecars."

Finding a left-hand-drive version of a period-correct 300 SEL proved a challenge in right-hand-drive South Africa. He found one that had been privately imported, a rare find in a country where the local Mercedes club estimates that only about twenty LHD models exist.

While he remained mostly true to the original, some compromises were made since he intended to run the car in vintage races. He had the engine bored out to 6.8 liters and swapped out the automatic for a manual. But he also ditched original touches such as the carpeting and the rear bench seat. Instead of plexiglass, the glazing is Lexan, and the roll cage is more modern in execution.

In addition to historic racing, Viljoen's Red Pig was displayed at the Mercedes-Benz dealerships in Pretoria and Johannesburg and at the AMG Performance Tour when it made a stop at the Kyalami Grand Prix Circuit.

Beyond its own replicas, Mercedes-AMG has done one-off tributes to the Red Pig on more modern models. In advance of the launch of S 63 AMG, Mercedes built the Thirty-Five concept in 2010 with a similar paint and decal scheme of the original race car. The show car also sported flared wheel arches for the 20-inch (51-cm) wheels, two AMG sport bucket seats with four-point harnesses, and an AMG steering wheel. Beneath the hood, however, was an M157 5.5-liter biturbo V-8 making 571 hp and 664 lb-ft of torque.

In 2011, when Hans Heyer's son, Kenneth, was set to compete in the 24 Hours of Spa in a Mercedes SLS AMG GT3, the car was given the same look as the Red Pig to honor the fortieth anniversary of the historic run. The Black Falcon privateer entry carried the number 35 and qualified nineteenth overall. Not quite able to achieve the same result as his father, nonetheless, Heyer, along with codrivers Thomas Jäger and Stéphane Léméret, brought the car home third overall in the top GT3 Pro Class.

More recently, Mercedes-AMG marked the fiftieth anniversary of the Spa result by building three special race cars: two AMG GTs and an SLS Gullwing in GT3 specification. The trio was presented as the "50 Years Legend of Spa" series of one-offs that carried the number 50 instead of 35.

While the SLS had been out of production since 2015, AMG took the final body shell from its warehouse and built up the special edition GT3 in Red Pig livery. Likewise it used a 2016 GT3 version of the GT sports car with chassis number 100 for that tribute model. The third was identical to the Mercedes-AMG GT3 racers participating in that year's twenty-four-hour Spa event. Each has a badge identifying it as "One of One," as well as a plaque with the signature of Hans Werner Aufrecht.

LEFT This meticulously crafted Red Pig replica is owned and vintage raced in South Africa by Grant Viljoen. *David Leadbitter photo*

OPPOSITE, TOP Hans Heyer (right) with son, Kenneth, at Spa forty years after his class win there. The younger Heyer competed in the 2011 event in a GT3 SLS sporting a commemorative paint scheme.

OPPOSITE, BOTTOM For the fiftieth anniversary of the Spa race, Mercedes-AMG built three tribute cars, one from a leftover SLS body and two AMG GT models, one built to GT3 racing spec. The trio is joined here by the Red Pig replica.

Mercedes-Benz
Mercedes-Benz
Mercedes-Benz
Mercedes-Benz
Mercedes-Benz
AMG AMG
35
SECA
AMG
35
DUNLOP

AMG
AMG
AMG AMG
35
50
SECA
AMG
35

U/min
bar
AMPERE
sec

2

MEETING OF THE MINDS

IT GOES WITHOUT SAYING that there'd be no AMG if not for Mercedes-Benz. The two principals, Hans Werner Aufrecht and Erhard Melcher, met while working there. In a way, the eventual acquisition and conversion into Mercedes-AMG neatly closes a loop that began with the employment of the very young, and at the time, unappreciated engineers.

But beyond just being the place where Aufrecht and Melcher came together, there was a unique set of circumstances that provided the impetus for the performance-obsessed pair to leave Mercedes and set up their own shop. This chain of events began in 1955 at Le Mans with the tragic death of works driver Pierre Levegh and more than eighty spectators when his car careened off the track and into the crowd. Mercedes pulled out of the race, finished out the Grand Prix season that year, and then announced that it was withdrawing factory involvement in racing "for a few years."

That official ban on racing stretched on for much longer, though enterprising enthusiasts within the company found ways to work around it by offering support to individuals involved in rallying and touring car races. Former Mercedes team driver Karl Kling, who headed the racing department after Grand Prix team manager Alfred Neubauer retired, was able to convince upper management of the benefits of supporting these nearly stock vehicles in such events.

Kling, who had traveled to Algiers in 1959 to observe the Trans African Rally, was convinced as a former race driver to enter the event rather than just spectate. At the wheel of a 190 D and with journalist Ranier Günzler navigating, he won the event.

During the late 1950s and early 1960s, the team of Walter Schock and Rolf Moll won the European Rally Championship driving a 300 SL. In 1960 they won the Monte Carlo Rally driving a 200 SE Fintail on their way to winning another European Rally Championship. Some of these efforts were conducted through intermediaries such as the Stuttgart Motorsports Club; others, like Shock and Moll, were supported directly by the factory.

Mercedes stepped up its direct efforts to win the grueling 2,756-mile (4435-km) Argentine Gran Premio Standard rally race for four years running, with Schock and codriver Manfred Schiek taking the first in 1961, the female team of Ewy Rosqvist and Ursula Wirth in 1962, while Eugen Böhringer won the 1963–64 editions in the new 300 SE. Böhringer would not only win rallies in Europe, but he also won touring car races for Mercedes at Nürburgring, Spa, and Macau. But at the end of the 1964 season, Mercedes management again sent down the word that the company was shutting down its direct role and that the sport department would revert to aiding privateers, mainly by providing suspension bits.

Part of this latest withdrawal hinged on the fact that some rally competitors were beginning to field factory-built limited-run homologation specials rather than the more stock-oriented machines that reflected favorably on the production lineup. But also for Mercedes, a change in top management played a role. Chairman Walter Hitzinger, a harsh Austrian who at one time headed that country's nationalized steel industry, was replaced at the beginning of 1965 by Joachim

Zahn, a tax lawyer recruited from the finance staff. Instead of being given the chairman title, Zahn was referred to as speaker of the board, which was more of a role described as "the first among equals," according to Beverly Rae Kimes's definitive Mercedes history, *The Star and the Laurel*.

The new management structure had plenty on its plate and racing was hardly a priority. During 1964, Mercedes had taken steps to set up its own subsidiary to sell cars in the lucrative North American market. In addition, new models needed to be engineered and sold. During this period of expansion, product development was the province of Karl Wilfert and Rudolf (Rudi) Uhlenhaut.

Wilfert is best known for his mentorship of Béla Barényi, holder of over 2,500 patents and a pioneer in vehicle safety. One of his crowning achievements was the development of crumple zones to manage the energy generated in collisions.

Uhlenhaut had come from the competition department, where, as a young engineer in the 1930s, he developed the W124 and W154 models that turned around the company's fortunes in grand prix racing. Uhlenhaut would go on to have a hand in the creation of the 300 SL, both road and racing versions, as well as the Grand Prix W196 300 SLR that would win in Formula 1, Le Mans, and the Mille Miglia. In addition to being an accomplished engineer, he was quick behind the wheel. Thanks to his thousands of miles of development work on the Nürburgring, legend has it that he posted faster times there than the great Juan Manuel Fangio. When Mercedes shut down its factory grand prix effort, Uhlenhaut turned his talents toward production-vehicle development.

PREVIOUS Mercedes-Benz used this engine test bench for six- and eight-cylinder engines in the 1960s. Hans Werner Aufrecht and Erhard Melcher likely met at one of these stations and argued about how to best obtain data.

ABOVE While Mercedes had effectively quit racing at the end of 1955, Karl Kling (in sunglasses by the driver's door), who headed the motorsports department that supported privateers, entered and won the Algiers-Cape Town Rally in 1959. The win kindled a resurgence in factory support for rallying and touring car racing.

S JE 985
RALLYE MONTE-CARLO

With Uhlenhaut's background, one would think that those within the company who wanted to see a return to factory racing would have a patron. But in a 1964 profile in *Esquire* magazine, Uhlenhaut was asked if racing was necessary to develop innovations that could be transferred directly to passenger cars. He replied that it is "not easy to answer because we did it and I can't say what we would have accomplished if we had done it differently. I should say you can get quite a lot of knowledge from racing. But my own personal impression is—mind [you] not everyone at Mercedes agrees with me—but my own impression is that it is not a necessity."

Later in the article, he admitted to no longer attending races, saying he'd "only been three or four times since we stopped racing. Terrible, isn't it? Well, I don't like all that standing around. Waste of time. When we were building the cars ourselves, it was a different thing."

But the ban only hardened the resolve of the engineers in the lower ranks to keep the competitive spirit alive. Engineers such as Aufrecht had joined the company precisely because of Mercedes' racing success. "Motorsports have always been the greatest [interest] to me," Aufrecht said. "I was just fascinated by them, the story of the Silver Arrows. [Juan Manuel] Fangio and [Karl] Kling were my idols. And Mercedes was something very special."

A native of Germany's Swabia region, Aufrecht was working as a test bench engineer in the experimental department (the renamed racing department) in 1964. Solingen-born Melcher came from the Rhineland. Fresh out of school with a mechanical engineering degree, he was assigned to engine development.

To say the pair clicked right off the bat would be highly inaccurate. Even though they were born just thirteen months apart, Aufrecht in December 1938 and Melcher in January 1940, they were quite different in appearance and outlook. Aufrecht was compact in stature and was intense like his older superiors. Melcher was tall and gangly, with longish hair and the laid-back attitude of the coming younger generation.

OPPOSITE Walter Schock, left, and Rudolf Moll won the European Rally Championship in 1960, a major boost in Mercedes' rally effort.

ABOVE Mercedes dominated Argentina's grueling Touring Car Grand Prix, a rally race over open roads, across four years (1961–1964) with a factory effort. Here, Eugen Böhringer and Klaus Kaiser take the checkered flag in the 1963 edition. They would again win the event a year later.

TOP There was limited factory involvement in European Touring Car racing in the early 1960s. Mercedes engineer Erich Waxenberger driving with Peter Lang in a six-hour event at the Nürburgring in 1963 drove this 300 SE to a third-place finish.

MIDDLE Eugen Böhringer wins his class in the 1964 ADAC 6-Hour at the Nürburgring.

BOTTOM Mercedes entered factory cars at the 1964 24 Hours of Spa. Böhringer, who set the fastest lap in the No. 100 car, pits ahead of the eventual race-winning No. 102 car driven by Robert Crevits and Taf Gosselin.

From the start, there were disagreements on how things should be run and stories of tense exchanges and terse notes left in test logs. Melcher recalls that "[w]e had a fight the first day we met because our temperaments are so different and because we had different roles."

Eventually they sorted out their differences and began work in secret on improving the performance of the 300 SE. The M189 3.0-liter inline-six beneath the hood produced 170 hp using a Bosch indirect injection. It was a definite improvement over its carbureted predecessor, the M186 3.0-liter inline-six that made just 115 hp. Still, the M189 needed more muscle to compete with the lighter entries in the touring car category.

Melcher came up with a more aggressive cam profile that allowed the engine to rev to over 7,000 rpm and lifted output to over 200 hp. Not only was it a healthy boost over stock models, but the modifications also outperformed the factory-backed Argentinian rally cars that boasted 195 hp. Additional modifications were made to lighten the car and prepare it for the track. All the after-hour and weekend efforts were beginning to pay off.

"With the 300 SE, we tried to build a car that was actually capable of also causing a furor in motorsports," Aufrecht recalls. Building the car was the easy part. Convincing the higher-ups that the car should be raced had its own risks.

After showing the car to Uhlenhaut, the development chief took the matter up with the board. The green light was given on the condition that if the car was successful, Aufrecht and Melcher could keep their jobs. If not, they would leave the company.

Manfred Schiek, a coworker and copilot of Walter Shock in Mercedes' 1961 victory in Argentina, was tapped to drive the 300 SE prepared by Aufrecht and Melcher in the 1965 German touring car series. He won the first race in May at the Nürburgring in a 220 SE competing in the 2,000–2,500cc class before switching over to the more powerful 300 SE.

The first outing for the 300 SE in a European Touring Car race held promise, but ultimately disappointed. Schiek, who was teamed up with Eugen Böhringer, qualified fourth behind pole-sitting John Whitmore in a Ford Lotus Cortina, a BMW 1800 TI driven by Huber Hahne, and a Ford Mustang with Roy Pierpont at the wheel. Schiek jumped out to an early lead, Whitmore had let him by to study his line. Soon, he caught up, but then the Mercedes would retire with clutch problems. Whitmore, teamed with Jack Sears, won the race with Pierpoint and Jochen Neerpasch finished second in the Mustang.

TOP The No. 102 car takes the checkered flag at the 1964 24 Hours of Spa.

LEFT World Champion Juan Manuel Fangio (right) congratulates Crevits (left) and Gosselin on their Spa win.

ABOVE A Mercedes ad touts the 1964 Spa win. It would be the last ad promoting a Mercedes touring-car victory.

ABOVE Böhringer wins a six-hour touring car race in Macao.

Returning to the German series, Schiek scored his first win at Avus in late June, taking the 300 SE to victory past a 3.8-liter Jaguar Mark II in the over 2,500cc class.

It was the third round, at the Norisring, where the big Mercedes impressed everyone with its sheer power. The four classes were divided into two races, the first for 1,300–2,000cc entries and the second for cars over 2,000cc, which incorporated the 2,000–2,500cc category. There would be a 1,000 DM prize for the fastest time over the course of a nineteen-lap race. Vic Elford in a Ford Cortina edged Josef Schnitzer in a BMW 1800 TI by just under nine seconds with a time of 34 minutes 15.5 seconds in the first race. Then the big cars ran.

According to *touringcarracing.net*, "It seemed impossible that the large and somewhat outdated Mercedes could beat the Cortina's time. Schiek tried anyhow and hammered down 8 laps in true [Eugen] Böhringer style. Then he spun in lap 9 at the entry of the S-curve, coming to a complete standstill and lost eight seconds at least. He continued ever more aggressive, nearly lost it again at the very same corner and finished in 34.13.7—he won!" In addition to taking home the prize for the fastest race, he beat the second-place Fiat 2300 S Coupe driven by Günter Schiemer by more than a lap, as well as a Jaguar Mark II and a Ford Mustang also competing in the over 2,500cc class.

The next two rounds were contested at airport circuits in Mainz-Finthen and Trier with Schiek prevailing over the 3.8-liter Jaguars. Schiek returned to a 2,000–2,500cc class Mercedes 220 for the German Grand Prize race at the Nürburgring on August 1, winning his class, while Friedrich Bryzmann won the over 2,500cc category in a Jaguar Mark II 3.8.

There would be no more races for the Aufrecht/Melcher-prepared 300 SE. The second to the last round was for smaller cars, a 500-kilometer (311 mi) contest again at the Nürburgring. The last race of the season at the Wunstorf Airfield was on November 3. Tragically, Schiek was killed on September 11, exactly two months shy of his thirtieth birthday, while competing in the Tour d'Europe rally. In an accident that occurred near Prague, he was driving a Mercedes 230 SL with Martin Braungart, who escaped with minor injuries. Schiek was awarded the driver's touring car

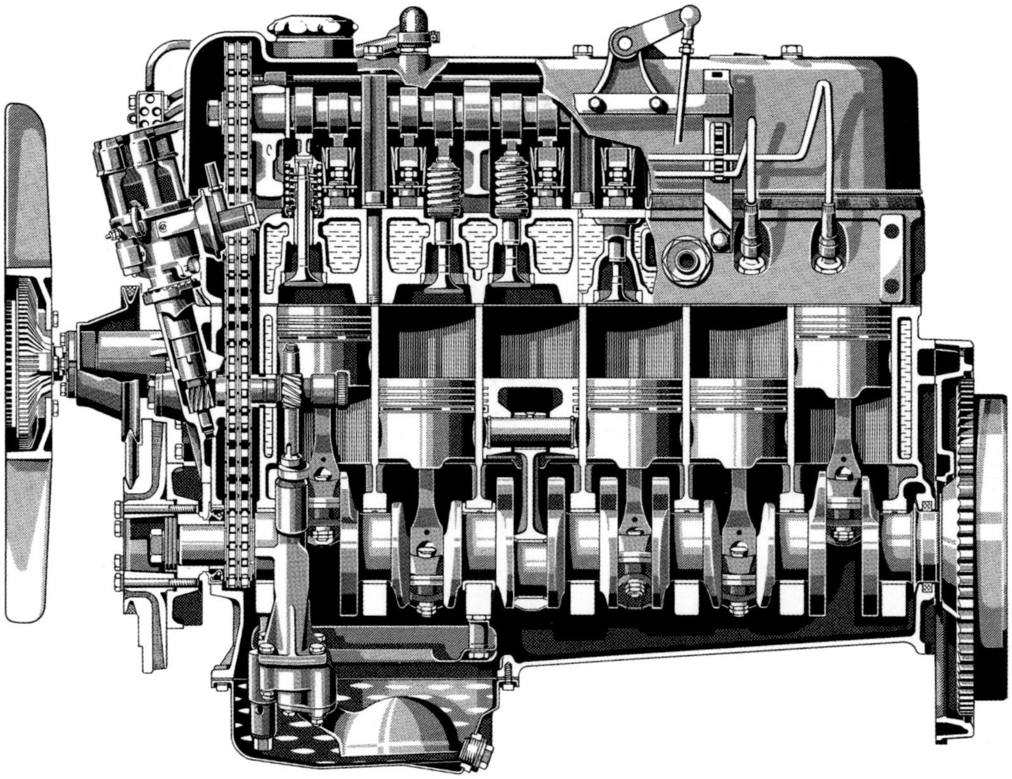

LEFT The 3.0-liter inline-six engine used in the Fintail benefitted from Melcher's magic touch. After its cam profile was changed, the hotter engine was fitted to a 300 SE with the intent to go racing.

BOTTOM Rudolf Uhlenhaut with his 300 SLR company car. Though he came up through the ranks in racing, he was somewhat skeptical of continued motorsports participation when he took over production car development. He gave Melcher and Aufrecht the go-ahead to campaign their 300 SE in 1965, but he also said their careers at Mercedes would end if they weren't successful.

LEFT Aufrect and Melcher tapped Manfried Schiek (pictured to the right of Mercedes' works driver Hans Hermann) to drive for them.

BELOW Even though Mercedes' "official" racing program wound down at the end of 1964, the company touted its successes in production car advertising.

OPPOSITE Schiek, center in white shirt, talks to Melcher, right, following his victory at the Norisring. Note the winner's laurel sticking out of the sunroof of the modified Fintail.

crown for his class posthumously and shared the overall championship with two other drivers. The factory decided yet again that it no longer could afford direct involvement in racing.

While Aufrecht and Melcher kept their jobs, they were not highly regarded by the old guard. Considered more garage tinkerers than race engineers, Aufrecht and Melcher continued to toil away in relative anonymity. Despite their successes during 1965, the company made no mention of the victories. Even though Uhlenhaut approved their foray into racing, it never really was a factory-sanctioned effort. Even to this day, the Mercedes archives have no mention of any of Schiek's racing activities after 1964.

Despite their full-time employment at Mercedes, as far as the duo's racing activities were concerned, they were considered outsiders. That they would eventually leave the company and continue to work on Mercedes cars was testament to their true belief in the brand.

During an interview on the Czech talk show *At the Swimming Pool*, Melcher said, "We wanted to go racing and show the factory that it is possible with this car to win races. Mercedes did not believe this. We want to show them that we can do it better. There were old men in the factory, [and] we were the young revolutionaries."

While the successful campaign of the 300 SE did not create the sensation that the Red Pig would at Spa six years later, it did expose the talents of Aufrecht and Melcher to some very important people. Mostly they were the privateers campaigning Mercedes cars in events ranging from local club meets to major touring car races. Those looking for a boost in performance for the heavier Mercedes sedans came calling.

One such customer was Albert Pfuhl, a wealthy businessman and gentleman racer from Darmstadt, whom Schiek introduced to the pair. Having done some tuning work on a 220 SE for him, Aufrecht and Melcher promised a free performance upgrade on a 300 SE. According to an account on *Mercedes-Fans.de*, Pfuhl acquired the car from Böhringer for 8,000 DM and the duo went to work.

Melcher, who had experience tuning motorcycle racing engines for his brother, Hans-Jürgen, busied himself designing a direct fuel injection system to find that extra power. The Melcher brothers, both large in stature, needed to extract more power from their mounts in order to compete with lighter riders. The same principles would apply to the heftier Mercedes sedans.

Melcher recalled that to find "the performance to beat the BMWs and the Jaguars, I covered all the furniture in Aufrecht's apartment in drawings. I drew on the direct injection [from the 300 SL] and improved it on the drawing board and built the fixtures. In Aufrecht's basement we built the first direct injection engine designed outside a large company and put it in a 300 SE." With direct injection, the engine now made 238 hp.

Pfuhl took two class wins in 1966, a 100-miler (161 km) at Hockenheim and another at the Mainz-Finthen airport races. As a result of those two finishes and strong outings in other events, other Mercedes drivers came calling for similar upgrades. In addition to bringing business to Aufrecht and Melcher, Pfuhl would continue to source his race and road cars from the duo.

Soon Aufrecht and Melcher found their evenings and weekends consumed with fitting 300 SE race cars with the direct injection system they developed in addition to holding down their day jobs at Mercedes. As they worked out of Aufrecht's basement and garage in Großaspach, Melcher recalled that "we did not do it for money, we did it for racing."

Higher-ups in the company took a dim view of the afterhours work. "There was always a prospect of getting fired," Melcher said in an interview in the book *AMG Reaching for the Stars*. Especially so, "when I had secretly ordered racing pistons from Mahle on my own authority."

Aufrecht, in a 2014 interview with *Motorsport Retro*, said, "We were working on cars after work. To begin with, we only focused on motorsport and its private teams, but then the drivers began to come to us and suggest, 'wouldn't it be great if you could build one of those motors of yours for street use?' So, we started to build engines for road-going cars. And then gearboxes, transmissions."

"And piece by piece," added Melcher, "we got into tuning!"

Aufrecht recalls that at the time, plenty of independents tuned Volkswagens and BMWs, "but never, ever a Mercedes. Back in those days you simply didn't tinker with a Mercedes, because it was already perfect."

But the timing was ripe for the two Mercedes engineers who knew what needed to be done. Melcher explained, "We benefited because BMW was building some wild cars even in their normal series and they [also] supported tuners. For Mercedes there was nobody who could do that."

"In the end, our customers more or less forced us to start a company," Aufrecht concluded.

Tale of the Fintail

BASED ON THE W109 300 SEL, the Red Pig is *the* Mercedes model that made AMG. But, as significant as that large car is to AMG's legacy, its predecessor, the W111/112 Fintail in 300 SE trim did its share in putting Hans Werner Aufrecht and Erhard Melcher on the map.

The Fintail's importance extends even further in Mercedes' production car and motorsports legacy for it represents the transition from the staid Ponton-bodied cars it replaced and the W108/109 series that followed.

Originally introduced in 1959, the W111 sedan came in three trim levels, the 220b, 220 Sb, and the 220SEb. All were powered by an iron-block M127 2.2-liter inline-six. The base model made 95 hp; the Sb, with twin Solex carburetors was rated at 110 hp; the top-line SEb with Bosch indirect fuel injection pumped out 120 hp.

The unit-body W111 featured safety features pioneered by Béla Barényi, including crumple zones, safety door locks, and padded dashes and steering wheels. Designed by Friedrich Geiger, the exterior featured prominent tail fins, though not as exaggerated as those found on American cars of the time. Cleaner, more modern coupe and convertible models built from 1961 to 1971 that minimized the tail fins were penned by French designer Paul Bracq.

The exclusivity of the Fintail was undercut by the introduction of the W110 models that were equipped with four-cylinder engines. While they shared the same body shape from the cowl rearward, these shorter-nosed models wore less brightwork. Their more fuel-efficient gas and diesel engines also made them ideal for taxi service, which also did little to burnish the image of the more senior six-cylinder models.

While the W111 models were raced and rallied with success, W112 300 SE introduced in 1961 represented a large step up in both power and handling. The M127 was replaced by the M189 3.0-liter inline-six. The iron block of the M127 gave way to a new aluminum alloy design that saved 88 pounds (40 kg). Bosch manifold injection was standard and helped produce 160 hp. That output was bumped to 170 hp in 1964 by using a higher compression ratio.

In addition to the upgraded engine, the W112 featured an air suspension, a four-speed automatic transmission, dual-circuit four-wheel disc brakes, and power steering.

In a January 1963 road test, *Car and Driver* observed that "[t]he mechanical over-elaboration of this car is not immediately apparent after the first driving experience. It is only after becoming familiar with it and its behavior that the full possibilities of the various elements in the chassis are realized. . . . For the European rally championship, Mercedes-Benz has so far relied upon the four-door 220 SE to bring home the points, but competition manager Karl Kling, after lengthy tests with the 300 SE, feels that this car, in spite of its automatic transmission, may do the job better. The advantages of its air suspension show up better when the road conditions get worse, especially when high average speeds are aimed at."

By the mid-1960s the fin craze had finally died out worldwide, and with the introduction of the W108/109, Mercedes also dialed back the styling on the W111 sedan for its final run from 1965 to 1968. Featuring the more restrained tail end look of the coupe and cabriolet, the last run of the Fintail, now called the 230 S, featured the M180 2.3-liter inline-six with a modest 118 hp.

Mercedes produced more than 344,000 W111/112 sedans over the 1959–1968 production run. With its unique styling and its spirited performance, the Fintail combined a touch of the exuberance of fifties styling with a dash of the coming horsepower wars of the sixties.

TOP The W112-based 300 SEL Fintail had an illustrious career in racing and rallying. The chromed-edged tailfins were very much a styling convention of the time, influenced heavily by American cars.

BOTTOM, LEFT The W112 incorporated both performance and safety upgrades over the Ponton model it replaced. The chassis was the first Mercedes to use crumple zones to reduce crash forces.

BOTTOM, RIGHT The rear axle on the W112 was a single-pivot swing design that also incorporated air springs, a feature that carried over onto future models.

AFFALTERBACH
AMG

3

AMG IS BORN

AFTER A YEAR OF WORKING nights and weekends, Aufrecht and Melcher soon realized that it was time to move on from Mercedes and start their own business. With the latest no-racing stance from management, they had little incentive to stay on. For Aufrecht, having initially achieved a lifelong dream of joining the racing department to test engines, the idea of doing dyno work on production-car engines held little appeal.

With a growing list of clients, the timing seemed right. But there would be a gamble in starting a new business. Germany had experienced its first major recession since the postwar recovery years. Auto production dropped to 2.3 million units in 1967, down from 2.8 million a year earlier. Melcher recalls that Opel laid off 6,000 workers.

Aufrecht understood the risk, but also believed Melcher's talent would be an essential component in the enterprise. Aufrecht explained that "Melcher had so much intelligence, so much genius, that I knew I would be successful with him."

Melcher said that "Aufrecht was the real driving force to start a business. He convinced me, pleaded with me, to do it. We saw an ad in the local paper for a mill in Burgstall." Part of larger Burgstetten, the village of Burgstall an der Murr is about 5 miles (8 km) south of Großaspach and 3.5 miles (6 km) east of AMG's home in Affalterbach.

The mill still exists, and the exterior appears unchanged since the AMG days. Located on the edge of town on Mühlestraße (Mill Street), the building sits on the Mühlekanal that channeled the river's flow to the mill's water wheel. The Murr river, one house over, separates it from an open area used for athletic fields. If you squint, you can almost see Fintail models perched on outdoor lifts as they were in the late 1960s. Melcher, when not wintering in the Canary Islands, still lives nearby.

"I had to go and look at it on my own as Hans Werner had just got married and was building a house," Melcher said in the *At the Swimming Pool* interview. "I was a bachelor and could take the risk. If things worked out, he would then join me later. It was possible for me to do this. I had no family. I was a young guy, kind of a hippie. I lived in cooperation with other people. I was not a normal engineer. I was an engineer, but I didn't live like an engineer. I had six or seven patents in the three years I was in the firm [Mercedes] and I got money for this. I could live off this for one or two years. I did not need much. It was 1967 and we were all revolutionary and crazy."

Thus, Aufrecht Melcher Großaspach Ingenieurbüro, Konstruktion und Versuch zur Entwicklung von Rennmotoren was born. Translated, it was the Aufrecht Melcher Großaspach engineering firm, design and testing for the development of racing engines. Eventually the name was shortened to AMG Motorenbau und Entwicklungsgesellschaft mbH—German for AMG Engine Production and Development Limited.

PREVIOUS Though AMG started with work in Großaspach and later occupied a mill in Burgstall, its eventual move to Affalterbach is a prominent feature on the company's crest. This badge is an enduring symbol of the talents and vision of Hans Werner Aufrecht and Erhard Melcher.

LEFT Melcher, right, attends to a client's car at a race. Word of mouth regarding AMG's ability to extract more engine power quickly spread in Germany's motorsports community.

ABOVE AMG's first shop was an old mill in Burgstall an der Murr. The outside lift is an indication that the operation was a bit primitive. Inside, the dirt floor garage had a pit dug out to allow access beneath vehicles.

In recalling those days for the *Motorikon* podcast, Melcher said, "I was immediately enthusiastic. It reminded me of my home in the Bergisches Land. There were turbines in the front, the river in the back and a rather dilapidated workshop. Aufrecht wanted something better. But I said, Ken Tyrell, he also works in such a wooden shed."

Melcher had quit Mercedes at the end of April, but he didn't officially register the company until that summer. He was soon joined by Aufrecht, and both had their brothers, Hans-Jürgen Melcher and Friedrich Aufrecht, join them in the company. The elder Melcher left about six months later, but Friedrich stayed on until his retirement from AMG in 2002.

"When we started tinkering with Mercedes models, our landlord, who owned the old millhouse, must have suspected we were doing something illegal. Back in those days you simply didn't tinker with a Mercedes, because it was already perfect. But I already knew back then that there was no future in being a millwright, and that our star was just beginning to rise," Aufrecht told *Mercedes-Benz Classic* magazine in an article about the pair. Melcher added, "That's just how you've always been—a man who only looks ahead, never backwards. Yes, we were something out of the ordinary here. I always listened to loud jazz when I was working. And whenever a customer asked how to get to us, I'd just say: 'follow the tire tracks.'"

The operation was so nondescript that their customers had a hard time finding it. And the conditions of the garage with its dirt floor were primitive. In a *Motorsports Retro* profile, Aufrecht said, "We had no money, so we had to improvise. We even dug out an earth pit so that we could work beneath the cars. Customers would come in and ask us if we knew where AMG was!"

Concentrating primarily on Fintail SE models with 2.5- to 2.8-liter sixes, Melcher said there was plenty of work in extracting additional horsepower for both competition and street use. "We had a lot of work," Melcher said, noting that a lot of what they did wasn't necessarily high tech, but that the pair were good mechanics with deep knowledge of Mercedes engines. Aufrecht specialized in the mechanical fuel injection systems, while Melcher machined parts and worked on valve and head modifications. In addition, some of their compatriots from Mercedes were moonlighting at AMG. These specialists also lent a high level of expertise to the operation.

At the time, AMG had the market to itself for two main reasons. First, there were no shops specializing in Mercedes. Melcher said, "We benefited because BMW was building some wild cars even in their normal series and because they supported tuners. From Mercedes, there was nobody who could do that."

Second, and perhaps most important, the brand no longer had the performance cachet it enjoyed a decade earlier thanks to its racing efforts and the production of cars such as the 300 SL Gullwing and Roadster.

Heinz-Ulrich Wieselmann, editor-in-chief of Germany's prestigious *auto motor und sport*, famously criticized Mercedes for building cars suitable for "executives, farmers and retirees." The popularity of four-cylinder Finback models as taxis, while underscoring the car's dependability, also did little to enhance the brand's reputation among enthusiasts.

In the official forty-fifth anniversary book on AMG, Aufrecht further explained that "[i]t's important to remember something: we actually wanted to work in car racing right from the beginning. That was our passion. Then, more and more racecar drivers came to us who wanted more performance in their road vehicles . . . we just hadn't thought that far ahead. . . . We didn't want to be tuners, we just transferred a bit of high-end racing technology to road vehicles. It must also be said, however, that our

S PB 54H

former colleagues in Untertürkheim [Mercedes' headquarters] considered us crazy at first. Tune a Mercedes! That was practically a sin! Behind our backs, we were condemned as traitors to the Mercedes-Benz brand, that's why they didn't take us seriously in Stuttgart at first. This mindset only started to change once our cars started being publicly described as sensational."

While Aufrecht and Melcher did what they could to burnish the performance credibility from outside of Mercedes, it was an insider, engineer Erich Waxenberger, who changed the course of history for both the three-pointed star and AMG. Like Aufrecht's and Melcher's clandestine race preparation of the 300 SE in 1965, Waxenberger worked behind the scenes to unleash the potential of Mercedes' first production car V-8.

While Americans had long understood the value of large displacement V-8 engines in producing power, Europeans, still rebuilding after World War II, concentrated on more efficient four- and six-cylinder gas and diesel engines. V-8s were at the heart of the muscle car wars in the United States. But in Germany, Mercedes viewed the development of its first production V-8 not so much as a street performance power play, but rather as part of a larger effort to recapture the company's heritage of building grand automobiles.

Introduced in 1963, Der Große Mercedes (the Big Mercedes) W100 limousine lived up to its billing. The short wheelbase version measured 126 inches (more than 10 feet) (3 m) between the axles and stretched out to nearly 18.5 feet (6 m) in overall length.

OPPOSITE, TOP Designer Paul Bracq's early renderings for a new grand Mercedes are far more futuristic than the 600 that went into production.

OPPOSITE, BOTTOM The Mercedes 600 or *Grosser* (Grand) Mercedes required V-8 power to haul its considerable heft when it was introduced in 1963.

TOP This comparison shows the difference in size starting at right with a W110 Fintail, the standard wheelbase 600 in the center, and the Pullman limousine on the left.

ABOVE The M100 V-8 displaced 6.3 liters and produced 250 hp. It was a mainstay in Mercedes' engine lineup until 1981.

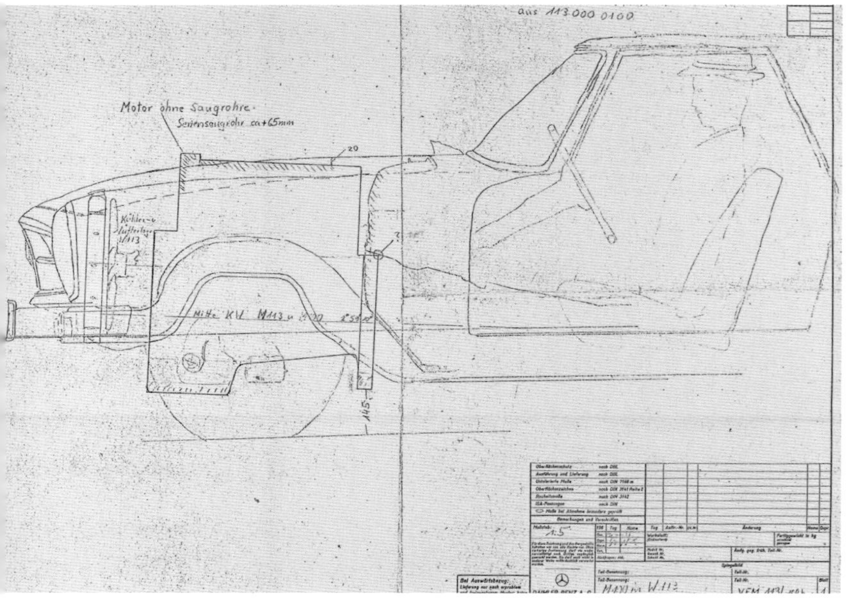

TOP LEFT With ample horsepower and torque on tap, the Mercedes 600 was capable of spirited handling in addition to its luxury ride.

TOP RIGHT Erich Waxenberger was the engineer in charge of Mercedes' experimental department under Rudi Uhlenhaut. Having begun his career in the 1950s with work on the 300 SL and SLR, he didn't hold Aufrecht and Melcher in particularly high esteem.

ABOVE As this drawing illustrates, the V-8 sat too high and too far forward, which upset the balance of the SL roadster.

OPPOSITE, TOP Chastened by the editor of *auto motor und sport* who felt Mercedes lacked performance and built cars for executives and farmers, Waxenberger took it upon himself to boost the company's image. His first attempt to mate the M100 with an SL didn't pan out.

OPPOSITE, BOTTOM LEFT The introduction of the W109 successor to the Fintail presented an opportunity to upgrade Mercedes' performance image.

OPPOSITE, BOTTOM RIGHT Better handling and more power from the inline-six engine in the W109 model alsotranslated to racing successes by privateers. Mercedes highlighted that point in its US advertising.

The long-wheelbase version, known as the Pullman, added another 27.5 inches (70 cm) to that measurement, while overall length was nearly 21 feet (6 m). It was available in four- and six-door configurations as well as a Landaulet open-top version usually reserved for heads of state.

With the 600's curb weight varying between 6,592 and 7,231 pounds (2,990 and 3,280 kg), the 178-hp M189 inline-six used on the previous 300-series Adenauer limo wasn't up to the task of powering this behemoth, so the 250-hp 6.3-liter M100 V-8 was developed specifically for the W100.

Waxenberger, a protégé of Rudi Uhlenhaut, started in the Passenger Car Testing department at Mercedes in 1953. Son of a DKW dealer and an amateur racer, Waxenberger moved up quickly in the company, working on chassis development of the 190 SL, 300 SL Gullwing, and the 300 SL Roadster. Taking Wieselmann's criticism to heart, which also reportedly included a face-to-face meeting with him and Uhlenhaut where the editor accused the thirty-five-year-old of being an old man, Waxenberger was looking to inject higher performance in Mercedes' relatively staid lineup.

One of his early plans to turbocharge the M189 inline-six in the 300 SE was shot down by management. An effort to shoehorn a V-8 into a 230 SL also didn't pan out. With 100 more horses than stock, the M100-equipped SL was fast, but a handful to drive. The larger engine would only fit in the engine bay positioned farther forward than in the standard inline six. That, plus the additional 165 pounds (75 kg) of mass, contributed to excessive front tire wear and handling issues. The project was ultimately abandoned.

But Waxenberger wasn't finished. He wrangled the body of the new W109 SEL rejected by the factory in Sindelfingen and set about transplanting the 600's V-8 engine into it. This included modifications to the steering linkage as well as the exhaust and intake manifolds to ensure that the engine could be squeezed into an engine bay designed for an inline six. The automatic transmission was replaced by a manual gearbox from a truck to add a touch more performance.

According to *automotiverarebirds.com*, Waxenberger took his secret project out for a test drive late one Friday night in 1967 hoping no one would notice. But Uhlenhaut had been working late and heard the rumble of the car as it passed by. When confronted later, Waxenberger confessed to the project. Uhlenhaut insisted on driving the car, but Waxenberger stalled because he felt it wasn't quite ready yet. After a bit more finessing, he finally let his boss drive the V-8-powered

S-VN 592

S PA 175H

The big new Mercedes-Benz 6-cylinder is not a sports car
So why have we raced it so often?
The big new Mercedes-Benz 6-cylinder models are among the finest cars in the world.
We know that. We proved it. We punished them on gruelling race tracks like the Nuerburgring. These cars have been really put through it. They've done thousands of miles – under test and under racing conditions.
We tested their powers of road-holding, cornering, braking, and their motor performance. To the limit.
They passed. We *know* these cars are good. Perhaps incomparably good.
You, of course, will want to prove that to yourself. Fix up a test run. See your Mercedes-Benz agent.
The Mercedes-Benz Class
MB 250 SE
This will interest you: Mercedes-Benz data
Model 200 4-cylinder, twin carburettor, 105 gr. HP/SAE to 5400 r.p.m., max. 99 m.p.h.
Model 200 D 4-cylinder Diesel, 60 gr. HP/SAE to 4200 r.p.m., max. 83 m.p.h.
Model 230 6-cylinder, twin carburettor, 118 gr. HP/SAE to 5400 r.p.m., max. 106 m.p.h.
Model 230 S 6-cylinder, twin carburettor, 135 gr. HP/SAE to 5600 r.p.m., max. 109 m.p.h.
Model 250 S 6-cylinder, twin carburettor, 146 gr. HP/SAE to 5600 r.p.m., max. 112 m.p.h.
Model 250 SE 6-cylinder, injection engine, 170 gr. HP/SAE to 5600 r.p.m., max. 118 m.p.h.
Model 250 SE Convertible 6-cylinder, injection engine, 170 gr. HP/SAE to 5600 r.p.m., max. 118 m.p.h.
Model 250 SE Coupé 6-cylinder, injection engine, 170 gr. HP/SAE to 5600 r.p.m., max. 118 m.p.h.
Model 300 SE 6-cylinder, injection engine, 195 gr. HP/SAE to 5500 r.p.m., max. 118 to 124 m.p.h.
Model 300 SEL 6-cylinder, injection engine, 195 gr. HP/SAE to 5500 r.p.m., max. 118 to 124 m.p.h.
Model 300 SE Convertible 6-cylinder, injection engine, 195 gr. HP/SAE to 5500 r.p.m., max. 118 to 124 m.p.h.
Model 300 SE Coupé 6-cylinder, injection engine, 195 gr. HP/SAE to 5500 r.p.m., max. 118 to 124 m.p.h.
Model 230 SL 6-cylinder, injection engine, 170 gr. HP/SAE to 5600 r.p.m., max. 124 m.p.h.
Model 600 8-cylinder, injection engine, 300 gr. HP/SAE to 4100 r.p.m., max. 127 m.p.h.
Model 600 Pullman 8-cylinder, injection engine, 300 gr. HP/SAE to 4100 r.p.m., max. 127 m.p.h.
MERCEDES-BENZ

TOP In the W109, Waxenberger finally found the right vehicle that could accommodate the 6.3-liter M100. He took the car racing in 1969, winning a six-hour event in Macau.

SECOND FROM TOP Emboldened by the victory at the Guia Circuit in Macau, Waxenberger began preparing entries for several touring car races in Europe. One of the early tests was at Hockenheim.

THIRD FROM TOP Uhlenhaut, white hair at center, attends the Hockenheim test, talking with Waxenberger who is leaning on the car.

BOTTOM Waxenberger and Kurt Ahrens codrove this 300 SEL 6.3 at Spa, qualifying the car sixth on the grid. However, the factory decided to withdraw just before the start of the race over tire concerns.

OPPOSITE Building on the new 300 SEL 6.3, AMG would offer tuned versions of the M100 engine that produced up to 320 hp.

sedan. Uhlenhaut was convinced and, in turn, he urged the management board to go ahead with the project to use the M100 engine in the W109 successor to the 300 SE Fintail sedan. The 300 SEL 6.3 was born, making its debut the following March at the Geneva Motor Show. Boasting 247 hp and nearly 370 lb-ft of torque, the 300 SEL 6.3 was capable of 0–62 mph (0–100 kph) in 6.6 seconds and had a top speed of 137 mph (220 kph).

But getting the car into production wasn't enough for Waxenberger, who wanted to go racing despite the official company ban. A right-hand-drive 300 SEL 6.3 was prepared and sent to Macau, where it was entered in a six-hour touring car race on May 18, 1969. Waxenberger codrove the car with Albert Poon, a wealthy Hong Kong resident who "owned" the car, thereby circumventing the edict of factory involvement in motorsport. A second car paired drivers Jan Bussell and Ted Moorat.

The Mercedes entries qualified one-two, with Waxenberger taking the pole. In the race, Poon drove for perhaps twenty minutes with Waxenberger taking the checkered flag ahead of a Porsche 911. The Bussell/Moorat 300 SEL 6.3 finished third.

Waxenberger had even greater ambitions despite the management board's stance against factory involvement in racing. He prepared three cars for the 1969 twenty-four-hour race at Spa the following July. They were entered under the auspices of the sporting department under Kling's successor, Baron Alexander von Korff, and the return of Mercedes to racing caused a minor sensation. The cars would be driven by Hans Hermann/Jackie Ickx, Finnish rally driver Rauno Aaltonen/Dieter Glemser, and Kurt Ahrens/Erich Waxenberger.

The SELs were quick in practice. However, the stock tires were chunking, something the team had not encountered in previous tests. Alternate tires were tried with similar results at the Belgian circuit. While concern over the tires is the "official" story, Melcher told *Motorikon* that "the engines didn't hold . . . the engines were revved too high, the connecting rod bearings broke, the camshafts broke. They kept quiet about that, they always just claimed that the tires didn't work, but you could change tires. They also knew they couldn't win the race. The BMWs and the Capris were so strong back then. And also, Alfa Romeo with the Giulia, they drove in a different class, but they were hellishly fast."

Although the cars qualified second, fourth, and sixth on the grid, the Daimler-Benz board, now aware of what was going on, decided that it would be best to withdraw, which occurred the morning of the race.

Waxenberger may have been down, but he wasn't out. Teaming with AMG, he had the engines bored out to 6.8 liters, installed fender flares, and fitted the cars with wider lightweight wheels and larger tires. Karl Ludvigsen, in *Quicksilver Century*, reported that "[e]arly in 1970 the improved car was tested at many of the circuits that made up the European touring car championship. It consistently matched or broke the existing lap records. The young engineers had made their point: a racing car was ready if DBAG (Daimler-Benz AG) wanted to race."

"But some of the older heads were wary," Ludvigsen continued. "Joachim Zahn was the company's chairman. . . . With a background in finance, he did not even pretend to be knowledgeable about cars and trucks. A sober and exact Prussian, Zahn seemed unlikely to lead the company into a new racing era. Competition enthusiasts in the firm curbed their expectations."

While the board decided against campaigning the cars that Waxenberger built, it created the template for the Red Pig. While Aufrecht and Melcher built their race car from a wreck, some accounts say two of the Waxenberger cars passed through AMG, one of which was acquired by Klaus Behrmann. That silver car raced in 1970–1971.

The third car, painted dark red, is on display at the Mobilia Museum in Kangasala, Finland. Purchased from the factory by Finnish businessman/journalist Urpo Lahtinen in 1970, he raced the car with Aaltonen. While it retained its 6.3-liter engine, AMG had bumped its output to 320 hp. It led a race at the Keimola Motor Stadium near Helsinki until a problem with the automatic transmission forced its withdrawal. It was later fitted with bumpers and registered for the street. It did compete in a drag race in Keimola in 1975 where it was the fastest street-registered car in the quarter mile. It ended up in the museum after Lahtinen's death in 1994.

The work by Waxenberger in conceiving and getting the 300 SEL 6.3 built was a monumental step in changing the image of Mercedes-Benz in enthusiast circles. It was also a boon to AMG, for it laid the foundation for its mastery of increasing the performance of V-8 engines. Just as Aufrecht and Melcher had done with direct injection of the M189 3.0-liter six, they would do so with the M100 and subsequent V-8s by developing a four-valve head that would create a whole new generation of Benz hotrods. The house of AMG was ready to roll.

M100 Meets W109: A Perfect Match

Erich Waxenberger may have just wanted to go faster, but his idea of putting the M100 V-8 into the newly introduced W109 Mercedes-Benz 300 SEL was a stroke of genius. It married Mercedes' first production V-8 with a new long-wheelbase version of what would become the S-Class. He would create a high-performance luxury sedan that won the raves of enthusiast publications and, more importantly, customers worldwide.

Road & Track proclaimed it as "Merely the Greatest Sedan in the World." Even higher praise came from *auto motor und sport*, which was still helmed by Heinz-Ulrich Wieselmann, who had earlier decried Mercedes' lack of performance. In 1968 the German magazine wrote: "We took delivery of one of the closely guarded first examples, a vehicle not yet even fitted with the '6.3' designation. The lack of model badge seemed to cause confusion to many a Porsche 911 and 911 S driver, normally accustomed to being kings of the motorway and who now suddenly found themselves being left looking flat-footed by the distinguished and relatively harmless-looking Mercedes. Should any of them be reading this, we would wish to point out that they have no cause to return their vehicles to the factory on account of deficient performance."

Mercedes' press release at Geneva boasted that "[t]he 300 SEL with 6.3-litre V-8 engine is a fast and comfortable tourer and is intended to bridge the gap between the 300 SEL and the 600. It will take up a leading position in the international market. As regards to the combination of optimal comfort and superb driving performance, this model should outclass all competition. It fulfills all wishes of the customer who expects top performance."

Of course, the success of this car started with the M100 V-8 for which planning began in 1955 along with the idea of building the 600. Mercedes Chief Engineer Fritz Nallinger originally envisioned a 6.0-liter aluminum-block engine. He also considered and later discarded the idea of building a 7.5-liter V-12. When work started in earnest, displacement of the V-8 was down to 5.0 liters by the time the engine finally was run on the test bench in late 1959.

It was through this development work that the size of the engine gradually grew, first to 5.8 liters, then to 6.0 liters. In these first stages of development, the block was constructed of aluminum with steel cylinder liners. The last go-around in increasing displacement to the production 6.3 liters entailed scrapping the aluminum block in favor of iron because the larger bore introduced some reliability issues.

The engine featured single, chain-driven overhead cams set in aluminum heads with two sodium-filled valves per cylinder. The Bosch fuel injection system was an eight-plunger mechanical design feeding the intake manifold. All M100 engines were hand built and dyno tested for 265 minutes, forty of which were under full load.

While power was rated at about 250 hp, it was the engine's ability to produce 371 lb-ft of torque that was critical in moving the mass of the 600, which tipped the scales between 6,500 and 7,200 pounds (2,948–3266 kg), depending on model. The robust torque also required an increase in the number of planetary gear sets from three to six in the transmission.

The 1963 debut of the 600 not only added the V-8 engine to the Mercedes lineup but was also part of a larger shift in Mercedes-Benz design. The clean lines adopted by designer Paul Bracq were similar to the crisp aesthetics of the fin-less 300 SE Coupe and Cabriolet he introduced a year earlier. This family look was then applied to the new W108/109 SE and SEL models when they were introduced in 1965.

The confusion caused by *auto motor und sport* among Porsche 911 drivers can be attributed to the little change in design between the standard six-cylinder 300 SEL models and the new 6.3-liter rocket. The V-8 SEL was distinguished by the 6.3 badge on the right rear decklid, the stacked halogen headlamps, a speedometer with a wider speed range, a standard tachometer, and a relocated clock. The rear-axle ratio was changed to a final drive of 2.85, but the single-pivot rear swing axle with its automatic leveling air suspension, four-speed automatic transmission, and power steering were unchanged from the six-cylinder models.

While expectations for the 300 SEL 6.3 were extremely low, with a skeptical management board foreseeing sales of about fifty per year, a total of 6,526 of them would be sold from 1968 to 1972. It was a brilliant move and helped to scale up M100 V-8 production, since only 2,700 of the engines would go into the low-volume 600 from 1963 through 1981.

TOP, LEFT The Mercedes-Benz 300 SEL 6.3 turned the heads of enthusiasts on both sides of the Atlantic. *Road & Track* called it "Merely the Greatest Sedan in the World" while *auto motor und sport* taunted 911 owners with its speed.

TOP, RIGHT Discreet 6.3 badging on the rear was the only tip that the 300 SEL was packing V-8 muscle beneath its hood.

BOTTOM Originally designed with six-cylinder power in mind, the engine bay needed some additional modification to accommodate a V-8.

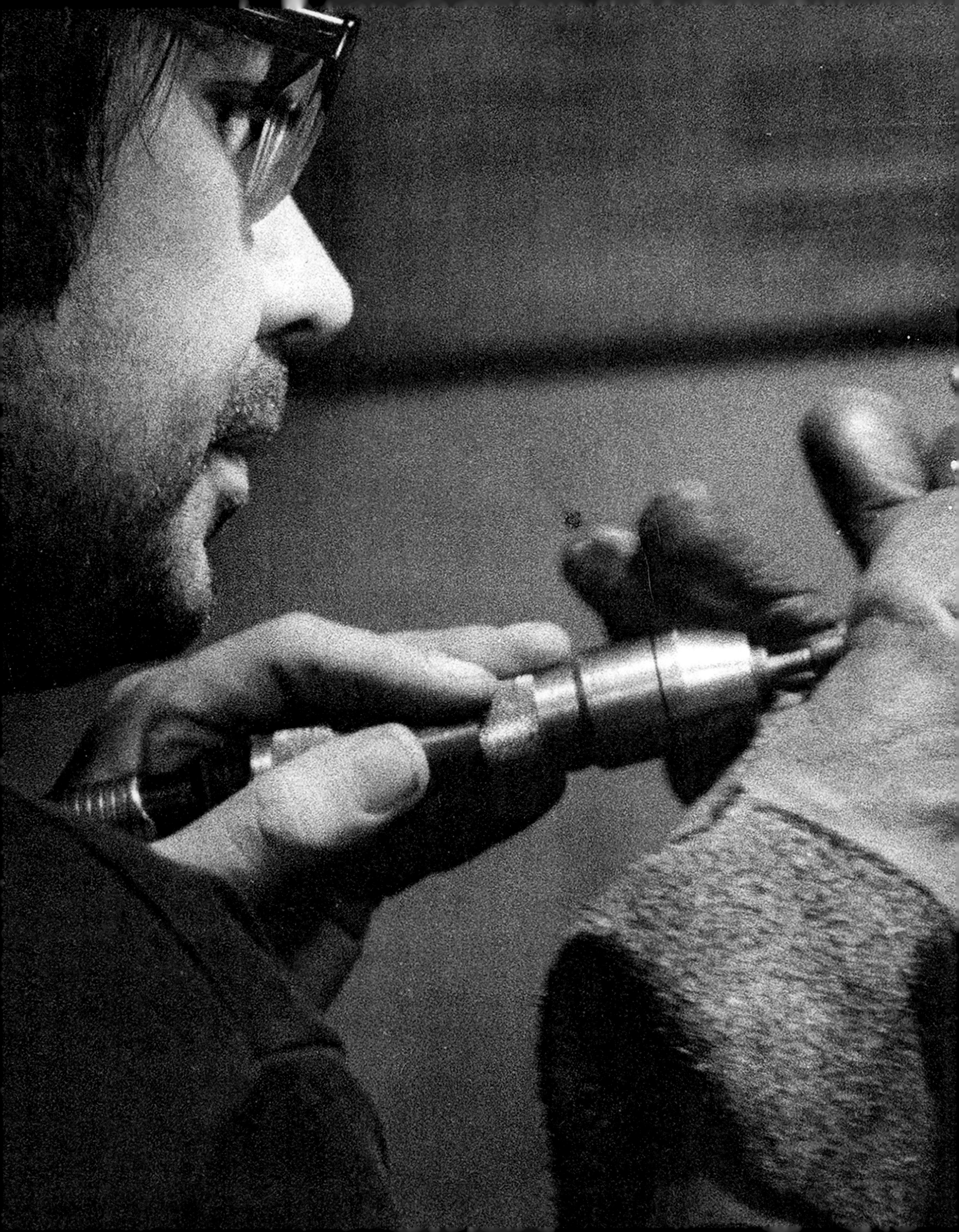

4

ONE MAN, ONE ENGINE

HANS WERNER AUFRECHT HAS A HABIT OF introducing himself by saying, "I'm the A in AMG." Erhard Melcher is certainly the M, but more than that, he might best be described as the man behind One Man, One Engine philosophy that sets AMG apart from its rivals. To this day, one technician builds an engine up from its many components.

It's become a standard of operational excellence attested by a badge attached to each engine built in Affalterbach that bears the name of the person who assembled it. The solo effort required to build an engine harkens back to Melcher's solitary approach to designing engine modifications and then creating the parts necessary to complete the project.

Hartmut Feyhl, an AMG employee who would come to the United States to build cars for the company and eventually started RENNtech, describes Melcher as "an amazing engineer." In an interview on the *Cars Yeah* podcast, Feyhl said Melcher was not just talented from an engine design perspective, but in "all the whole aspects of the car, aerodynamics, suspension, and of course primarily on top of it, engines, camshafts, valvetrains. He was machining the castings by hand in his milling machine and lathe, making the camshafts by hand, grinding it, machining it, you name it. Every single part that he could not buy off the shelf he basically designed it and made it himself."

"When I came to AMG, most of the time it was just Aufrecht in the office. Melcher was often in the forest, lying in the shade and thinking about the ideal pitch of the camshafts," joked Albert Pfuhl in a *Mercedes-Fan* interview.

"We complemented each other perfectly," Melcher said in a *Motorikon* podcast. "I was the player and developer and he [Aufrecht] was always the doer. That was a good mix."

Melcher summed up the early business nicely in the *AMG-45* anniversary book, saying, "With us, customers found respectable-looking, long-lasting Mercedes models with good safety features that could also be driven fast. Some customers entered these cars in hill climbs and rallies. In AMG trim, they could compete with the sports cars of the time—and they still had all the advantages of a Mercedes-Benz.

"Although we mostly tuned road cars which belonged to race drivers in the beginning, it wasn't long before ordinary car owners started coming to us, too," Melcher added. "It was the smaller Mercedes that was built starting in 1968, the so-called Stroke-8, that gave us our real breakthrough. Our order volume started doubling from year to year. The new, distinct Mercedes W114 and W115 brought us our first wave of success."

While the 300 SEL with its 6.3-liter V-8 engine was grabbing all the headlines, it was an expensive and relatively rare piece. *Road & Track*'s November 1968 road test lists an MSRP of $13,995 at a time when the average car sold for about $4,000. An AMG conversion bumping output from 250 to 320 hp plus suspension upgrades would cost up to $6,000.

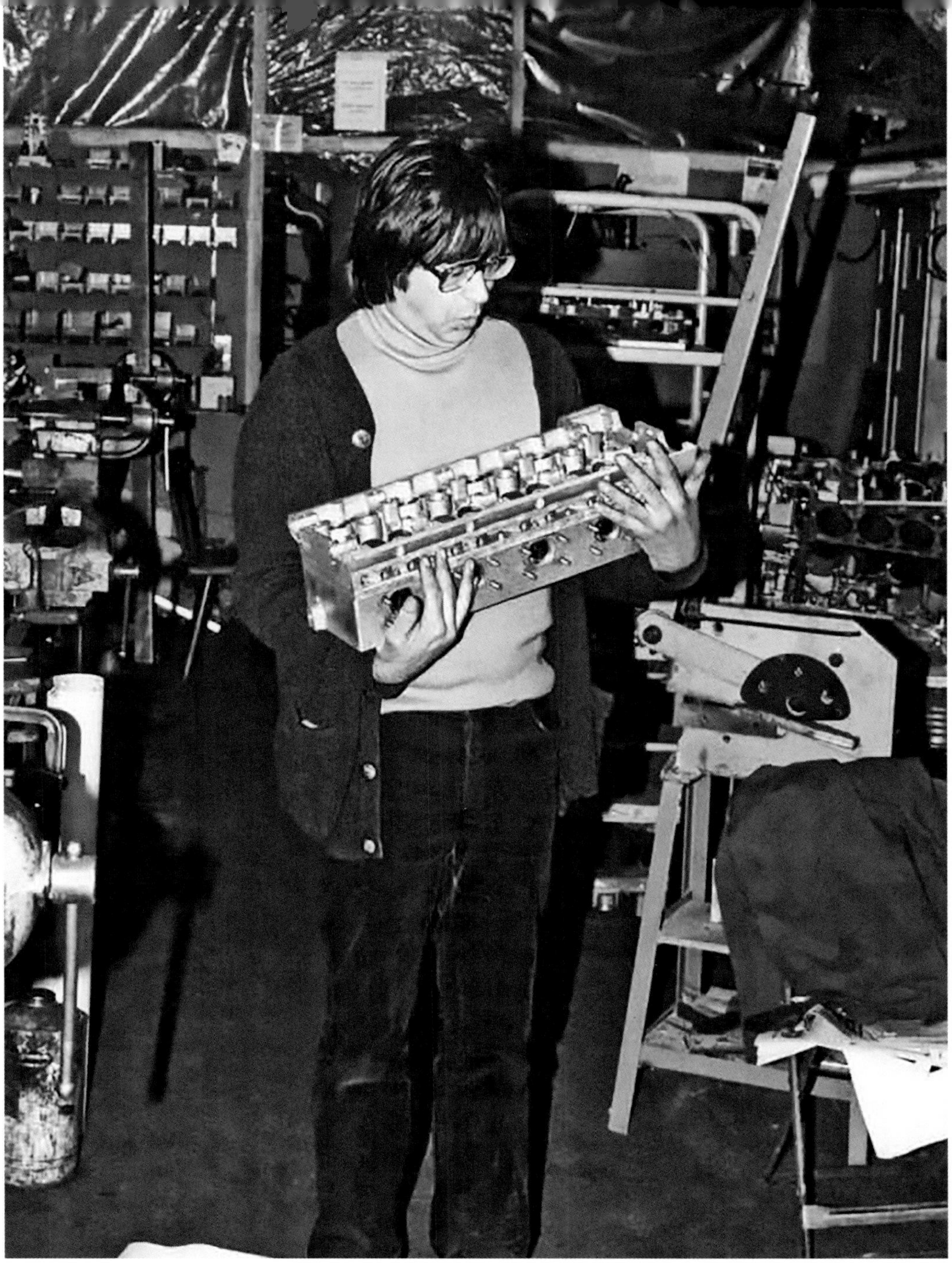

PREVIOUS As a skilled racing motorcycle engine builder, Melcher viewed the challenge of tuning a six-cylinder engine not so much as a whole, but rather how he could boost the performance of each individual cylinder and repeat the process.

LEFT Melcher's genius in engine development was recognized by Aufrecht, who believed that AMG would not succeed without the input from his gifted collaborator.

Work continued on the carryover W111/112 Fintail successors as well as M189 six-cylinder W108 models. But it was the new W114/115 models introduced in 1968 (the /8 or Stroke-8 designation derived from its introduction year) that would become a mainstay. Slightly smaller than the W108 and powered by 2.5- and 2.8-liter inline-sixes and later a 3.5-liter V-8, the new model offered the greatest potential for spirited performance at a relatively affordable price.

The Stroke-8 was the precursor to the midsize E-Class sedans of today and had the distinction of being the first postwar Mercedes to use an all-new suspension. A semitrailing rear arm setup replaced the single-pivot swing axle. Disc brakes were standard at all four corners and the wheel diameters grew from 13 to 14 inches (33–36 cm).

Designer Paul Bracq further refined the clean look developed for the W108. The Stroke-8 dispensed with any pretense of rear fins, the greenhouse was enlarged, and the visibility enhanced by thin pillars. He retained familiar cues such as the chromed grille and the stacked headlamps.

The six-cylinder W114 models, offered in displacements of 2.3, 2.5, and 2.8 liters (AMG would only modify the two larger engines), were further differentiated from the W115 by sporting a pair of bumperettes flanking the license plate frame beneath the main front bumper.

Performance upgrades for the 2.5-liter inline-six were modest, with only a 10-horse gain in output over the stock 130 hp. The larger six would see as much as a 40 hp gain over the base 145 hp. These modifications, which included reworked cylinder heads, would cost anywhere from

TOP LEFT The introduction of the W114/115 midsize coupe (above) and sedan opened the door to a new class of slightly smaller and more affordable cars that could benefit from AMG's ability to boost horsepower and improve handling.

TOP RIGHT With crisp lines, stacked headlamps, and a larger glass area, the W114/115 sedan was called the Stroke-8 in reference to its 1968 introduction.

OPPOSITE, TOP Dispensing with fussier designs of earlier models such as the Fintail, designer Paul Bracq ushered in a new era of Mercedes styling. The new models coming would share similar cues, lines, and proportions across the model range.

OPPOSITE, BOTTOM LEFT The 2.7-liter M130 inline-six in the W114 (the W115 were primarily four-cylinder gas- and diesel-powered), was a popular choice for enthusiast upgrades. AMG tuning boosted output from 145 to as much as 186 hp.

OPPOSITE, BOTTOM RIGHT Also introduced along with the Stroke-8 was the 3.5-liter V-8 from the S-Class. The M116 had the potential of producing up to 286 hp after a visit to Burgstall.

$300 to $1,800 depending on state of tune specified. When the 3.5-liter V-8 was added in 1971, customers could opt for an upgrade to either 268 or 286 hp. In addition to the engine work, AMG offered stiffer shocks as well as the option of a five-speed automatic or manual gearbox over the standard four-speed automatic.

But the volume of work and the pressures of being a partner in the rapidly growing business soon took its toll on Melcher. Although he had done preparatory work on the engine that would go into the Red Pig, he didn't stay on to see the car race at Spa.

Melcher related to *Motorikon* that "I wanted to leave. My father had died at 64; I was very miserable. I had had a [motorcycle] accident." The business had gotten more bureaucratic "and it all became too much for me. Then I left in the spring of '71, but left behind the light connecting rods, the light engine parts. I practically did all the preparatory work for the [Red Pig's] engine. And camshafts too, we ground them on this machine. That was a drudgery, grinding a racing shaft out of a production shaft. It all went very slowly."

While he was skilled at engine development, Melcher found going to events too stressful—even though he had worked as a mechanic for his brother who raced motorcycles. Working with limited budgets, he couldn't bench test the engines before races to determine durability. Melcher always worried that something would go wrong. Having left the company that spring, Melcher was not at Spa but heard about the result over the radio.

In taking a break from AMG, Melcher studied industrial design for two semesters at Wuppertal in his native Rhineland. He returned to AMG as a contractor and later set up his own company MKB Manufaktur in Burgstall. He continued his collaboration with Aufrecht and AMG developing a four-valve head for the V-8 engines, four- and six-cylinder engines used in DTM racing, and an engine that was used in Formula 3 racing.

By the time Melcher resumed his collaboration with AMG, Mercedes had introduced a new model that would become a mainstay in the tuner's catalog for nearly two decades. The R/C107 roadster and coupe successor to the 280 SL were introduced in 1971 and AMG immediately set about offering performance upgrades.

Based on the Stroke-8 platform, the 350 SL two-seat roadster had a folding cloth top or a removable hardtop while the 350 SLC was a four-place coupe riding on a 111-inch wheelbase (2.8 m), about 4 inches (10 cm) longer than the roadster. Erich Waxenberger's dream of adapting V-8 power to the SL chassis came true with the R/C107, which now sported Mercedes' M116 3.5-liter engine. AMG revisions to the heads and cams would boost output from 215 to 240 hp.

In 1974 the M110 inline-six would bow in the 280 SL and SLC and AMG would bring a modest gain of 15 horses to reach 192 hp with minor adjustments to the injection system and new cams. A higher output modification used reworked heads, which pushed output to 207 hp. The top tier featured 222 hp via refined combustion chamber profiles as well as extensive modification to the exhaust.

AMG continued to offer modifications on the M116 V-8 as it grew to 3.8 liters in displacement through 1985 as well as on the M117 V-8 through its various iterations that ranged from its initial 4.5 liters up to 5.4 liters in displacement. Among these models are the AMG 450 SL/SLC, 450 SL/SLC 5.0, and the AMG 500 SL/SLC, which was produced from 1980 to 1989. AMG built a 5.0-liter

R EK 310
M AA 3506

version of the SLC coupe in 1980–1981 as well as 5.2- and 5.4-liter versions of the 500 SL roadster from 1980 to 1985.

The other major development at the time was the introduction of the W116 successor to the W108/109, which had put AMG on the map. This new flagship sedan was the first to officially carry the S-Class designation for Mercedes when it was introduced in 1972.

The new S-Class would be the last car rendered by Friedrich Geiger, who had started his career at Mercedes in 1933 and designed the legendary 540K. The S-Class featured a sleeker shape defined by strong character lines, plus the squat grille and horizontally oriented headlamps introduced with the R/C107 roadsters and coupe. It was initially offered with two variants of the M110 2.8-liter inline-six, carbureted in the 280 S and fuel-injected in the 280 SE, and the M116 3.5-liter V-8 in the 350 SE.

Modifications by AMG boosted the dual-carburetor inline-six to about 175 hp, almost on par with the injected version. The injected 2.8-liter powerplant would see its output increase from about 180 hp to as much as 230 hp after a visit to Burgstall. Similarly, the M116 V-8 could be boosted from 200 to 235 hp, though those conversions were rare.

Instead AMG saw more of the M117 4.5-liter V-8 models that started to appear in 1973. AMG was able to increase output from 222 to 280 hp. Of course, that work came at a price, about $4,500 over the cost of the car.

History would soon repeat itself, as Mercedes dusted off the M100 V-8 with its 6.8-liter displacement and put it beneath the hood of a long-wheelbase version of the S-Class in 1975. This new model, christened the 450 SEL 6.9, would gain 60 hp with AMG tuning, jumping from 286 to 346 hp.

Both the improvements by Mercedes and AMG came at a considerable price. The standard S-Class featured a hydro-pneumatic suspension and dry-sump engine lubrication, advancements that helped push the US price to nearly $40,000 when the car finally hit our shores in 1977. The average car at the time cost $5,813. If you add that to the 450 SEL 6.9 sticker, you'd have the all-in price of an AMG conversion.

AMG used this period to concentrate on road cars because changes in touring car rules had all but sidelined the efforts to race large displacement sedans like the Red Pig. So Aufrecht began to cast about for other alternatives to keep the motorsports flame kindled at AMG. The Interserie formula was created in 1970 as a European version of

OPPOSITE, TOP Replacing the venerable Pagoda, the R/C107 SL Roadster and SLC Coupe presented additional opportunities for AMG. When these models were introduced in 1971, AMG offered enhanced versions of the base 2.8-liter inline-six as well as pumped up the four V-8s of 3.5, 3.8, 4.5, and 5.0 liters over a fourteen-year run.

OPPOSITE, BOTTOM The SLC Coupe not only was a 2+2 Grand Tourer, but it also would be successfully campaigned in both rallying by the factory and in several touring car races by AMG.

TOP LEFT The successor to the W108, the basis of AMG's claim to fame in the Red Pig, was the W116, which was the first model to officially carry the S-Class banner.

TOP RIGHT AMG now had the top of Mercedes' range covered by offering packages for the SE and SEL sedans and the SL and SLC roadster and coupe.

ABOVE The M117 4.5-liter V-8 had its intake enlarged and new cams fitted by AMG to increase output to 280 hp.

TOP Echoing the previous generation 300 SEL 6.8, the M100 V-8 was used in the W116 to create the 450 SEL 6.9. AMG would coax 346 horsepower out of the engine.

SECOND FROM TOP AMG dabbled briefly with the idea of competing in the European Interserie, an analog to the North American Can-Am Challenge, with a McLaren M8F fitted with an M100 V-8. It's shown here sitting outside the Burgstall garage. However, Melcher's attempt to coax more than 600 horsepower paled in comparison to what Porsche extracted from its 917. As a result, the project was shelved.

THIRD FROM TOP Albert Pfuhl, who had been a patron of AMG, ended his relationship after a dispute over who would pay for crash damage involving his potential Interserie entry. Waxenberger took Pfuhl (left) under his wing, letting him drive for the factory's rally program. In this 1978 photo, Daimler-Benz CEO Joachim Zahn (center with glasses) and board member Werner Breitschwerdt (left) attended a reception celebrating a race success. The pair would pull the plug on the rally program two years later.

BOTTOM Friedrich Aufrecht is shown here building a race engine by himself, much in the same way upgraded engines were built for customer cars. This image is on the wall in Affalterbach where AMG engines are individually assembled by one technician.

North America's CanAm Challenge series. According to *Mercedes-Fans*, Albert Pfuhl had a Lola T70 that was outfitted with an AMG V-8; however, it crashed in testing. A dispute over repairs led to Pfuhl falling out with his longtime supplier of performance vehicles.

Aufrecht then purchased a McLaren M8F for the 1972 season and replaced its big-block Chevrolet engine with an M100 6.8-liter V-8. Hearing that the Porsche 917-10 would have a turbocharged flat-twelve making upward of 1,000 hp, Melcher began experimenting with turbo boost on the V-8. The first, a triple turbo setup, was abandoned in favor of a single unit. But even then, running it at constant boost, the unit could only generate 0.5 bar of pressure, compared to the 1.5 bar of the Porsche. The engine fell far short of its goal of producing 600 hp. Reverting to the 6.3-liter in normally aspirated form, Melcher was able to coax 500 hp from the engine, but that was still far short of the power needed in order to be competitive. After AMG failed to get the car prepared for a race at the Nürburgring and then logging DNFs at Imola and Silverstone, the AMG McLaren M8F project was shelved.

AMG wouldn't build another race car until later in the decade. Change was coming to the auto industry that would soon alter the course of AMG's business. With stricter fuel economy and emissions regulations, manufacturers were focused more on cleaner, more efficient engines rather than outright performance. It would be left to the independent tuners to provide a boost not just in speed, but also handling. And not only did the finished product have to go faster, but it would also have to look the part.

One Man, One Engine Today

ERHARD MELCHER'S SOLITARY APPROACH to developing engines could be viewed as the foundation of the One Man, One Engine philosophy. In reality, the small size of the operation in its initial stages and the number of different engine upgrades precluded the use of mass assembly. It was just simpler to have one mechanic work on one engine at a time.

Overseeing the engine shop was another Aufrecht, Hans Werner's brother, Friedrich, who spent his entire career at AMG building engines for race and road cars. Visitors to the engine assembly building at AMG are greeted by two large images on the wall. One shows the assembly of a current four-cylinder engine by technician Daniel Brysch. The other is Friedrich, putting together an M110 I6 in the 1980s.

Today AMG builds its M177/176 4.0-liter biturbo V-8 on the first floor of this modern 107,000-square-foot facility, while on the second floor, technicians assemble the M139 turbo inline-four. Off in the corner, one master engine builder, Michael Kübler, crafts V-12 engines for Pagani. It takes Kübler three to four days to produce an engine for the Italian exotic.

V-12 engines, no longer used in AMG-badged products, but still appearing in the S-Class and Maybach models, had their assembly moved to a Mannheim plant in 2019 to make room for the four-cylinder operation. Other engines used by AMG, including the M260/264 2.0-liter inline-four, the M256 3.0-liter inline-six, and the M276 3.0-liter V-6, are produced in Mercedes-Benz engine factories.

continued

About 300 workers employed on three shifts operate around the clock, five days a week. It's still called One Man, One Engine, but currently there are two women who worked through the ranks of engine builders to become line supervisors, and another assembles engines.

The technicians move their engine-stand carts along a U-shaped track as they add components to complete their individual build. But there are key differences in the V-8 and inline-four engine processes. The V-8 line is more old school with the workers stopping at various stations where they select components, scan them into the system, and use one of 400 torque wrenches and tools hanging from the ceiling to bolt things together.

In addition to the nineteen different stations, there are five test areas along the line that check for leaks in both the cooling and lubrication systems as well as other scans that ensure quality as part of the AMG Trace program that tracks both the components and the assembly process.

Following along the line, you can see this blend of modern technology and hand-built craftsmanship as technicians scan in various codes and also use their feel to correctly position pistons in the cylinder or toss a bolt that doesn't seem to be properly taking the torque from a power wrench. One of the most labor-intensive parts of the process is installing the wiring. Looking like an octopus, the harness is carefully spread open by the technician who connects the 180 wires using seventy clips.

After all the tests, including a cold-cranking operating that takes the engine up to 1,000 rpm, the final element is added: an AMG badge with the signature of the person who built it. It takes between three and four hours to produce an engine, roughly two per day per shift. If it's not done, the engine is covered and pushed off to the side for completion by the same worker the next day.

Upstairs, the M139 four-cylinder engine process is similar but with some rather significant upgrades. Instead of the 400 wrenches and tools hanging from the ceiling at stations around the line, the cart on which the engine is being built is equipped with changeable power tools. All the components are prescanned and put into an automated bin that follows along.

There are test stations along the track, some combining several operations, such as leak detection in the crankcase and cooling system. Even though the four-cylinder has over 700 parts, nearly double the number used to put together the V-8, workers can assemble an engine in two-and-a-half to three hours. Also, there are two variations on the engine, the 416-hp version for transverse applications and the more powerful 469-hp longitudinal-mounted unit used in the GT and C 63.

Outside the assembly hall is a wall showing the pride and passion of AMG in its work there. Samples of all the individual signed badges of all the employees who ever worked the line are displayed. The top row includes plates with black background designating the master craftsmen charged with building the engines powering the iconic Black Series models.

While AMG has been modifying engines since 1967 and building complete engines when it was designated a manufacturer in 1984, the recognition of afforded by these signed plates dates back only to 2002. Since then, it has grown to be one of the defining features of the brand.

AMG
AMG

5

FROM BURGSTALL TO AFFALTERBACH

THE OLD MILL HAD OUTLIVED ITS PURPOSE. With the business ever expanding, AMG needed larger quarters to house its growing team of employees. The range of services offered by the company also figured into the equation.

No longer were customers looking solely for a boost in power. They were coming to AMG to seek out better handling with new suspension components, more stopping power with larger brakes, and better grip with larger wheels, tires, and even aerodynamic body kits. In addition to these hardware upgrades, these clients were also seeking a higher level of customization that required paint booths and upholstery facilities.

From the earliest of days, Aufrecht was often quoted as saying, "You can't really improve a Mercedes, but you can make it different." Focusing on the looks of the car became inevitable in AMG's evolution.

Making many of the vehicles in the Mercedes-Benz lineup "different" through body kits, custom wheels, and paint and personalized interiors opened up an entirely new dimension for the company. And it dovetailed neatly with the burgeoning trend in the 1970s of the Euro Look.

Much of that look came from tuners such as AMG, as well as Alpina and Schnitzer doing BMWs, Cosworth with Ford, and Steinmetz at Opel. All were involved in motorsports one way or another. Their modifications included stripping the cars down to lighten them. That included removing excessive chrome, lowering the bodies, fitting larger wheels and tires, beefing up suspensions and brakes, and adding chin spoilers and rear wings. Racing was the driving force behind the Euro Look and customers wanted it for their road cars.

These changes tended to be more understated in their execution as opposed to the American aftermarket, where much of the influences grew out of drag racing. These more extroverted creations in the United States sported jacked-up rear ends, unmuffled side pipes, and wild paint jobs.

German tuners, such as AMG, preferred to fly under the radar so as not to attract the attention of the authorities. Not only did the cars have to pass rigorous vehicle inspections to be licensed, but aftermarket parts also needed government approval.

Aufrecht told *Car and Driver* that "[f]rom 1967 to 1977, we did only engine and suspension development, so we are coming from the *Technik* way . . . we have always been involved in racing. The important thing is that we are always coming from the sports and *Technik* way and we show it at the track."

But as the business grew, the move to Affalterbach allowed AMG to expand its catalog of offerings. Aufrecht said, "In the mid-1970s, we increasingly got requests that customers wanted exterior modification in addition to technology, and we met them. We do the whole car; we make the *Technik*, the *Optik* [meaning exterior appearance packages] and also the interior."

To get to that point, however, required some additional paperwork. "In the 1970s, the law required a certificate of safety from the car manufacturer in order to, for example, approve wider wheels," Aufrecht said in *AMG at 45*. "Mercedes-Benz didn't want to officially support this for various reasons, even though many Daimler employees would have been happy to help us. We

needed to find another way to get government approval, and in 1977, we found one. Some aluminum wheels met with regulation approval and were being accepted for the first time: Porsche wheels, 7.5 × 15, that we had modified with a different pitch circle. We used low-profile tires on them, and these were a big success as an accessory. We then received official approval for body accessories. That meant that we had broken through on development and from then on, we were earning enough money to expand AMG."

If Burgstall was off the beaten path, Affalterbach is a bit more findable, though it's still a small town in the middle of farms and orchards. Aufrecht landed on a small industrial building that offered more working space than the mill. Better still, there was room to grow the operation. The original workshop has since become part of a small complex with a courtyard that has a showroom and a private lounge upstairs for clients.

The corrugated walls of the original building were painted a rust color. The corrugated pattern remains on it, as well as on all the new buildings, but they are now painted silver in keeping with Mercedes-AMG branding. Affalterbach remains a small close-knit community of about 4,000 residents. Until recently, the town didn't even have a hotel. Most of the workers would come from the surrounding communities or from Stuttgart itself, some 15 miles (24 km) south.

The new setting added a new sense of legitimacy for the concern, while the rural nature also allowed Aufrecht's wife Rosie and daughter to keep and maintain horses. There's still an equestrian facility that borders the AMG complex. There is also a strong sense of family that goes back generations to when about forty employees moved from Burgstall to the new facility.

Moving to Affalterbach in 1976 could not come soon enough, for the European market for aftermarket conversions was exploding. A slew of German muscle cars began to appear on the Autobahn with monochromatic paint schemes, alloy wheels shod with low-profile tires, road-hugging ride heights, and all manner of driving lights, wings, and spoilers. A whole new category of performance upgrades was born and was about to expand worldwide.

At Affalterbach, AMG would utilize the larger facilities to boost the performance and handling of customer cars by installing engine kits and suspension pieces. Clients also were offered exterior appearance upgrades and personalized cabin treatments. And these modifications would be applied to a much wider range of Mercedes-Benz vehicles. Two major introductions in the decade, the W123 successor to the Stroke-8 and the W126 replacement for the W116 S-Class, would become mainstays in the AMG catalog.

The new midsize W123 Mercedes would improve upon the trailing link rear suspension of the previous model by adding a double-wishbone front independent setup. Engines, for the most part, carried over. But new body styles were added after the sedan bowed in 1976. The following spring, there would be a coupe, and that fall, the first factory-built wagons in the T series debuted at the

PREVIOUS Embracing the monochromatic Euro look, the W123 sedan with the full AMG treatment includes body-colored bumpers and wheels which contrast with the blacked-out moldings and grille.

TOP LEFT After the move to Affalterbach, AMG began to offer a wide range of both performance and appearance upgrades.

TOP RIGHT AMG's new home provided the additional space needed to install engine and suspension kits, customize interiors, and add aerodynamic body bits.

ABOVE Nothing was out of the question when it came to exterior treatments as this gussied-up G-Wagen shows.

OPPOSITE This early, rather crude brochure tells the AMG story highlighting both its Burgstall operation and the new facilities in Affalterbach. The old mill was still used to build racing engines.

IAA show in Frankfurt. Proving to be one of the most popular Mercedes models, some 2.7 million W123s were built over the nine-year production run that ended in 1985.

While the engines were similar to previous models, the calibration wasn't quite the same, as Mercedes had begun the transition to using unleaded fuel. AMG likewise had to go back to the drawing board to find additional power in the M110 inline-six. It did so by reworking the heads to change the combustion chamber profile, thereby increasing the compression ratio to 9.0:1. Other changes included redesigned camshafts, lighter cam followers and porting, and polishing of the intake and exhaust manifolds. The result was 205 hp, a net gain of 28 from the stock M110. AMG further enhanced its performance by offering a five-speed Getrag manual gearbox.

AMG also built a limited number of 280 E sedans with the M116 4.5-liter V-8. These rare cars were rated at 217 hp and were equipped with four-speed manual transmissions. The price of the engine conversion alone was $40,000 compared to the $16,000 for a complete engine and suspension upgrade on an M110-powered model.

Mercedes would add to an engine lineup that had as its base unit the 2.3-liter M102: the new M123 2.5-liter inline-six positioned just below the 2.8-liter M110. Customers could opt for varying levels of performance upgrades from as little as 15 hp with new cams installed in as quickly as one day to more involved modifications that included revamped heads, freer breathing intake systems, and less restrictive exhausts. The M102 was offered on sedans, coupes, and wagons, as was the M110. The new M123 kit was available on the sedans and wagons only.

While Melcher was no fan of four-cylinder engines, much less diesels, in his absence AMG had developed modifications for the OM115 four-cylinder turbo diesel and the larger OM116 inline five-cylinder oil-burner. The standard 240 D would go from 65 to 100 hp, while the five-cylinder would see a 40 hp gain to 120. Torque would increase from 127 to 188 lb-ft. The diesels were offered on the W/S123 sedans and wagons.

The *AMG at 45* history relates that "these transformations could be further extended by means of a sport suspension that included lowering the vehicle height by 30 millimeters [1 inch], a sweeping spoiler look, and small but dignified details in the interior such as the more manageable leather-covered steering wheel. Whoever wished to do so could even replace the standard

Wer ist AMG?

Hans Werner Aufrecht

Die drei Buchstaben AMG stehen seit dem Jahre 1967, dem Gründungsjahr des Unternehmens für **A** wie Hans-Werner Aufrecht, **M** wie Erhard Melcher, der frühere Geschäftspartner und **G** für Großaspach, den Geburtsort Hans-Werner Aufrechts. Angefangen hatte alles in einer alten Mühle im württembergischen Burgstall, wo das Unternehmen bis 1976 seinen Sitz hatte.

Start in der alten Mühle, Burgstall
As it was in the beginning – the old mill in Burgstall
Début dans le vieux moulin de Burgstall

Seit 16 Jahren also befaßt sich AMG ausschließlich mit der Veränderung von Fahrzeugen aus dem Hause Daimler Benz. Aufgrund des großen Kundeninteresses hat sich die Firma – vor allem in den vergangenen 5 Jahren – von einem kleineren Tuningbetrieb zu einem mittelständischen Unternehmen entwickelt, das heute weltweit arbeitet. Neben Stützpunkten in der Bundesrepublik Deutschland bestehen Vertretungen im europäischen Ausland (Schweiz, Österreich, Großbritannien, Niederlande, Frankreich, Italien, Finnland), in den Golfstaaten, den Vereinigten Staaten von Amerika, Japan, Indien und Indonesien.
Diese Entwicklung ging parallel zur Trennung der Geschäftsinteressen der Partner Aufrecht und Melcher. Während Aufrecht durchaus seine Zukunft in der Ausweitung des jungen Unternehmens sah, wollte sich Melcher seine ihm eigene Individualität bewahren. 1970 kam es zur Trennung in aller Freundschaft. Und Erhard Melcher ist der AMG heute als freier Mitarbeiter und Lieferant von Nockenwellen verbunden.

What is AMG?

AMG was founded in 1967. What do these three letters stand for? **A** is for Hans-Werner Aufrecht, **M** is for Erhard Melcher, his former partner and **G** is for Großaspach, where Hans-Werner Aufrecht was born. It all began in an old mill in the Württemberg village of Burgstall, where the company was located until 1976.

AMG's sole activity for the past 16 years has been modifying Daimler Benz vehicles. As a result of the great interest shown by customers, the company has – particularly in the past 5 years – developed from a small tuning workshop to a medium sized company which today operates throughout the world. Along with bases in the Federal Republic of Germany, there are agencies in other European countries, (Switzerland, Austria, Great Britain, Holland, France, Italy, Finland), in the Gulf States, the USA, Japan, India and Indonesia.
At the same time as this development was taking place, the business interests of the two partners Aufrecht and Melcher followed different paths. Whilst Aufrecht saw his future in the expansion of the young company, Melcher wanted to preserve his own individuality. In 1970, the two partners separated on the best of terms. And today, Erhard Melcher is still connected with AMG on a free-lance basis and as a supplier of camshafts.

Qui est AMG?

Les trois initiales AMG représentent, depuis l'année 1967, l'abréviation de trois noms: **A** pour Hans-Werner Aufrecht, **M** pour Erhard Melcher, l'ancien partenaire commercial, et **G** pour Grossaspach, le lieu de naissance de Hans-Werner Aufrecht. Le tout débuta dans un vieux moulin de la commune wurtembergeoise de Burgstall, où l'entreprise avait son siège jusqu'en 1976.

AGM s'occupe donc exclusivement, depuis 16 ans, de la modification des voitures de marque Mercèdes Benz. En raison du vif intérêt présenté par la clientèle, la firme se transforma, surtout au cours des 5 dernières années, du petit atelier d'adaption en une entreprise de classe moyenne travaillant aujourd'hui à l'échelle mondiale. En plus de bases disséminées en République Fédérale d'Allemagne, elle possède des agences en Europe (Suisse, Autriche, Grande-Bretagne, Pays-Bas, France, Italie, Finlande), dans les Etats du Golf, aux Etat-Unis d'Amérique, Japon, Inde et Indonése.
Cette évolution se réalisa parallèlement avec la séparation des intérêts des partenaires Aufrecht et Melcher. Tandis qu'Aufrecht considérait que l'avenir résidait dans l'extension de la jeune entreprise, Melcher désirait conserver sa propre individualité. On se sépara donc en toute amitié, au cours de l'année 1970. Et Erhard Melcher entretient toujours d'excellentes relations avec AMG, par sa collaboration libre et comme fournisseur d'arbres à cames.

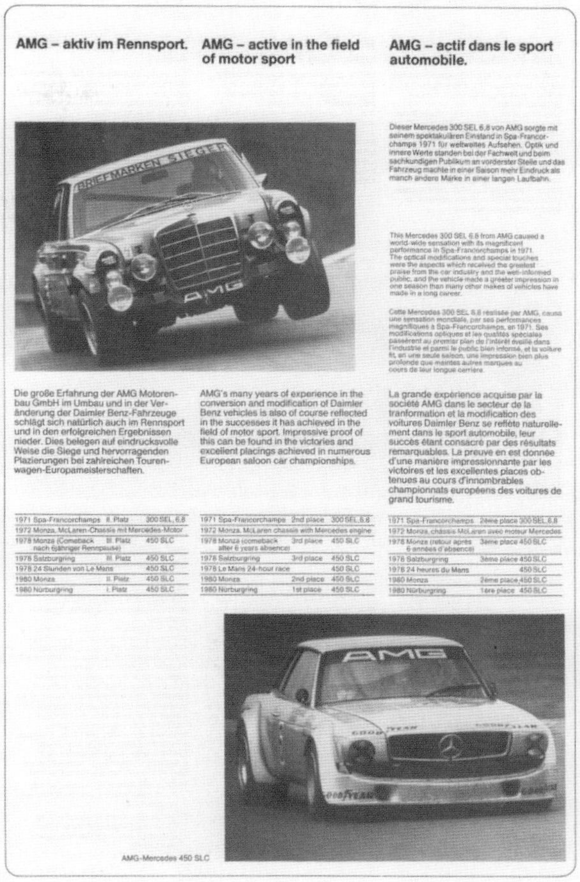

AMG – aktiv im Rennsport.

Dieser Mercedes 300 SEL 6,8 von AMG sorgte mit seinem spektakulären Einstand in Spa-Francorchamps 1971 für weltweites Aufsehen. Optik und innere Werte standen bei der Fachwelt und beim sachkundigen Publikum an vorderster Stelle und das Fahrzeug machte in einer Saison mehr Eindruck als manch andere Marke in einer langen Laufbahn.

Die große Erfahrung der AMG Motorenbau GmbH im Umbau und in der Veränderung der Daimler Benz-Fahrzeuge schlägt sich natürlich auch im Rennsport und in den erfolgreichen Ergebnissen nieder. Dies belegen auf eindrucksvolle Weise die Siege und hervorragenden Plazierungen bei zahlreichen Tourenwagen-Europameisterschaften.

1971 Spa-Francorchamps	II. Platz	300 SEL, 6.8
1972 Monza, McLaren-Chassis mit Mercedes-Motor		
1978 Monza (Comeback nach 6jähriger Rennpause)	III. Platz	450 SLC
1978 Salzburgring	III. Platz	450 SLC
1978 24 Stunden von Le Mans		450 SLC
1980 Monza	II. Platz	450 SLC
1980 Nürburgring	I. Platz	450 SLC

AMG – active in the field of motor sport

This Mercedes 300 SEL 6.8 from AMG caused a world-wide sensation with its magnificent performance in Spa-Francorchamps in 1971. The optical modifications and special touches were the aspects which received the greatest praise from the car industry and the well-informed public, and the vehicle made a greater impression in one season than many other makes of vehicles have made in a long career.

AMG's many years of experience in the conversion and modification of Daimler Benz vehicles is also of course reflected in the successes it has achieved in the field of motor sport. Impressive proof of this can be found in the victories and excellent placings achieved in numerous European saloon car championships.

1971 Spa-Francorchamps	2nd place	300 SEL 6.8
1972 Monza, McLaren chassis with Mercedes engine		
1978 Monza (comeback after 6 years absence)	3rd place	450 SLC
1978 Salzburgring	3rd place	450 SLC
1978 Le Mans 24-hour race		450 SLC
1980 Monza	2nd place	450 SLC
1980 Nürburgring	1st place	450 SLC

AMG – actif dans le sport automobile.

Cette Mercedes 300 SEL 6.8 réalisée par AMG, causa une sensation mondiale, par ses performances magnifiques à Spa-Francorchamps, en 1971. Ses modifications optiques et les qualités speciales passèrent au premier plan de l'intérêt éveillé dans l'industrie et parmi le public bien informé, et la voiture fit, en une seule saison, une impression bien plus profonde que maintes autres marques au cours de leur longue carrière.

La grande expérience acquise par la société AMG dans le secteur de la tranformation et la modification des voitures Daimler Benz se reflète naturellement dans le sport automobile, leur succès étant consacré par des résultats remarquables. La preuve en est donnée d'une manière impressionnante par les victoires et les excellentes places obtenues au cours d'innombrables championnats européens des voitures de grand tourisme.

1971 Spa-Francorchamps	2ème place	300 SEL 6.8
1972 Monza, châssis McLaren avec moteur Mercedes		
1978 Monza (retour après 6 années d'absence)	3ème place	450 SLC
1978 Salzburgring	3ème place	450 SLC
1978 24 heures du Mans		450 SLC
1980 Monza	2ème place	450 SLC
1980 Nürburgring	1ère place	450 SLC

AMG-Mercedes 450 SLC

Wer sind die AMG-Kunden?

AMG-Kunden sind immer Individualisten, denen gemeinsam ist, ihre anspruchsvollen Forderungen an ein Automobil erfüllt zu sehen.
Dies sind einmal Menschen, die in ihren Berufen außerordentlich aktiv sind und Außergewöhnliches leisten. Stark engagierte Leute mit einer überdurchschnittlichen Vorliebe zur Individualität und der Neigung ihrer Selbstverwirklichung auch im sportlichen Umgang mit einem exclusiven Automobil zu finden. Und schließlich und selbstverständlich selbständige Unternehmer, die sich ein teures Auto leisten wollen und können.

Who are AMG's customers?

AMG's customers are always individualists and have one thing in common – they desire to see the high demands they make of a car fulfilled.
They are people who lead a very active and successful professional life. People devoted to their work who have a distinct preference for individuality and who get a great deal of satisfaction from driving a sporty exclusive car. And, of course, people with their own businesses who desire and can afford an expensive car.

Qui sont les clients de AMG?

Les clients de AMG sont tous des individualistes, qui ont une caractéristique commune – ils désirent voir concrétiser leurs exigences sévères posées à une voiture de grande classe.
Il s'agit ici de personnes très actives, qui obtiennent un grand succès au cours de leurs occupations professionnelles. Des personnes très engagées, avec une préférence marquée pour l'individalité et une tendance prononcée à la joie de posséder une voiture sportive exclusive. Et enfin bien entendu des entrepreneurs qui désirent et peuvent se permettre d'acheter une voiture luxueuse.

AMG-Mercedes-Tuning heute in Affalterbach
AMG Mercedes tuning today in Affalterbach
AMG-Mercedes Tuning aujourd'hui, à Affalterbach.

Was und wie verändert AMG an Daimler-Benz-Automobilen?

Waren es bis 1974 hauptsächlich technische Veränderungen wie Motor- und Fahrwerk-Verbesserungen, kamen ab 1974 mehr und mehr auch optische Akzente hinzu.
So verändert AMG den Wünschen entsprechend – ästhetische und technische Vernunft vorausgesetzt – letztlich all das, was der Kunde verändert sehen möchte. Aufgrund der langjährigen Erfahrung mit Daimler-Benz-Fahrzeugen (Hans-Werner Aufrecht war vor seiner Selbständigkeit im Hause Daimler Benz tätig) besitzt AMG ein technisches Know how, das es rechtfertigt, sich mit derartig umfassenden, ja auch ausgefallenen Kundenwünschen zu befassen, sie in Angriff zu nehmen und zur vollen Zufriedenheit zu erfüllen.
Im wesentlichen setzt sich die Aufgabenbreite aus zwei Sachgebieten, die allesamt miteinander verbunden werden können, zusammen:

1) Technische Veränderungen im Sinne gesteigerter Fahraktivität;
2) Optische Veränderungen im Sinne einer Individualisierung des Fahrzeuges abgestimmt auf den Eigner bzw. Fahrer;

How does AMG modify Daimler Benz cars?

Up to 1974, AMG carried out mainly technical modifications such as improvements to the engine and chassis. From 1974, however, visual aspects have been steadily increasing in importance.
AMG thus modifies everything that the customer desires changed – provided that this does not go beyond the bounds of aesthetic and technical common sense. As a result of its many years of experience with Daimler Benz vehicles (Hans-Werner Aufrecht was employed at Daimler Benz before setting up his own business), AMG now possesses sufficient technical know-how to justify its work in dealing with customer wishes which are so extensive and sometimes so extravagant and in carrying out the work to the full satisfaction of everyone. AMG's range of services covers two main areas, which can be combined:

1) technical modifications to improve vehicle performance;
2) visual modifications to cater for the individual style of the owner or driver;

Quelles sont les modifications apportées par AMG sur les voitures Daimler-Benz?

Jusqu'en 1974, il s'agissait principalement de modifications apportées sur le moteur et le châssis. A partir de 1974, on y ajouta de plus en plus divers aspects optiques.
C'est ainsi que, répondant à la demande – et à condition de conserver l'esthétique et le bon sens technique –, on modifia pratiquement tout ce que le client voulait modifier. En raison de sa longue expérience acquise avec les voitures Daimler-Benz (Hans-Werner Aufrecht travaillait chez Daimler-Benz, avant de se mettre à son compte), AMG possède un "savoir faire" technique qui l'autorise à répondre à de tels voeux de transformation si étendus, voir même étranges, à l'entière satisfaction de ses clients. AMG s'occupe essentiellement de 2 domaines d'activités qui peuvent cependant être combinés les uns aux autres:

1) les modifications techniques en vue d'une augmentation des performances de conduite;
2) des modifications optiques en vue d'une individualisation de la voiture, adaptée à son propriétaire ou à son conducteur;

Die Möglichkeiten der unter 1) und 2) genannten technischen und optischen Veränderungen sind derart vielseitig, daß an dieser Stelle auf eine ausführliche Darstellung verzichtet werden muß. Wir übermitteln insoweit beigefügt unseren AMG-Prospekt sowie unser grundsätzliches Fahrzeugveränderungsprogramm. Diese Unterlagen sollen und können nur richtungsmäßig aufzeigen, in welcher Weise wir derartige Veränderungen herbeiführen können. Weiteren und anderen Wünschen sind, wie vorerwähnt, keinerlei Grenzen gesetzt. Bei Durchführung sämtlicher Arbeiten achten wir besonders darauf, daß das vom Hause Daimler Benz bekannte Qualitätsniveau keinesfalls unterschritten wird; wir sind stets bemüht, das Beste und Mögliche zu fertigen und zu liefern. Dabei kommt uns, soweit es die unter 1) aufgeführten technischen Veränderungen betrifft, unsere langjährige Rennerfahrung zustatten. Wir sind bestrebt, sämtliche Fahrzeugumbauten mit Allgemeiner Betriebserlaubnis bzw. TÜV-Gutachten anzubieten. Vor der Prüfung durch den TÜV haben wir diese Teile und Umbauten selbst ausgiebig getestet, was uns aufgrund einer erteilten Erprobungsausnahmegenehmigung, die uns insoweit mit einem Herstellerwerk gleichstellt, besonders gut möglich ist.

There are so many possible technical and visual modifications that we cannot go into full detail here. However, we enclose our AMG brochure as well as our basic range of vehicle modifications. These documents can only give a brief outline of how we are able to achieve such modifications. As we have already mentioned, as far as other wishes are concerned, the sky's the limit.
In carrying out our work, we always pay particular attention to maintaining the well-known standard of high quality which characterizes Daimler-Benz cars. We always endeavour to supply our customers with the best possible work. Here, as far as the technical modifications mentioned under 1) above are concerned, our many years of experience in the field of motor sport stand us in good stead. We always try to supply all our modified vehicles to meet the appropriate official regulations. Before the vehicles are officially tested, we subject the parts and modifications to stringent tests ourselves. We are able to do this particularly well thanks to the fact that we have been granted exemption from certain test regulations. In this respect, we have the same status as a vehicle manufacturer.

Les possibilités de transformations techniques et optiques signalées selon 1) et 2) sont si variées que nous devons renoncer à en faire une description détaillée dans le cadre du présent exposé. Nous transmettons donc à ce sujet notre prospectus AMG ainsi que notre programme fondamental de modifications apportées aux voitures. Ces documents n'ont pour but que d'indiquer en principe les grandes lignes d'exécution de telles modifications, en soulignant qu'aucune limite n'est posée à d'autres désidérata différents. Au cours de l'exécution de tous les travaux, nous veillons particulièrement à ne pas affaiblir le niveau de qualité bien connu de la maison Daimler Benz; nous nous efforçons toujours de fabriquer et de livrer le meilleur possible. En ce qui concerne les modifications techniques mentionnées selon 1), nous profitons aussi de notre longue expérience des courses automobiles. Nous nous efforçons aussi de proposer toutes les voitures modifiées avec l'autorisation générale de conduite ou avec l'expertise d'agréement du "TÜV" (Service de Surveillance Technique). Avant la vérification par cet organisme, nous procédons à des tests détaillés de ces pièces ou transformations, ce qui nous est possible grâce à l'attribution d'une autorisation exceptionnelle d'essais, qui nous range à pied d'égalité avec un constructeur d'automobiles.

AMG-Prüfstände 1967 u. 1983
AMG test benches in 1967 and 1983
Bancs d'essai AMG en 1967 et 1983

S DY 6121

AMG

S HV 9822

AMG

AMG

4-speed manual transmission with a 5-speed transmission from Getrag—either with a longer (for low-rev economical driving) or shorter (for sporty performance) gear ratio. Indispensable to many was a feature that has long become characteristic of a genuine AMG: the matte-black finish of the chrome components—available for 2,900 DM [about $1,200]."

At the top of the line, the W116 S-Class would be replaced by the W126 variant in 1979, followed in 1981 with the C126 coupe version. The sedans came in both standard and long wheelbase chassis, while the coupe was now based on the S-Class underpinnings, moving from the SL-based C107 platform. Much attention was paid to aerodynamics in the Bruno Sacco design because it was part of a plan to reduce fuel consumption by 10 percent over the previous model.

Four different engines were offered in Europe, the M110 inline-six in carbureted and fuel-injected trim and a choice of 3.8- or 5.0-liter V-8s. Both the respective M116 and M117 engines now had aluminum blocks that did not require steel cylinder liners thanks to a new silicone coating process to combat wear. A turbo diesel model, the 300 SD, also was introduced in 1981 with the 3.0-liter inline five-cylinder engine destined solely for the North American market.

AMG would boost the carbureted M110 to 176 hp and, through various stages of tune, offer up to 230 hp from the fuel-injected version of the inline six. The 3.8-liter V-8 would see an increase from 215 to 253 hp, while the 5.0-liter could be raised from 240 to as much as 295 hp depending on the extent of the modifications. Other upgrades included stiffer springs and shocks, 16-inch (41-cm) alloy wheels, as well as a wide range of spoilers, side skirts, and a rear apron. AMG also offered its signature matte-black finish of chromed accents.

OPPOSITE, TOP Mercedes continued to revamp the lineup introducing its midsize W116 replacement with the sleeker W123.

OPPOSITE, SECOND ROW, LEFT The W126 replacement for the S-Class put even more emphasis on aerodynamics.This look would also influence the W124 successor to the W123.

OPPOSITE, SECOND ROW, RIGHT When Mercedes added a wagon version of the W123, it wasn't long before a full AMG version appeared.

OPPOSITE, THIRD ROW, LEFT The AMG version of the W123 sedan used a black spoiler and window surrounds to contrast with the white paint treatment.

OPPOSITE, THIRD ROW, RIGHT AMG's look also would evolve with the S-Class marking the return of some brightwork on the grille and window surrounds.

OPPOSITE, BOTTOM The W126 SEC coupe, shown here in AMG spec, added a much-needed large two-door positioned between the W123 and the SLC.

ABOVE In the late 1970s, AMG produced a restomod version of the legendary 300 SL using a 4.5-liter variant of the M117 V-8. AMG would produce a limited run of similar cars in the 1980s with 6.0-liter engines, most of which went to the Middle East.

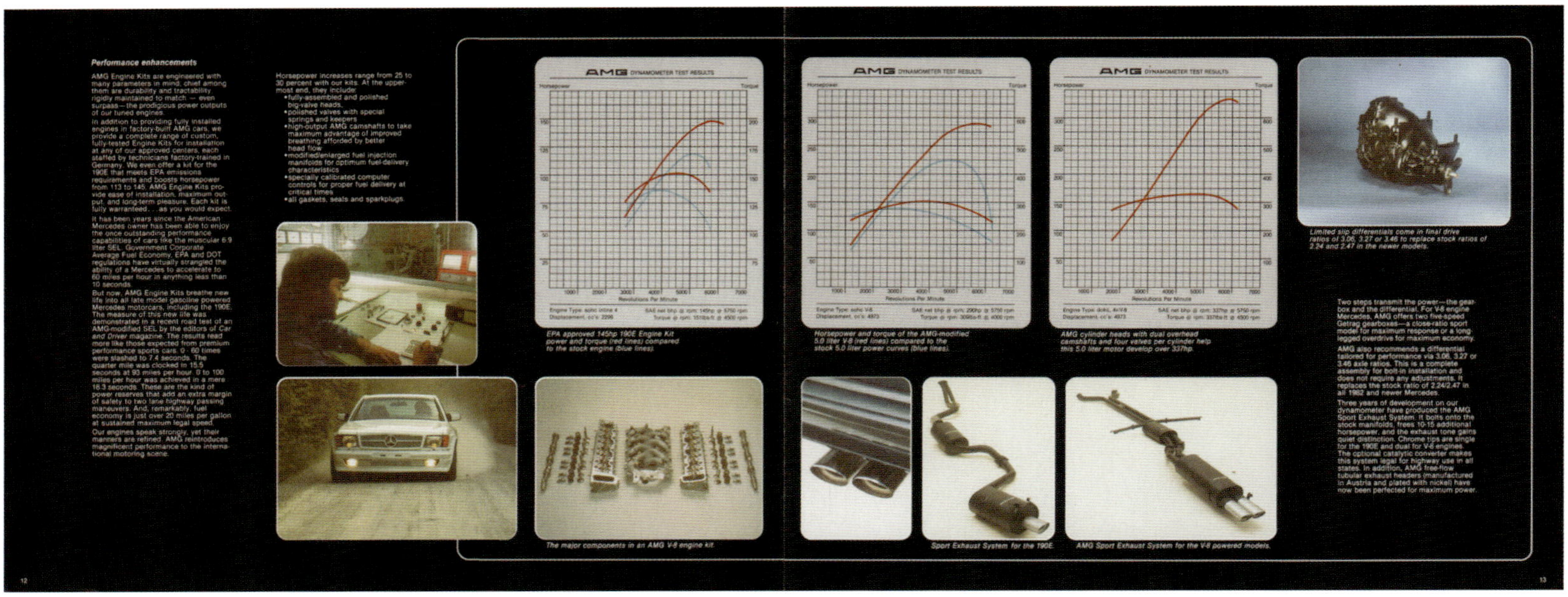

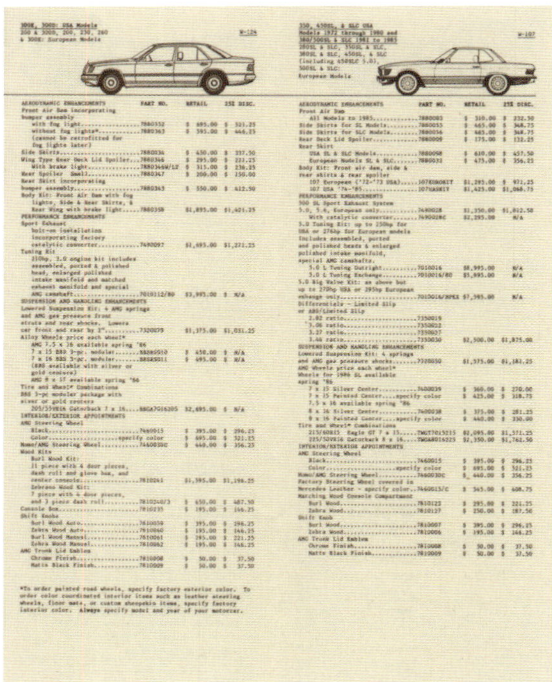

ABOVE Pages from a 1986 brochure go into great detail on what goes into the making of AMG products. The pricing list gives an idea of what these conversions cost.

LEFT The complete range of engine, suspension, and aerodynamic pieces are shown in the 1987 catalog.

OPPOSITE A 1987 brochure shows the metamorphosis of an E-Class from stock to fully modified.

The S-Class coupe became a star in its own right with the help of AMG. The first iterations of the 500 SEC after it launched in 1981 benefitted from an increase in power from 240 to 276 hp. Three years later, AMG would develop a four-valve version of the M117 V-8 pushing output to 340 hp. The new head developed by Melcher not only included doubling the valve count but also the use of dual overhead cams with higher lift and longer duration. These versions also could be equipped with Getrag five-speed manual transmissions. In addition to the stiffer suspension and larger 16-inch [41-cm] wheels, AMG also would outfit the cars with premium ten-speaker audio systems,

AMG: It [illegible] as Good as it Looks!

In 1967, AMG set up shop in an old German mill. The idea was to build special Daimler-Benzes, but the company was tiny and the flow of customers was no more than a trickle. In twenty years, the flow has swelled from a trickle to a flood.

Set in Burgstall in Wuerttemberg, West Germany, the old mill at first saw only two men arrive each morning. Their enterprise was hardly even an idea, barely more than a dream. One man was Hans-Werner Aufrecht, a former Mercedes-Benz development engineer. He was determined to create the fastest Mercedes to be found. His partner was Erhard Melcher. The initials of their last names gave the AMG logo its start, and the first letter of Aufrecht's hometown of Grossbach provided its finish. Melcher has since left AMG, but he still supplies many of its precision engine parts.

Today, the company's blocky three-lettered emblem, still faithfully applied exclusively to cars born under the three-pointed star, is famous around the world in its own right. Even in countries producing fine luxury and performance automobiles of their own, the machines from Daimler-Benz enjoy recognition as the finest automobiles in the world. From AMG's ordinary beginnings, the company dedicated itself to making the best even better.

As each machine—large or small, elegant or sporting—arrives in its owner's hands from Mercedes, each is different. Each calls for a different approach to every area of potential improvement. In essence, each customer calls upon AMG to make the most of a singular perception of a single *Mercedes*—to enhance its nucleus, to polish its strong points, and to alter and solidify its aura.

At AMG, even the sky is no limit. AMG takes pride in having invented and popularized the monochrome look, visually unifying the entire body with a single striking splash of color. Now virtually every builder of production and specialty cars offers similar monochromatic treatments. However, each AMG customer remains free to select almost any combination of inner workings and outer trimmings. Technical practicality remains the only guideline to individual expression.

Daimler-Benz builds no throwaway designs. Every car conceived and designed in the think-tank atmosphere of Daimler-Benz headquarters in Stuttgart, West Germany, is a product of brainpower dedicated to automotive excellence. Every aspect of packaging and performance comes under intense scrutiny. Every test and alteration along the way is dissected and improved many times. Eventually, the first prototype powers past the brainstorming stage. It rises off the drafting tables, flickers from the computer banks, rumbles from the steel foundries, bubbles from the glass and petrochemical laboratories, grows its inner lining in the upholstery shop, and comes together in the assembly center. Finally, the prototype goes on the road. Once gone, it goes endlessly, at first by itself and soon with others something like it, each slightly different as improvements are made, all funneling toward the ultimate realization of the fully evolved goal.

Whatever that goal represented in the beginning and whatever it becomes in the end, one thing never changes—the determination within Daimler-Benz that the end result be as fine as Daimler-Benz can make it. That it be better than the rest. An abstract goal becomes an energetic sculpture in steel and glass and paint and plastic and leather and rubber. This animate sculpture, like every Mercedes, gleams with achievement and honors that tradition incomparable in every human endeavor: to be the best.

And so it is with AMG. With its constant increase in expertise, reputation, and clientele, AMG has bloomed from two employees to almost 150 at the main headquarters alone. Known as AMG Motorenbau und Entwicklungs GmbH, the flourishing company long ago forsook the old mill for an expansive compound in the Swabian village of Affalterbach, near Stuttgart. The only connection with the past remains the Old World skills of the workers, who also embrace the new world of technological advances.

AMG's success brought modern management adept at tapping outside suppliers and serving today's worldwide customer base. Then came a large computerized bookkeeping department. Roomy administration quarters. Space for ever-increasing research and development and durability testing. Spacious parts warehousing for the exclusive product line. Major shop areas organized to handle both prototype and customer work. Pleasant reception and meeting areas. Airy showrooms displaying AMG automobiles and products. And comfortable sales offices for determining details on individual orders.

Whether purchasing from the source in Affalterbach or from one of its distributors around the world, AMG customers take almost as much pleasure in designing their cars and anticipating their completion as in their driving. But in the end, the driving and savoring the result reigns supreme.

Luckily for AMG's chassis and engine tuning, the company headquarters open onto an array of Swabia's most challenging back roads. They curl in a labyrinth through layered hills, forests, and fields, snaking over streams, past lakes, and soon into mountains. The devious terrain and the roads that cling to it so tenaciously quickly reveal any shortcoming in prototype suspensions. Drivetrains must deal with the endlessly changing terrain, powering constantly up and down an extraordinary speed range. Brake units repeatedly bear the brunt of the assault on basic physics. Near Affalterbach lie unlimited autobahns where tremendous speeds are the norm. Safe and efficient aerodynamic aids are critical for high-speed stability and low drag. High engine output and maximum durability are critical to speed and longevity. Engine assemblies must shrug off [illegible]ghest high-rpm challenge as if it were no more than [illegible]yday business—which is precisely what it is in Germany. And doubly so in AMG's neck of the Swabian woods. Even the luxury components crafted for AMG's special interior treatments must meet the company's high standards for functional longevity.

AMG counts itself lucky that the environment that creates the problems lies just beyond its doors. For AMG's work force, there is an equally important advantage to headquartering at the very edge of this scenic and tortuous real-world test area—it keeps the boss happy. When there is driving to be done, Hans-Werner Aufrecht likes getting on the road quickly. To this day, he handles all of AMG's primary development driving, and he makes all AMG decisions regarding vehicle dynamics. His credo, now the company credo: "To make AMG cars feel as good as they look."

Amid the pressures of business, Hans-Werner Aufrecht's road work remains his pleasure. He savors every kilometer rushing beneath him. It is more than a self-indulgence. Working the controls, pressing on with the simultaneous inner joy and analytical detachment of a test pilot delving deep into the recesses of the performance envelope, he takes sensory messages flashing up from his hands and feet and the seat of his pants and stores their subtle magic in his memory bank, folding new insights into the treasury of his experience. So AMG's technical improvements in dynamics unfold at the same pace as Herr Aufrecht's testing: fast.

Always fascinated with outright performance, AMG gloried in racing in its early and middle years, but discontinued competition in 1980 when business began to take more time than racing allowed. By 1986, AMG's larger business staff allowed the company to engineer a return to racing that shook its disbelieving rivals. AMG screamed back to the fore in the viciously contested German Touring Car Championship, winning twice on the daunting fourteen-mile Nurburgring circuit that still threads through the Eifel Mountains and once on the hyperfast Avus loop in West Berlin. As AMG had never forgotten, much of what is learned on the track applies to roadgoing performance as well. And vice-versa.

Every AMG component must pass not only AMG's rigorous testing but the strict requirements of the TUV, West Germany's tough counterpart of the U.S. Department of Transportation and EPA. Components intended specifically for North America are manufactured to satisfy its particular requirements.

The international AMG network encompasses distributors that provide showrooms, installation-and-service centers, and parts-storage warehousing in Austria, Italy, France, Great Britain, Finland, India, the Persian Gulf States, Indonesia, Japan, and the United States.

Since its establishment in 1981, AMG of North America has grown rapidly to encompass a network of dealers in most major metropolitan areas throughout the United States. At AMG

Top to bottom below: a Mercedes 300E in AMG metamorphosis.

Pieces of Eights . . . Sixes and Fours

AMG
3.2 LITRE · 245 hp

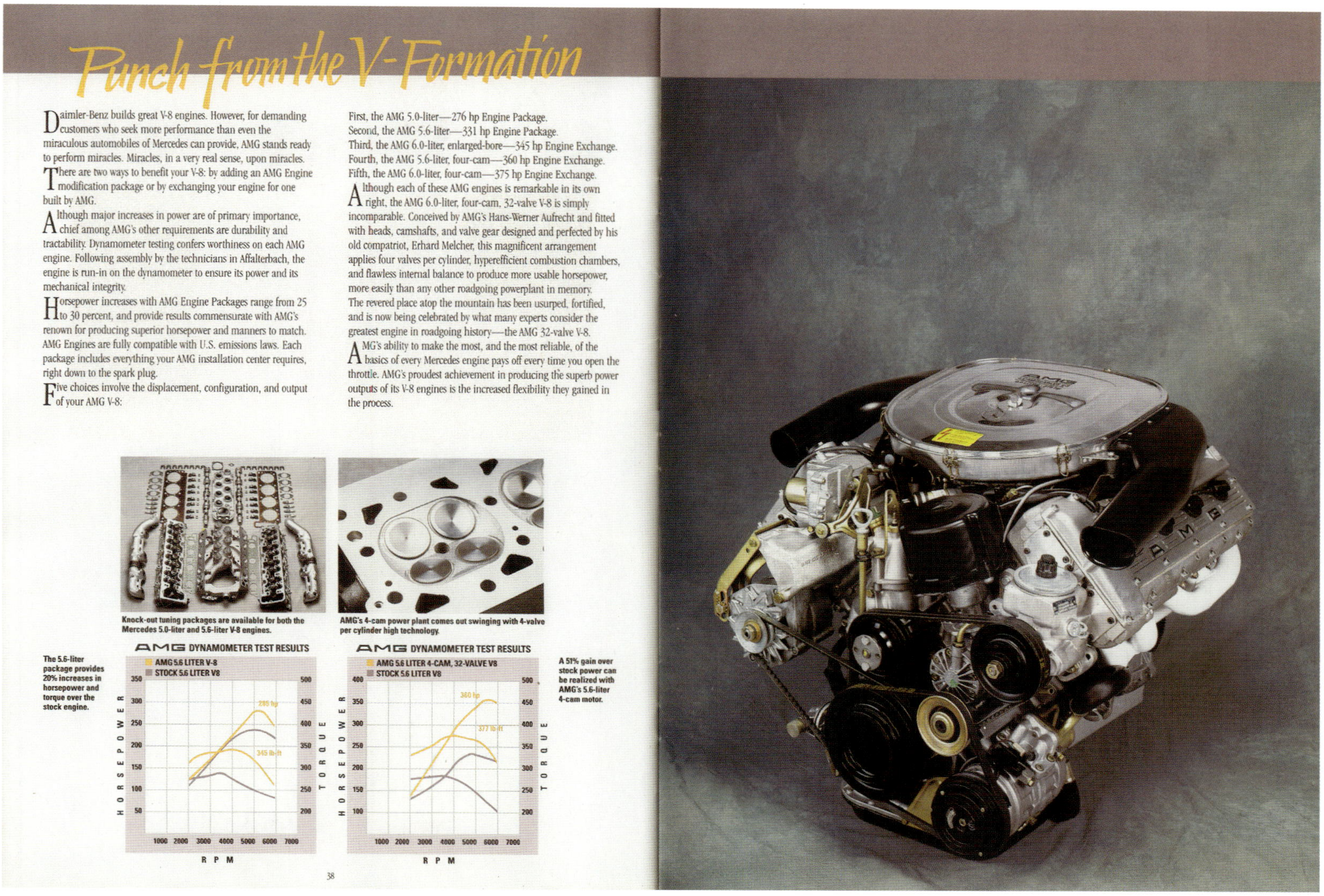

Punch from the V-Formation

Daimler-Benz builds great V-8 engines. However, for demanding customers who seek more performance than even the miraculous automobiles of Mercedes can provide, AMG stands ready to perform miracles. Miracles, in a very real sense, upon miracles.

There are two ways to benefit your V-8: by adding an AMG Engine modification package or by exchanging your engine for one built by AMG.

Although major increases in power are of primary importance, chief among AMG's other requirements are durability and tractability. Dynamometer testing confers worthiness on each AMG engine. Following assembly by the technicians in Affalterbach, the engine is run-in on the dynamometer to ensure its power and its mechanical integrity.

Horsepower increases with AMG Engine Packages range from 25 to 30 percent, and provide results commensurate with AMG's renown for producing superior horsepower and manners to match. AMG Engines are fully compatible with U.S. emissions laws. Each package includes everything your AMG installation center requires, right down to the spark plug.

Five choices involve the displacement, configuration, and output of your AMG V-8:

First, the AMG 5.0-liter—276 hp Engine Package.
Second, the AMG 5.6-liter—331 hp Engine Package.
Third, the AMG 6.0-liter, enlarged-bore—345 hp Engine Exchange.
Fourth, the AMG 5.6-liter, four-cam—360 hp Engine Exchange.
Fifth, the AMG 6.0-liter, four-cam—375 hp Engine Exchange.

Although each of these AMG engines is remarkable in its own right, the AMG 6.0-liter, four-cam, 32-valve V-8 is simply incomparable. Conceived by AMG's Hans-Werner Aufrecht and fitted with heads, camshafts, and valve gear designed and perfected by his old compatriot, Erhard Melcher, this magnificent arrangement applies four valves per cylinder, hyperefficient combustion chambers, and flawless internal balance to produce more usable horsepower, more easily than any other roadgoing powerplant in memory. The revered place atop the mountain has been usurped, fortified, and is now being celebrated by what many experts consider the greatest engine in roadgoing history—the AMG 32-valve V-8.

AMG's ability to make the most, and the most reliable, of the basics of every Mercedes engine pays off every time you open the throttle. AMG's proudest achievement in producing the superb power outputs of its V-8 engines is the increased flexibility they gained in the process.

Knock-out tuning packages are available for both the Mercedes 5.0-liter and 5.6-liter V-8 engines.

AMG's 4-cam power plant comes out swinging with 4-valve per cylinder high technology.

The 5.6-liter package provides 20% increases in horsepower and torque over the stock engine.

A 51% gain over stock power can be realized with AMG's 5.6-liter 4-cam motor.

38

and even a television for the rear seat passengers. The all-in price for the top conversion cost nearly $80,000.

In 1985 Mercedes upped the displacement of the M117 to 5.6 liters, boosting stock output to 300 hp. Still employing only two valves per cylinder, the engine would be tweaked by AMG to produce 320 hp and 367 lb-ft of torque. Bolting on the four-valve heads developed by Melcher took that engine to 360 hp and 376 lb-ft of torque. The next step was to bore the engine out to 6.0 liters. With two valves per cylinder, the AMG tuning resulted in 331 hp and 387 lb-ft of torque. The ultimate tune was fitting the thirty-two-valve dual-overhead cams for 385 hp and 417 lb-ft of torque. Installing this engine in what would become the 560 SEC 6.0 cost around $30,000.

The coupe versions of the W124 and W126 also would add a new dimension to AMG's exterior modifications that moved beyond spoilers by offering wide body kits for the 300 CE and 560 SEL. Only about two dozen of each were built. They featured significantly wider front and rear fender flares to accommodate bigger wheel and tire packages. The modifications gave both a much wider stance and a more aggressive look. Both versions are highly prized premerger collectibles.

The success of AMG as a pioneer in Mercedes tuning is perhaps best captured by author Trevor Legate in *The Ultimate History of Mercedes-Benz*. He wrote, "The company's influence in the aftermarket tuning business was confirmed when no less than 176 exhibitors at the 1981 International Motor Show in Frankfurt tried to follow their lead by announcing themselves as specialist tuners of Mercedes product." From a small, two-man operation working out of an old mill in Burgstall, AMG had grown to become not just a benchmark in tuning, but also would soon become Mercedes-Benz' partner in performance.

OPPOSITE The M103 I6 was bored out from 2.6 to 3.2 liters and offered up to 300 hp in the 190E and 300 E sedans.

ABOVE The M117 V-8 could be specified in either two- or four-valve configurations in 5.6- or 6.0-liter displacements. This is the engine used in the W124 Hammer and the 560/600 SEC AMG.

Wheels of Fortune

IT'S ESTIMATED THAT the global aftermarket-wheel business is worth more than $6 billion. Wheels and tires are one of the first things replaced by car buyers looking to upgrade the look or handling of their vehicles. AMG has been at the forefront of this business, which grew out of the need for improved roadholding to go with the engine upgrades that racing required.

Recall that the Red Pig used wheels cobbled up from the experimental Mercedes C111 prototype. These five-spoke wheels evolved into AMG's "Penta" design, a rim with a pentagon-shaped hub. The Penta name was used originally in 1979 on wheels made by the British firm ATS. The AMG Penta wheels appeared across the entire range of R/C107, W116, W/C/S123, W201, and W/C126 models up through the early versions of the 560 SEC AMG Widebody.

The next big change in wheel design was the more aerodynamic Monoblock. It featured a large face with five slots that gave the appearance of short, fat spokes. The Monoblock Aero I and II also were made by suppliers such as O.Z. and BBS and came in one-, two-, or three-piece configurations. These were the first to carry the AMG logo stamped on the wheel's face.

AMG wheel offerings have expanded to hundreds of designs and finishes, including chrome, brushed or machined aluminum, gloss and matte painted surfaces, and even carbon fiber. Bastian Baudy, head of Mercedes-AMG design, said there is more that goes into the process than just looks. "The performance attitude of these wheels is more than just styling, it's about light weight and brake cooling. These wheels have way more impact on these performance cars than all the other [regular production] cars."

With the advent of the Mercedes-AMG brand, the aftermarket for wheels and other appearance and suspension upgrades has evolved significantly. While customers can order AMG wheels from Mercedes-Benz dealers, the *Optik* or appearance items that Aufrecht used to greatly expand his business is now a trim level from the factory.

Part of this shift can be seen in the AMG logo itself, which at one point acquired several slashes ahead of the lettering. The slashes were adapted from Mercedes' own Sportline trim level that added wheels, exterior aero bits, and sporty interior upgrades.

The Sportline trim level lives on as the AMG Line, which offers a sportier step up from standard vehicle offerings just short of full-on performance modifications done to AMG-specific vehicles in the model range. AMG Line models are distinguished by their diamond-pattern grille treatments, AMG wheels, and chromed exhaust tips. Cabins are fitted with AMG sport seats, a flat-bottom sport steering wheel, aluminum pedals, and AMG-branded floor mats.

The latest twist in AMG Line is the Night Edition package, which is a throwback to the early days of the Euro Look. The package, offered on the C-/E-Class, GLE, and GLC, features blacked-out trim, wheels, and grille, along with the interior upgrades that come with AMG Line trim.

TOP LEFT The original five-spoke wheels on the Red Pig were modified wheels similar to those used on Mercedes' C111 Wankel-powered supercar. The five-spoke look would become an AMG staple. Along the way, the original five-spoke wheels picked up the Penta name from a supplier that made the wheels for AMG.

TOP RIGHT A big change in wheel design debuted with the C 36, the first full collaboration between Mercedes and AMG. The new rims were called Monoblock wheels.

MIDDLE LEFT A variant in AMG wheel design appeared with this six-spoke take used on the EVO II.

MIDDLE RIGHT Many AMG wheel designs still play off the five-spoke theme but have also been joined by new looks that incorporate split-spoke and turbine wheel looks.

BOTTOM Mercedes previously offered appearance packages under the Sportline trim That trim level would be changed to AMG line and the slashes from the Sportline badge incorporated into the AMG logo..

BOSCH
SECA
100
OCTANE
AMG
BILSTEIN

sport

sportLine

AMG

NOKIA
Lohr
DEKRA
6
Wir fahren ab auf
BERLIN
2000
Deutsche Aerospace
AEG
debis
BRIDGESTONE
BAUMLER
International men's fashion
BOSCH
Shell
E. Lohr
MAMPE
MAMPE

6

FROM ROAD BACK TO TRACK

AMG'S BUSINESS THRIVED on its aftermarket performance and appearance upgrades as well as its work in supplying engines to racing teams. It hadn't run a race since 1971, though in 1978 and again in 1980, it did compete in a handful of European Touring Car Championship races, campaigning a 450 SLC.

The best result came in 1980 when Clemens Schickentanz (who co-drove the Red Pig at Spa) teamed with Jörg Denzel to win a four-hour Nürburgring race. Denzel would give Hans Werner Aufrecht pause when he came in from the lead with one lap remaining. According to *touringcarracing.net*, he asked if the champagne had been put in the refrigerator "just in case." Aufrecht admitted, "At first, I wanted to hit him."

After that one-off return to competition, the 1980s would see AMG return to racing in earnest. And unlike the 1971 campaign with the W109 300 SEL equipped with an M100 V-8, AMG would rely on a new compact-class car powered by a four-cylinder engine called the 190 E 2.3-16.

In the wake of a turbulent 1970s, which saw two oil crises, economic upheavals, and a raft of new emission and fuel economy regulations, the auto industry set out on a course of downsizing their passenger cars to address these challenges. The smaller cars would be more fuel efficient, cleaner, and more affordable. Even luxury car makers such as Mercedes-Benz were not immune to this shift in the automotive landscape.

In fact Mercedes started development on its first modern compact-class car in the early 1970s, taking nearly a decade to create the 190. This car proved to be a hit, with over 1.8 million produced over a run that extended from 1982 to 1993. It also would open the door for AMG to become a major player in touring car competition, primarily the Deutsche Toureinwagen Meisterschaft (DTM) series as well as making power packs and other aftermarket performance upgrades for this entry-level Mercedes.

Designed by Bruno Sacco, the W201 190 was a scaled-down version of the upcoming W124 executive class model. The look, which also would migrate to the S-Class, invariably contributed to the "Baby Benz" moniker. The 190 also used the same four-cylinder engine as base E-Class models. The M102 four-banger came in 2.0- and 2.3-liter displacements, the latter 190 E models equipped with Bosch K-Jetronic mechanical fuel injection.

Well before AMG would become involved with the 190, the story takes a turn, across the English Channel to another engine specialist also founded by two men: Cosworth Engineering. Established by Mike Costin and Kevin Duckworth, Cosworth had built a sterling reputation in building racing engines for Formula 1 and IndyCar single-seaters and rally and touring cars, as well as providing performance upgrades for road cars for a wide range of manufacturers.

Mercedes turned to the company to develop a four-valve head for the M102, hoping to use the engine in a rally car variant of the 190. Work had gotten underway to develop an entry to compete in Group B, a new category created by the FIA for both Grand Touring (GT) racing and rallying. The rules were scheduled for implementation in 1982.

The unlimited nature of Group B, which allowed for composite bodies, all-wheel-drive, and turbocharged engine technology proved to be a difficult challenge for the 190, even though the factory had gone as far as building a prototype of a two-door hatchback to better fit the anticipated competition. The normally aspirated rear-drive 190 would be pitted against the likes of the Audi Quattro, Ford RS200, Renault 5 Turbo, Lancia Delta S4, and Peugeot 205 T16, all of which were turbocharged and featured all-wheel drive.

These plans changed dramatically during a December 18, 1980, motorsports reception, a mere four days after the conclusion of the season-ending Ivory Coast Rally, which Mercedes had won. According to Karl Ludvigsen's *Mercedes-Benz Quicksilver Century*, Walter Breitschwerdt, head of Mercedes R&D (which oversaw the competition department), announced that the company would no longer compete in the series. In dropping the bombshell, Breitschwerdt said that at the behest of the board of management, "we have decided to invest our available development capacity completely in research work to meet environmental demands, as a priority and thus are withdrawing from rallying."

This edict went further in that it applied to all motorsport efforts. While top management continued to debate the value of factory-backed competition, engineers continued their clandestine work to develop the new engine. The focus shifted to creating cars that would compete in Group N and Group A, new road racing categories established by the FIA for vehicles that more closely resembled their stock counterparts.

Originally conceived as the Deutschen Produktionswagen Meisterschaft (German Production Car Championship), the new series was organized under Group A rules and launched in 1984. Two years later, its name changed to the Deutsche Toureinwagen Meisterschaft (DTM).

But before racing could begin, the necessary modifications needed to be made to the 190 E production model to incorporate the work by Cosworth on the sixteen-valve head. While Mercedes would not have direct factory involvement in racing, it would produce a competitive car for privateers. In 1983, at the Frankfurt Motor Show, the 190 E 2.3-16 made its debut.

With twin overhead cams and sixteen valves, the revised M102 inline-four made 183 hp and 174 lb-ft of torque compared to the stock eight-valve model's 136 hp and 151 lb-ft of torque. US versions, due to emissions, would be throttled back to 167 hp and 162 lb-ft of torque. The cars also were offered with a new five-speed manual transmission, with so-called "dogleg" shift patterns where first gear was positioned to the left and back.

The changes to the bodywork were subtle yet related to making the car more aerodynamic for the track. The lower front fascia was more upright and featured a chin spoiler. Body-colored side cladding and rocker panels also aided aero efficiency. At the rear, a longer rear fascia and a small trunk-mounted wing contributed to the car's slippery 0.32 coefficient of drag.

Other modifications included stiffer spring and damper settings, quicker steering complemented by a smaller diameter wheel, bolstered sport seating for four, and a larger fuel tank. The center console also was fitted with an oil temp gauge, voltmeter, and stopwatch. All models were offered in just two colors: Blue-Black and Smoke Silver.

Even before the car's auto show debut, Mercedes had made history with the 2.3-16 earlier that summer when it set a raft of speed and distance records at the Nardo test track in Italy. A

PREVIOUS AMG's return to motorsports took the form of this quartet of vehicles developed in the late '70s and through the '80s. They include a 450 SLC (center), an AMG 500 SEC (behind), and two legendary DTM models: the EVO II (left) and C 63 DTM (right).

TOP LEFT Entered in the European Touring Car Championship in 1978 and again in 1980, the AMG 450 SLC had its best showing in the latter attempt, winning a four-hour race at the Nürburgring.

TOP RIGHT Even as AMG busied itself with the W201-based 190 in DTM, it tried but failed to homologate this 500 SEC for Group A competition. It finally saw two races in 1989, but it failed to finish at the Ring and Spa twenty-four-hour races.

Polcirkeln
Napapiiri
Arctic circle
Cercle polaire
Norrbottens län
A CM 836

team of three cars running around the clock set records for covering 50,000 kilometers (31,068 miles) in 201 hours, thirty-nine minutes, and forty-three seconds at a sustained speed of 154.06 mph (248 kph). Other records set included two for covering distances of 25,000 kilometers (15,534 miles) and another for 25,000 miles (40,234 km). There were also nine class records set by the 190 E 2.3-16 sedans.

The first taste of competition came in the 1985 French Production Car Championship. Snobeck Racing Service had switched from Alfa Romeo to the Mercedes 190 E 2.3-16 and won two of the twelve rounds. The following season Mercedes would participate in the DTM. That year, the first 190 E also appeared in the German series fielded by Leopold Gallina with an engine tuned by Hartmann Motorsport. However, Gallina joined the series only over the last three rounds and didn't finish in any of them.

For the 1986 season, Mercedes provided unofficial back-door support to a number of teams. Chief among them was AMG, which supported the RSM Marko team. Volker Weidler won two rounds at the Nürburgring and Avus to bring Mercedes its first victories in the series.

In 1987, with the introduction of the BMW M3 and further development of the turbocharged Ford Sierra Cosworth, the 190 E 2.3-16 was falling behind the competition. In race trim, the cars were producing at best 270 hp compared to the higher outputs of the competition. Even though Mercedes had up to seven entries in the series, the best result all season was fourth by Jörg van Ommen for the AMG Marko RSM team in the second round at Zolder.

Meanwhile, major changes came to Daimler top management. Edzard Reuter replaced Breitschwerdt on the management board. Acting with CEO Werner Niefer and Mercedes passenger car head Jürgen Hubbert, the trio decided to lift the ban on racing and provide direct factory support to the five teams involved in DTM. According to Ludvigsen's *Quicksilver Century*, Hubbert believed, "There is no better racing series than DTM for a manufacturer to present the sporting qualities and the dynamism of cars that are close to the standard specification."

OPPOSITE, TOP Bruno Sacco, head of Mercedes design, with a W201 mockup. The W201 was initially conceived during the fuel crises of the 1970s.

OPPOSITE, BOTTOM A development mule of the W201 looks like any other compact car of its era. Only later would the look evolve into what would be called the "Baby Benz."

TOP In production the 190 sported a new aerodynamic look that would be shared across the Mercedes-Benz lineup.

ABOVE Mercedes turned to British engine specialist Cosworth to tune a higher output version of the standard 2.3-liter four-cylinder engine as part of its bid to return to motorsports.

BELOW & OPPOSITE, TOP Prior to the launch of the more powerful 190E 2.3-16 at the Frankfurt Motor Show, Mercedes took the car to Nardo in Italy and set a string of long-distance speed records.

OPPOSITE, BOTTOM Meant for both road and track, the 190E 2.3-16 sported a rear wing and aerodynamic extensions to the front and rear fascias and the rocker panels.

AMG was prepared to accept that additional support and for the 1988 season prepared cars that produced 300 hp. The five teams fielded fourteen cars, with AMG as the official partner of Mercedes. The effort delivered double victories at Avus and the Hungaroring with Johnny Cecotto at the wheel. Still, the turbocharged Ford Sierra Cosworth, despite being hampered by air restrictors to balance performance, was tough to beat as driver Klaus Ludwig took the championship.

Looking for more power, a new 2.5-liter version of the M102 engine was introduced later that year. With its longer stroke, the new engine also had a lower compression ratio, but standard horsepower rose to 195 hp. It turned out the changes were not well-suited for racing, which favored shorter stroke, higher revving engines. As a result, it was back to the drawing board for a larger bore and new head arrangement to deliver the extra power the racing teams sought.

Group A rules had a provision that allowed for an evolved model if that car accounted for 10 percent of the 5,000-unit run needed for homologation. In other words, if a manufacturer was able to deliver at least 500 examples of this modified car to the market, it would be permitted to race. As a result, the Mercedes-Benz 190 2.5-16 Evolution was born.

With a larger bore and shorter stroke, the new engine would spin to 9,000 rpm and produce 330 horsepower. The 502 street versions, though rated at the same 195 hp as the 2.5-16, could be taken to 225 hp when specified with the optional AMG power pack. In addition to more muscle under the hood, Mercedes took advantage of the rules to add larger wheels and much improved aerodynamics thanks to a large front spoiler and a taller rear wing. Introduced at the Geneva Motor Show in March 1989, the Evolution was campaigned later that year by AMG, Snobeck Racing Service, and MS Racing.

The reigning champion, Klaus Ludwig, had moved from the Ford camp to the AMG Mercedes team and contributed to five of the eight Mercedes victories that year, the other two by Kurt Thiim. While both Ludwig and Thiim notched victories in the 190 E 2.3-16, Roland Asch scored the first win for an EVO I in mid-May when the car was finally homologated after 502 retail deliveries. Four of Ludwig's top podium finishes were in the EVO I.

Despite Ludwig's strong showing, poor finishes in the eleven-round series (two races each round) prevented him from cracking the top 10 in points. The crown went to Roberto Ravaglia driving a BMW M3 Evo for Team Schnitzer. Thiim was the top Mercedes driver, finishing fourth in the driver's championship.

WELTREKORD
50000 KM

S JZ 1823

TOP AMG preparation boosted the output of the 190E 2.3-16 to 300 hp. With Johnny Cecotto at the wheel, the car picked up its first wins a Avus and the Hungaroring in 1988.

MIDDLE DTM rules allowed additional performance modifications if 500 road-worthy homologation models were built. The Evolution was born, with Roland Asch taking the first victory in the car at Avus.

BOTTOM The Evolution, or EVO I, was distinguished by its deeper chin spoiler and taller rear wing.

The long list of manufacturers and tight racing made for a compelling show. The 1989 season attracted 581,000 spectators and a worldwide television viewing audience of 153 million. Mercedes was ready to up the ante with an even wilder evolution of the 190 E 2.5-16 introduced at the 1989 Geneva Motor Show.

The EVO II road-going homologation version boasted a bump in horsepower to 235 with the AMG power pack now standard equipment. In race trim, output was approaching 350 hp. Other technical innovations included an adjustable ride height through the use of hydropneumatic struts and, in racing versions for the first time, the adaptation of anti-lock braking (ABS) and driver's side airbag.

The revolutionary part of the Evolution was its wild aerodynamic package. Developed by Professor Richard Eppler from the University of Stuttgart, the EVO II sported a shovel-nose front splitter, huge flares on the front and rear wheel arches, stepped rocker panels, and a large apron rear bumper with a lower spoiler. The rear decklid was fitted with an even taller wing with additional flaps and spoilers on the trailing edge of the trunk and as well as an additional aero device set atop the rear window.

It's widely reported that BMW R&D chief Wolfgang Reitzle, upon seeing the EVO II, remarked, "It's totally stupid. The laws of aerodynamics must be different between Munich and Stuttgart. If that rear wing works, we'll have to rebuild our wind tunnel." Supposedly they did. The run of 502 road cars sold out immediately, fetching nearly $70,000 apiece.

Similar to the previous year, the new EVO II didn't make its track debut until the third round, at the Nürburgring, where Ludwig brought it home fourth in the first race. Ludwig had scored a win in the EVO I in the second round, while Thiim won the first two races at Zolder, also in the original Evolution. It wasn't until the ninth meeting that season that Thiim scored the first EVO II win and the final five victories that year for the AMG team. Hans Stuck, in a V-8-powered all-wheel-drive Audi, won seven of the twenty-two races to take the championship.

Even though AMG and Mercedes had their struggles, the popularity of DTM was having a large impact on the visibility of the brand. While a few hard-core enthusiasts in America became aware of AMG because of the Hammer, its stature was greatly enhanced globally through the more than 500,000 spectators who attended events and the hundreds of millions who had seen a race on television. The series, in addition to attracting major manufacturers, also was drawing top drivers such ase Ludwig and Stuck, as well as F1 racers such as Jaques Lafitte, Keke Rosberg, Christian Danner, and Alessandro Nannini. Perhaps the closest analog in US racing terms would be the glory days of late '60s and early '70s Trans-Am with the likes of Parnelli Jones,

Mark Donohue, Dan Gurney, and Sam Posey battling it out at the wheels of Ford Mustangs, Chevy Camaros, and Dodge Challengers.

The October 1990 agreement tying AMG even closer to Mercedes led to its development of all the cars for the factory teams as well as making the kits to upgrade the old models to EVO II spec. In addition to its own team, AMG was now providing technical assistance to Snobeck, MS Racing, and Zakspeed, which had left F1 to join the DTM.

In the ensuing season, Ludwig scored five victories, taking both races in the two rounds at the Nürburgring as well as an International Touring Car round at Brno. In the ITC, AMG and Mercedes took the respective team and manufacturer crowns.

The landscape soon shifted dramatically, as the DTM decided that for 1993 it would adopt new Class 1 specifications for the series. The rules would limit displacement to 2.5 liters and cylinder count of up to six while allowing additional modifications from stock trim. Opel decided not to compete in 1992, using that time to focus on adapting its new Calibra to Class 1 specs. Audi, which started the season, dropped out midway through. BMW announced it wouldn't compete in 1993. The evolution of the existing cars stopped. There would be no more 500-unit runs of EVOs forthcoming. Still, AMG continued to improve the cars, which now boasted redlines of 10,000 rpm and outputs in excess of 380 hp.

The 1992 season saw Mercedes dominate, winning sixteen of the twenty-four races. The AMG team took top honors on Ludwig's driver championship run of five wins. He was closely followed

TOP The second, more radical installment in the series, the EVO II, was introduced at the Geneva Motor Show in 1989. The fender flares help accommodate bigger wheels and a wider track. Rocker extensions are part of the aerodynamic package that was developed in a wind tunnel.

BOTTOM LEFT In contrast it was all business in the cockpit of the racer.

BOTTOM RIGHT The radical changes in the EVO II are evident in the progression from the original 190E 2.3-16 (car furthest from camera).

AMG
BOSS
DEKRA
6
LANSON
versichert
telcon
LANSON
Shell

DEKRA
SONAX
3
BRIDGESTONE
BÄUMLER
SONAX
Shell

AMG
BRIDGESTONE
NOKIA
RECARO
AMG
AMG
BERLIN 2000
BRIDGESTONE
NOKIA
BOSCH
BÄUMLER
men's fashion
BOSCH
Shell

Castrol
KÄRCHER
Castrol
BOSCH
BÄUMLER
BOSCH
BRIDGESTONE
BÄUMLER
Shell
Shell
Diebels Alt
Diebels Alt
Diebels Alt
BÄUMLER
Shell
MICHELIN
Shell
BERLIN 2000
BRIDGESTONE
BÄUMLER
Shell
Shell

by teammate Bernd Schneider, who won four races. Other AMG notables included Ellen Lohr, who became the only woman to win a DTM contest with her victory in May at Hockenheim. Keke Rosberg also scored a win for AMG, while Kurt Thiim and Roland Asch notched two wins each for Zakspeed.

With no homegrown competition for Mercedes, the DTM looked in dire straits for the 1993 season. The company had frozen development of the racing version of its new C-Class replacement for the 190, as it was waiting to see if the series would survive. In the end, Alfa Romeo showed up with its 155, which was equipped with a 2.5-liter V-6 that could rev to 11,000 rpm, make 420 hp, and boasted all-wheel drive.

AMG had little time to prepare for the upcoming season, looking to adapt the EVO II to the new specifications. Among the alterations approved in the rules was a shift to dry-sump lubrication, which allowed the engine to be mounted lower in the body and the use of a double wishbone rear suspension instead of the stock multilink setup. Mercedes factory support was down to two teams, AMG and Zakspeed, which fielded six instead of the previous season's eight cars.

While Alfa dominated the championship, with Nicola Larini winning half of the twenty races, the Mercedes factory teams won eight races in all. Schneider and Asch took two each, while Ludwig and Thiim each won a race. Asch's win at Avus near the end of the season marked the fiftieth victory in the series for the 190.

For the 1994 season AMG went all-in with a W202 C-Class that used all the latitude that the Class 1 regulations afforded. At the heart was a new 2.5-liter V-6 based on the 90-degree design used in the E 420's M119 V-8. The M106 V-6 featured an aluminum block and heads, tipping the scales at just over 240 pounds (109 kg). Revving to nearly 12,000 rpm, the engine would make over 400 hp in race trim. While both Opel and Alfa would employ all-wheel drive, Mercedes didn't offer a production car version with such a system, and as a result, it kept its rear-drive configuration for the track.

The car itself was anything but stock. The front clip was removed and only the rear structural support was used. A new front subframe accommodated the engine and double-wishbone front suspension, while the six-speed sequential shift gearbox was mid-mounted to balance the weight distribution. A tube-frame roll structure reinforced the cabin. At the rear, double wishbones were used for the suspension, and all four corners employed pushrod activated springs and dampers.

The body panels were made of carbon fiber, and while there was plenty of exotic tech at work, the car wasn't as wild looking as the EVO II. It did have a dramatically lower ride height, but the rules said all aerodynamic devices, except for the decklid-mounted rear wing, were limited to the areas of the car below the level of the axle hubs. As a result, the top half of the car looked very much like a stock C-Class and the bottom had an aggressive chin spoiler, a large lower inlet, a variety of vents and ducts along the rocker panels, and a huge rear diffuser under the rear fascia.

OPPOSITE, TOP EVO II had one of its first outings in a DTM race at the Norisring, the car driven by Kurt Thiim.

OPPOSITE, MIDDLE LEFT Klaus Ludwig takes the checked flag in 1992 on his way to winning the driver's title. In addition to Ludwig clinching the driver's title in 1992, Mercedes dominated to win the manufacturer's title.

OPPOSITE, MIDDLE RIGHT DTM attracted F1 drivers such as Keke Rosberg, who is shown here (left), with Ellen Lohr, the first woman to win a race in the series.

OPPOSITE, BOTTOM The AMG-prepared cars had a long list of stars behind the wheel. From left are Jacques Laffite, Jörg van Ommen, Bernd Schneider, Klaus Ludwig, Kurt Thiim, Roland Asch, Ellen Lohr, and Keke Rosberg.

ABOVE The EVO II was the first race car in Mercedes' stable to use anti-lock brakes. Here Roland Asch wins a heat at the Kyalami track in South Africa.

TOP An all-new C-Class would replace the W201 190. The sleek styling continued to bear a strong family resemblance to the E- and S-Class.

MIDDLE While there would be no more Evolution homologation specials, new rules provided more leeway in performance and aerodynamic upgrades. The C-Class DTM still had a big wing, but many of the other aero enhancements were confined to hub level and below.

BOTTOM Bernd Schneider and Mercedes dominated in 1995, winning the driver's championship over chief rival Alfa Romeo.

OPPOSITE Hans Werner Aufrecht, seen here conferring with driver Kurt Thiim, set up HAW AG in 1999 to build limited edition models and race cars for AMG.

AMG would field four and Zakspeed two of the new C-Class models. The close working relationship with Mercedes paid huge dividends. Then AMG manager Domingos Piedade explained in Ludvigsen's book that "this was the first time that we were ever able to design and build a racing car from scratch. And for the first time, we had proper product planning. We had Mercedes-Benz production, pre-development, research, and so forth working directly with our AMG R&D operation."

While Opel had returned full-time to the series, Mercedes' real nemesis was Alfa Romeo. Nannini won three of the first four races, with Kurt Thiim winning the third race in a Zakspeed C-Class. Alfa would go on to win eleven of the twenty rounds with Mercedes taking nine. Klaus Ludwig would win the driver's championship. Thanks to strong runner-up finishes, Mercedes was able to rack up enough points to take home the manufacturer's title.

The 1995 season was divided between DTM and ITC (International Touring Car) competition with each hosting respective seven and five meets with two races each round. AMG returned with even more power in the C-Class, which now made 440 hp and featured paddles for the sequential shift gearbox. AMG and Zakspeed fielded four cars each, with three other cars spread between two privateers. Klaus Ludwig left AMG for Opel to team with Keke Rosberg on Opel Team Rosberg.

Bernd Scheider stepped into the spotlight and dominated, winning five races in the ITC and six in the DTM to take the driver's crown in both. Mercedes took eight wins in DTM and seven in ITC, including one by Schneider's D2 AMG teammate, Dario Franchitti. On the strength of that showing, Mercedes won the manufacturer's cup in both DTM and ITC.

A move to consolidate DTM and ITC under the aegis of F1 impresario Bernie Ecclestone raised the costs and the stakes dramatically. The ITC would now consist of twelve rounds contested in eight countries around the globe, six of which would be in Germany. In addition to the German DTM circuits, races would be held in Italy, France, Great Britain, Portugal, Finland, Brazil, and Japan. Again, the three main protagonists were Mercedes-Benz, Alfa Romeo, and Opel.

While AMG was now getting 500 hp from the C-Class, Opel finally had found its stride, and along with Alfa, all three divvied up the spoils. Opel came out of the box strong, winning six of the first ten races, while taking nine over the course of the season. Alfa won eleven, while Mercedes took a total of seven. In the end, Opel's Manuel Reuter beat Schneider for the driver championship by thirteen points. In the manufacturer's standings, Opel came out on top, followed by Alfa Romeo and Mercedes-Benz.

The sky-high budgets, with little return on the lucrative television package controlled by the FIA, led to both Opel and Alfa Romeo throwing in the towel on the series. With no competition, Mercedes-Benz also ended its program. The DTM and ITC were finished for now.

With its many setbacks and successes, the DTM played a major role in tightening the bond between AMG and Mercedes. Aufrecht recalls that through the racing program Mercedes-Benz chairman Werner Niefer came to him and said, "Let's do this, together."

The HWA Way

In October 1998, in anticipation of DaimlerChrysler's majority stake in AMG going into effect, Hans Werner Aufrecht created HWA AG, a new entity in which Mercedes would outsource some of its motorsport activities and special vehicle projects. The move allowed Aufrecht to spend more of his time on his true passion, motorsports.

But first, with the demise of the DTM and ITC, HWA initially busied itself with such projects as helping AMG build the street versions of the Le Mans GT1-class CLK GTR, most notably producing the roadster versions of that model.

In 2000, however, DTM returned, this time calling itself the Deutsche Toureinwagen Masters. HWA built and campaigned the four factory cars, all Mercedes CLK coupes powered by 4.0-liter V-8 engines with a max output of 470 hp. Bernd Schneider won the driver's championship for AMG in 2000, 2001, and 2003.

For the 2004 season, the four-door sedan body of the C-Class was adopted using the same 4.0-liter V-8 engine package. AMG's success with its HWA partner continued, with Schneider taking the title in 2006, Gary Paffett in 2005, and Paul di Resta in 2010. In 2012 the series reverted to coupes using the C-Class silhouette. The car was renamed the C 63 DTM in 2015 and that year Pascal Wehrlein drove it to a championship.

Paffett again took the driver's title and Mercedes the manufacturer crown in 2018, a season that would mark the end of the Mercedes-AMG factory effort. HWA instead focused on a Formula E program that began in 2019 under the HWA Speedlab banner. According to HWA, during this eighteen-year span, it collected eleven drivers' crowns, fourteen team championships, and a dozen manufacturers' titles while tallying over 180 race wins. Mercedes-AMG returned to DTM in 2021 supporting privateers using Mercedes-AMG GT3-spec models.

continued

TOP Mercedes-AMG returned to DTM in 2000 with CLK DTM racers prepared by HWA. Bernd Schneider would again drive the new 4.0-liter V-8-powered car.

ABOVE In 2004 AMG adopted the C-Class four-door body style in DTM, which retained the V-8 engine.

Today, the HWA facility, adjacent to the AMG complex in Affalterbach, is the home to an assembly line that has built more than 700 Mercedes-AMG GT race cars for use in GT3 and GT4 races in different series that span the globe. The engines are built at AMG and then transferred over to HWA, which assembles the cars from tube frames and composite body panels.

HWA also has in-house designers and engineers that enable it to take on projects for small-volume makes as well as an in-house effort to re-create one of the most iconic AMG cars of all time, the EVO II. According to HWA Chief Technology Officer Gordian von Schöning, "We have wanted to create a modern version of the EVO II for some time, and it is not a task we undertake lightly considering the car's legendary status with enthusiasts and its history in the DTM. Our philosophy with the HWA EVO is to build an extremely dynamic but fully usable road car that can withstand the rigors of extreme track driving while retaining the spirit of the original car."

The HWA EVO II starts with a W201 190 E donor car and essentially strips it down to create a new vehicle. The front clip is removed and additional body strengthening welded into place in the cabin and rear end. In addition to a double-wishbone racing suspension, the car gets new carbon-fiber door skins and hood, and front and rear fenders that seamlessly integrate flared wheel wells are grafted onto the structure. The wheel

arches accommodate front 19- (48-cm) and rear 20-inch (51-cm) wheels, as opposed to the original 17-inch (43-cm) wheels found on the EVO II. The look is capped off by a towering rear wing.

Beneath the hood, instead of a beefed-up 2.5-liter four-cylinder, is an all-new 3.0-liter twin-turbo Mercedes V-6 tuned to produce over 440 hp, or up to nearly 500 hp with an optional power pack. "We wanted to create a highly agile and drivable car for both the road and track, and the compact V-6 biturbo proved an ideal starting point to achieve those values," explains Christian Liebeton, the HWA EVO powertrain project leader. The use of dry-sump lubrication also allows the engine to be mounted lower and further back in the body for better weight distribution.

Aside from the massive wheel and tire package and the LED running lights that frame the headlamps, the HWA EVO remains remarkably true to the original. While all but two of the original 502-unit run of the EVO II were painted Blauschwarz (blue-black), HWA will offer the car in a variety of colors. Also, the interior, which is fitted with four-passenger Recaro seating, features configurable digital instrumentation, including a screen that mimics the analog look of the original EVO II.

HWA plans on building only 100 cars priced at nearly $750,000 each. The first model built sold at auction for about $1.4 million.

TOP The next change involved reverting to the C-Class Coupe, which was now called the C 63 DTM. Pascal Wehrlein drove it to a championship in 2015, while Gary Paffett repeated the trick in 2018, the program's final season. Pictured in 2016 are Maximillan Götz in the white car with Paffett alongside and Lucas Auer behind.

ABOVE HWA is building restomods versions of the legendary EVO II. While it is faithful to the original, the EVO II features larger wheels and fender flares, and an all-new 3.0-liter biturbo V-6. Modern details such as LED lighting further differentiates the HWA EVO II from the original.

7

THE HAMMER DROPS

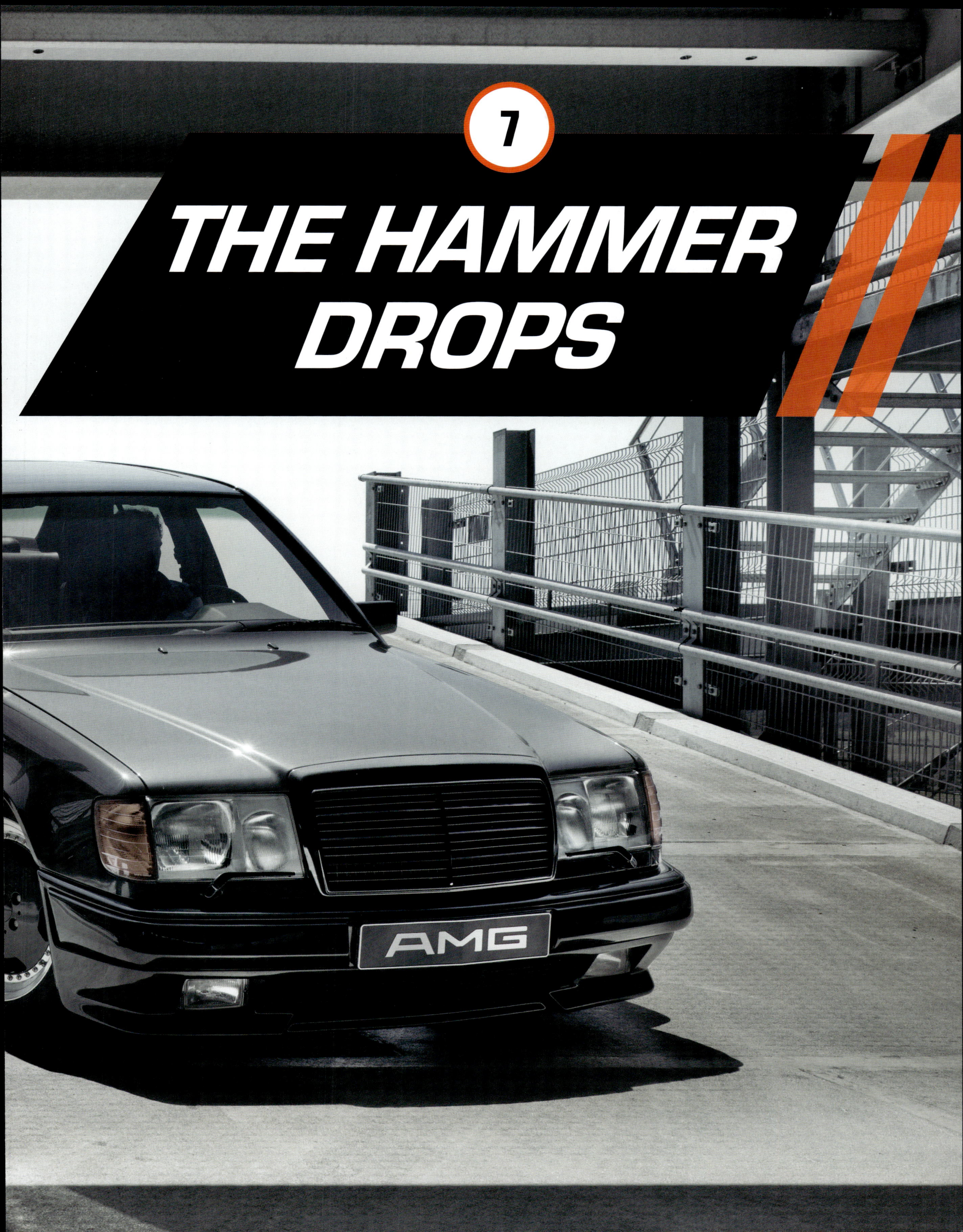

THE IDEA WAS SIMPLE: to create a road-going Mercedes-Benz that could go 300 kph (186 mph). That quest was very much a sign that times were changing. The auto industry had begun to emerge from the torpor of the 1970s, when performance took a back seat to fuel efficiency and stricter emission regulations.

The 1980s dawned with stable oil prices and supplies; catalytic converters were cleaning up emissions, and an economic recovery put money back into consumer pockets. Automakers were primed to flex some newfound muscle, not just with traditional sports cars, but also with luxury sedans, a concept not foreign to the maestros at AMG.

The first volley in the performance car wars was from BMW when it started production of the E28 5 Series M5 in 1984. Adapting the inline-six M88/3 engine from the M1 sports car, the M5 boasted 282 hp and was billed as the fastest production sedan on the planet.

Up the road from Munich, in Affalterbach, the M5 introduction did not go unnoticed. AMG was quick to pick up on the challenge but needed the right car and the right engine to achieve its goal of a 300 kph (186 mph) sedan. The current midsize W123 was dated, having been introduced in 1976. It would soon be replaced by the W124, which shared its inspiration from the compact W201 190 series, including its five-link independent rear suspension.

Bruno Sacco's design would play a key element here. The clean flowing lines of the W124 contributed to a wind-cheating coefficient of drag that would be as low as 0.28 on some models. Still, the W124 would come from the factory with four- and six-cylinder engines, hardly the stuff of 300 kph dreams.

Taking a page from Waxenberger's bold move of using the 600 limo's V-8 to create the 300 SEL 6.3, AMG transplanted the S-Class 5.0-liter V-8 into the new midsize W124. But AMG, being AMG, wouldn't leave well enough alone. Melcher had designed a new four-valve head for the M117 block, boosting output from 240 to 340 hp. Only a handful of cars were fitted with this engine and its subsequent 5.2- and 5.4-liter upgrades. Shoehorning the V-8 into the midsize W124 engine bay took some effort, including a reworking of the car's bulkhead as well as the rear end to incorporate the beefier differential from the larger W126 S-Class.

If incremental power is good, more is definitely better. When Mercedes introduced the 5.5-liter version of the M117 (sometimes referred to as a 5.6-liter engine since it was used in the 560 SL and SEL models), AMG adapted the engine using its heads to reach 360 hp. It upped the ante even more to 385 horses by boring the engine out to 6.0 liters. These 5.5- and 6.0-liter versions of the W124 came to be known as the AMG Hammer.

PREVIOUS In black, the AMG Hammer had a menacing look. Early models were equipped with 5.4- and 5.6-liter engines.

OPPOSITE The four-valve M117 would eventually grow to 6.0 liters in displacement, making 365 hp.

AMG

S ET 6527

Phantomdarstellung C124

It was the complete package due to the past decade's work by AMG to upgrade suspensions, brakes, and wheel/tire fitments to sharpen road manners. And the look was menacing, again thanks to AMG's broad experience in equipping cars with spoilers and blacked-out accents such as window surrounds, door handles, and grilles. Because of this monochromatic look, AMG cars counterintuitively stood out from all the rest of the cars of that era that displayed their brightwork like ostentatious jewelry.

Still, hitting that 300-kph (186-mph) mark was elusive. Hartmut Feyhl, who worked on the development of the car in Affalterbach before moving to America to build US versions, recalled that it was as much about the aerodynamics as making more horsepower.

In a video interview with *Curated,* an AMG collector/specialist organization, Feyhl said, "the 124 chassis was the first real aerodynamic car with wind tunnel development from Mercedes." AMG built on that aerodynamic foundation by covering up the underside of the car. By "filling everything in between the suspension," Feyhl explained that AMG gave the Hammer sort of a flat bottom that made "a nice difference."

On the mechanical side, AMG experimented with gear ratios and settled on the automatic transmission from the 500 SL to handle the additional power. Still, 300 kph (186-mph) remained elusive. More attention was focused on the 6.0-liter engine, with additional porting and polishing that Feyhl said added about 10 horses.

OPPOSITE, TOP The Hammer was conceived as an answer to the BMW M5. Its mission: hit a top speed of 300 kph (186 mph). *John Lamm photo*

OPPOSITE, BOTTOM Starting point for the Hammer was the new W124 E-Class. Its clean design prioritized sleek aerodynamics.

ABOVE The W124 series also included a coupe and a wagon, both of which also benefitted from AMG's V-8 power.

CAR AND DRIVER
DECEMBER 1986 • $2.50
Speed Reading!
178-mph AMG Hammer
238-mph Mazda RX-7 Turbo
165-mph Porsche 928S4
PLUS: Citroën CX, Renault Medallion, Mercedes 300TD, Alfa Romeo Milano, 1886 Benz, and a token Honda

TOP *Car and Driver* was an early adopter of the Hammer designation. Its test of a 5.6-liter Hammer appeared in the December 1986 issue.

MIDDLE The monochromatic scheme not only included the grille but also Mercedes' three-pointed star stand-up hood ornament. *John Lamm photo*

BOTTOM Parked beside a stock E-Class Mercedes, the AMG sits lower and wider, thanks to suspension modifications and larger wheels and tires. In addition to the lower chin spoiler, the Hammer also was fitted with a shutter system on the radiator, which enabled the car to surpass 300 kph (186 mph). Despite such high-speed trickery, road-holding was just as much a priority as top speed in the Hammer. *John Lamm photo*

OPPOSITE, TOP The red AMG Hammer pictured here was used in the *Road & Track* official test. It was the first Hammer completely built in the United States by Hartmut Feyhl. While touted for its outstanding performance, at the end of the day, the Hammer was above all a luxury sedan. Chromed monoblock wheels add a touch of elegance. *John Lamm photo*

OPPOSITE, BOTTOM The twin tailpipes emerging from the rear muffler was part of a US-compliant exhaust system fitted to models built in Chicago by AMG North America. The rear 6.0 badge indicates that this Hammer had the largest version of the M117 V-8. *John Lamm photo*

"I mean, we just tried everything and just couldn't get to 300 kph," he recalled. Melcher, who had developed the engine, discovered that Porsche had introduced the 928 S that had the same horsepower as the standard version, but was 15 to 20 kph (9–12 mph) faster. "They [Porsche] did a lot of aero work, including closing off the radiator. They had an automatic shutter system, which [manufacturers] have now again these days. But back then, Porsche was the only one.

"So, we tried that one on the Hammer, not an automatic one, we had a button inside. I was driving it on the autobahn with an engineer next to me. So, we got to like 290 with the radiator open." Feyhl pushed the button to close the shutters. "It was like an afterburner coming on. It was really giving it another shot up to 303 or 304 or maybe 305 [kph]. So that was it, wow."

"Wow!" That was the reaction of the US buff books when they got their hands on the car. Just as journalists came up with the Red Pig moniker, it was the press that called the new car the Hammer. *Car and Driver*'s December 1986 road test opens with: "Don't ask 'What's in a name?' Hammer means in German precisely what it means in English, and this car's name says exactly what it is: a hard-hitting tool. AMG crafts it to pound everything else flat." Wisely AMG quickly adopted the Hammer designation for sales and marketing purposes.

The car that so impressed *Car and Driver* was an early gray market model that Feyhl came over to the States to upgrade to the current 5.5-liter state of tune, which was 355 hp and 388 lb-ft of torque. The test results reported 0–60 mph (0–97 kph) acceleration of 5.0 seconds, a quarter-mile time of 13.5 seconds at 107 mph (172 kph), and a top speed of 178 mph (286 kph).

The numbers were startling for a four-door sedan. Its top speed was higher than a Ferrari Testarossa's. Its 0–60 mph time (0–97 kph) was on par with the Ferrari as well as the Porsche 911 Turbo and

AMG
6.0
AMG
AMG
BEVERLY HILLS MOTORING

AMG
mph
km/h
UNLEADED

AMG

Lamborghini Countach. The 0.88g it pulled on the skid pad put it between the 911 Turbo and Countach in roadholding. All this is from a car with seating for four by Recaro, wood trim, an automatic transmission, and Mercedes build quality.

But the price it commanded was steep. The $137,000 as tested price was more than double what it would cost to buy a 911 Turbo and still $10,000–$20,000 more than the Ferrari and Lamborghini rivals.

The magazine concluded, "The Hammer is the most scintillating sedan we have driven. The *C/D* staff drools as one. Even after federalizations, AMG's meanest should match pure speed with any factory's wildest—and make such speed more usable to boot."

Eight months later, *Road & Track* came to a similar conclusion after testing a red Hammer, this one with the 6.0-liter engine making 365 hp. This car also had the distinction of being the first Hammer built up in the United States.

Feyhl came over to America to not just prepare the first test cars given to the press, but also to work with Richard Buxbaum, who, since 1980, had been distributing AMG cars and parts through AMG North America, which was based in Westmont, a Chicago suburb. It was Feyhl, using engines, suspension, and interior bits, who produced all thirteen cars that were sold here. Also, around this time, Andy Cohen, through Beverly Hills Motoring Accessories, was the source for AMG products on the West Coast. He supplied the Hammer test car to Newport Beach–based *Road & Track* for its August 1987 story.

The magazine said, "You'll probably never see another like it because more than likely you'll never see a Hammer. Unless you buy one of your own. Turnkey ready, a Hammer costs $161,422, but if you already own a 300 E and want to have it converted into a Hammer, deduct $39,000 from that figure. That leaves only $122,422, which breaks down like this: Mercedes-Benz 5.6-liter engine with KE Jetronic [fuel injection] $17,000; modification to 6.0-liter DOHC, $39,950; Hammer conversion package (heavy-duty rear subframe, W126 rear differential with Gleason-Torsen limited slip), $33,302; AMG suspension kit, $1,495; AMG wheels with Pirelli P700 tires,

OPPOSITE, TOP A new speedometer topping out at 190 mph (306 kph) was part of the Hammer package. Note the plaque letting the driver know that unleaded fuel is required. *John Lamm photo*

OPPOSITE, BOTTOM Since AMG provided only performance upgrades, the interior of the W124 Mercedes was stock, meaning it retained the luxury trim associated with the brand. *John Lamm photo*

TOP LEFT Some additional finessing was required by AMG to fit the M117 V-8 into an engine bay originally designed to accommodate an inline-six powerplant at best. *John Lamm photo*

TOP RIGHT The engine carried AMG specific numbering. This is engine 247 displacing 6.0 liters built in 1985. *John Lamm photo*

$5,050; AMG aero body kit, $4,125; installation and painting of body and parts, $3,500; labor, $18,000.

"At full pop or at the discount price, you're buying exclusivity," *Road & Track* concluded. "There are only 13 Hammers in the world including this car, the only one of its kind in America. But more than exclusivity, you're buying the fastest Mercedes in the world, an automobile with the body of a 4-door sedan and the soul (and performance) of an exotic."

Cohen, who passed away in 2019, offered some interesting insights back in 2011 on the *Bring a Trailer* auction site. According to Cohen, "Ever[y] Hammer was a 300E based car, either four door (most common) or coupe or the one wagon. No [W]126 [S-Class] body styles were ever Hammers. There were a handful of SECs and SEL's with 4-valve motors built by AMG in Chicago, but they were not known as Hammers; there were just [W]126 cars with the 4-valve motor."

Cohen explained that "the Hammers required so many extensive modifications to accommodate the big engine in the car that only came with a 6-cylinder motor from the factory. The Hammers were basically a 300E body with all W126 components installed to be able to handle the power of the engine and also be able to handle and stop properly. [W]126 cars were different as it was pretty much a bolt in modification to put a 4-valve motor in a SEC or SEL. We even bought a 560 SEL with just a few hundred miles on it from Phil Hill and AMG Chicago shipped us a 4-valve motor. Hartmut flew out to California and installed the engine and transmission and other pieces in the SEC, and I sold it to a local client. There were also a handful of wide body SECs built in Chicago with 4-valve motors."

"All of the 4-valve engines that they installed were built at AMG in Affalterbach, West Germany, at the AMG plant, and they came complete and were installed at that facility by Hartmut," Cohen added. "Hartmut worked at AMG in Germany before he moved here to work at AMG North America, so it really was like Germany being here in the U.S. with this setup. The reason the Hammers were built in North America was that by that time you could not import a Hammer from Europe due to anti-gray market regulations. So, the decision

Since its launch in the 1980s, the Hammer's appeal as an exotic collectible has grown exponentially. *John Lamm photo*

was made to build the cars at AMG North America with virtually all of the parts that were used in Germany, with the same craftsman, Hartmut Feyhl. A U.S. Hammer was identical to a German built one except for the U.S. VIN number."

"One more thing was that *every* AMG engine built at the time was put on an engine dyno at AMG and run at redline for a long time and then checked again before being put in the car. That is why there were minimal engine problems when these cars were new," Cohen pointed out.

The Hammers Feyhl built in America included seven sedans, five coupes, and one wagon. AMG North America did a single cam, two-valve 6.0-liter conversion of a wagon, which isn't considered to be a genuine Hammer. That car, in John Phillips's 1990 *Car and Driver* test drive, was dubbed the Mallet.

Worldwide, the best estimate about the number of cars built is somewhere between fifty and sixty. Because of the ever-changing nature of each conversion, each vehicle is in its own way a unique work of art. For instance, the wagon was commissioned by Paul Fingold, a Canadian friend of Buxbaum's. As evidence of the close nature of the community, Fingold went on to purchase Beverly Hills Motoring Accessories from Cohen.

Fingold's blue wagon is currently owned by Jonathan Hodgman. He runs Blue Ridge MB, a shop outside of Atlanta that specializes in pre-merger AMG vehicles. The wagon started life as a 1987 300 TD diesel. The car, built for Fingold's wife, Malka, was fitted with the AMG-built DOHC M117 6.0-liter V-8. Among the custom features was an exhaust system that incorporated a Porsche catalytic converter. While Feyhl installed the drivetrain, a specialist from AMG in Affalterbach was sent over to handle the electrical system.

The car made its debut at Road America in Elkhart Lake, Wisconsin, at an AMG event in June 1987. The gathering was reportedly featured on an episode of *Lifestyles of the Rich and Famous*. During the showing, it was discovered the custom exhaust headers were hitting the firewall at idle. Feyhl is said to have climbed into the engine bay with a hammer to provide clearance. It's that bespoke nature of the Hammer that only adds to its allure. "No two are alike," Hodgman explained. "You could see improvements made along the way, like better brake line routing."

By 1990, when AMG signed its exclusive sales agreement with the Mercedes-Benz factory that allowed its dealers to sell vehicles and install parts, distributors such as AMG North America, as well as similar operations in Canada and Japan, were abruptly terminated. Feyhl moved to Florida to open RENNtech, continuing his work in performance upgrades on Mercedes vehicles.

"Once Mercedes became officially involved, everything started to become more polished as the might of their engineering and abilities crept in pretty quick," Hodgman said in an interview with *Marqued.com*. "Things became more standardized, something built in a proper facility, and stopped being race cars built in the back garage. Really, they stopped being one-off bits of madness to something more conventional, more corporate."

But Hodgman's work on the cars gave him insight into AMG's success. Rather than just an engine specialist making hot rod Mercedes, the company took a holistic approach to the upgrades. "They would change one thing, [and] there were many other things that had to be changed to make it work," he said. "If they didn't, you have a very unbalanced package. They [Mercedes factory cars] feel so nice out of the box, it's very easy to take them backward, very hard to go forward. You can ruin a balanced car." AMG, in Hodgman's estimation, would "elevate the car to a new level. The cars have personality, they have a soul. It's quite a trick, you have to be careful not to screw it up."

Though limited in number, AMG got the Hammer right. And it did for AMG's reputation for road cars what the Red Pig achieved nearly two decades earlier in the realm of motorsports. With the formal recognition from the factory long sought by Aufrecht in hand, AMG began its evolution from tuner to manufacturer.

OPPOSITE The Hammer's success arguably led to Mercedes' teaming with Porsche to build the E 500.

ABOVE Although AMG offered wagon versions of the Hammer globally, only one was built in the United States.

Premerger Cars: AMG's Holy Grail

Exclusivity has been a major asset for the AMG brand. And nothing is more rare than certain premerger models converted by Affalterbach and several other authorized shops around the world. The collector car world certainly sat up and took notice when a 1988 Mercedes AMG Hammer coupe crossed the block for $761,800 in August 2022.

Of course, the car had history. Besides being one of only five Hammer coupes converted by AMG North America by Hartmut Feyhl, it was also the notorious "Cocaine Hammer," a car impounded by the US Drug Enforcement Agency. It turns out the first owner, who took delivery from Andy Cohen's Beverly Hills AMG West operation, had gone to Las Vegas where he was pulled over and found to have cocaine and other contraband in the car.

The authorities apparently had a good time with the ride, clocking up 1,500 miles (2,414 km) while it was in their possession. Ultimately it was sold to pro baseball player Rob Deer, who owned the car for two years. It changed hands back and forth between two collectors and was for the most part garaged. Despite being thirty-four years old, the coupe came to auction with just 19,417 miles (31,249 km) on the odometer.

According to *Sports Car Market*, the result "is the definitive premerger AMG sale. The price here effectively takes the elusive Hammer from an expensive way to buy a fast and rare W124 to a blue-chip exotic within striking distance of a seven-figure valuation."

"This was the first auction in 12 years where a real, driving, usable Hammer was offered," the magazine reported, concluding that "while a multitude of AMG products have recently sold through the big auction channels, this was all just a ramp up for a market that was foaming at the mouth for the ultimate premerger AMG car."

Until that sale, the market had seen Hammers trading hands in the $300,000 range, which led to the speculation that the Cocaine Hammer would sell for about $320,000 until the bidding took off. Even though it's a big number, you must consider that most of the original Hammers sold in the United States for well over $160,000. This particular coupe, retailing for $190,000, would sell for $420,000 in current dollars.

While the high price can be viewed as a one-off due to the car's rarity and the fact that two parties got into a fierce bidding war before the (ahem) hammer dropped, it's definitely a case of a rising tide lifting all boats, including models that aren't considered to be genuine Hammers.

In addition to using the Melcher-designed heads on M117 V-8s in W124 sedans, AMG used the same powerplants in C126 500 SEC coupes with widebody kits. About fifty of these were built. Also, there are some W124 and C126 models from the early 1990s that may have the M119 four-valve Mercedes engine bored out to 6.0 liters instead of the M117 engines.

The rising value of the 560 SEC AMGs is tracking with the gain in value of the Hammer. Four months after the sale of the Cocaine Hammer, a Mercedes-Benz 560 SEC 6.0 AMG sold for $720,000. Another sold in March 2024 for $582,500.

According to *Hagerty.com*, the premerger AMGs are resonating with younger enthusiasts. The classic car insurer says its policy data shows more than half of these early cars are owned by millennials. Just over a third are Gen X owners, while boomers account for the rest, about 14 percent.

John Wiley, who manages Hagerty's valuation analytics, believes that while the AMG market is maturing, values will continue to grow. "With people bidding deep into six figure amounts on these early AMG cars, they're requiring documentation and those unique AMG features," Wiley explained. "In other words, exactly what serious collectors look for when buying valuable vehicles. With the youthful demographics, this market looks like it has room to run."

Blue Ridge MB's Jonathan Hodgman, who was born in 1978, typifies the interest of this younger demographic. "We lusted after these when we were kids, and now, we can get them," he says. "Nostalgia is a hell of a drug. Once you get a taste, it's strong."

Ride on the Wide Side

For the young and physically fit girl who frequents the beach and employs the glowing sun and scanty attire to display her breathtaking perfection, California coined a descriptive term—hard body. Just as AMG created a singular name to describe the breathtaking muscular aggressiveness and flawless mein displayed by the ultimate AMG SEC—Wide Body.

Like the girl on the beach, the Wide Body leaves no doubt about its outlook on life, both aware of their natural gifts, but one playful, the other forceful. And both beautiful.

Every line of the Wide Body has been born for a reason. No line goes its way without consideration for all others. And while subtlety is the key in every detail, the overall effect is one of extraordinary strength. From the integrated front air dam to the measured kick of the carefully contoured rear spoiler lip, every detail of the Wide Body contributes as much to aerodynamic efficiency as to the ability to fit much wider wheels—9.0 inches in front and 10.0 inches at the rear, all four with a 16-inch diameter—and much more adhesive tires. Their high-performance, low-profile sidewalls and gluey tread blocks and compounds make the most of the broad support. In turn, AMG's chassis engineers make the most of the Wide Body's handling potential, delivering exceptional stability, roadholding, and peace of mind, even at autobahn-rate speeds.

At lesser speeds, the AMG SEC Wide Body capitalizes on its looks by displaying a lingering look at its breathtaking natural perfection. Just like the girl at the beach.

SEC Wide Body conversions enable the use of AMG's 9.0-inch wheels front and 10.0-inch wheels in the rear.

The artful blending of the expanded fenders accentuate this SEC's dazzling demeanor.

22

TOP The Hammer was available as a coupe like this CE 300 6.0 AMG.

LEFT & ABOVE Although not a Hammer because it uses the C126 S-Class underpinnings, the Widebody SEC as seen in these photos from a 1987 AMG catalog has become a collectible for its use of the M117 V-8.

LB PA

8 OFFICIAL BUSINESS

THE 1990S PROVED TO BE A PIVOTAL decade for AMG, as it began its transition from outside tuner of finished vehicles to a full-fledged division within the Mercedes-Benz family. Replacing its global network with distribution through Mercedes dealers added new complexities, since now all of AMG's work would be covered by factory warranties.

While the deal also opened the door to the huge North American market, getting the new network up to speed while losing the outlets that existed before led to several lean years at AMG. Company lore has it that Aufrecht had to sell one of his cars to cover the cost of the annual Christmas party one year. Meanwhile AMG also had to absorb the cost of establishing its third production facility and increased workforce, which now numbered 400, quadruple of what it had been just five years earlier.

Now with this new factory relationship, AMG prepared to launch the first vehicle jointly developed with Mercedes with the North American market specifically in mind. That car would be a variant of the second generation "Baby Benz," the new W202 C-Class that replaced the W201 190.

The Mercedes-Benz C 36 AMG made its debut at the Frankfurt Motor Show in 1993, going on sale in the United States by 1995. AMG would start with partially built C 280 Sport models shipped from the C-Class factory in Bremen to the Affalterbach final assembly point.

Instead of using the 2.8-liter inline-six of the C 280, AMG started with the larger 3.2-liter M104 block from the E 320 and increased the bore and stroke to reach a displacement of 3.6 liters. A stouter crankshaft from a 3.5-liter OM diesel sold by Mercedes was machined and rebalanced to accept forged aluminum pistons and longer connecting rods. The short-skirt piston heads also helped increase compression from 10:1 to 10.5:1. Larger, better-breathing cylinder head ports used sodium-filled valves to dissipate heat.

The reworked engine also borrowed high-lift cams and a larger variable-length intake manifold from the E 320. In addition to reprogramming the engine management software, the C 36 also benefited from revised exhaust cam timing, greater valve overlap, and a freer-flowing exhaust system. True to AMG tradition, these engine builds were done by a single technician.

The changes had a profound impact on performance. The stock C 280 Sport made 190 hp and 199 lb-ft of torque. The larger C 36 engine boasted 276 hp and 284 lb-ft of torque (although North American models made slightly less at 267 hp).

AMG adapted the four-speed automatic transmission from the V-8-powered E 420 to better manage the increased output from the C 36's inline 6. The differential also was beefed up using components from the E-Class.

The C 36 also saw changes to its suspension, including higher rate gas-filled dampers, thicker anti-roll bars front and rear, and a lower ride height. The brakes also were upgraded with vented front discs and four-piston calipers from the SL, replacing the solid front discs of the C 280 Sport.

Rear brakes were still solid discs, but larger in diameter, coming from the E 420. Additionally the car was equipped with a quicker steering ratio and the front track increased by nearly 5 inches (13 cm).

While the mechanical modifications were extensive, the exterior, unlike the wild 190 EVO II, was quite restrained. The look of the new C-Class bore many similarities to the larger E-Class executive sedan. A traditional six-segment grille was flanked by flush headlamps with a three-pointed star hood ornament perched above.

The lines were simple and clean, with a raised power dome on the hood and a profile defined by a character line that connected the front and rear of the car. Along the lower third of the car, the C 36 displayed its AMG pedigree. The bumper and front fascia had a bolder look with a more pronounced chin spoiler, larger intakes, and fog lights at each corner.

The body-colored rub strip on the front bumper wrapped around the side and rear end while additional body-colored cladding added to the muscular look. Lower rocker sills helped reduce lift, and at the rear, a cutout in the lower bumper fascia housed chrome exhaust tips. Carbon fiber accented the upper B-pillar. A rear-deck-mounted spoiler was available as an option.

Depending on the market, the C 36 interior was upholstered in velour, or, as in the case of North American models, leather. These models also featured wood instead of fake carbon-fiber accents used in Europe and elsewhere. AMG-specific features included a white-faced 160-mph (258-kph) speedometer and a two-tone leather treatment on the steering wheel and sport seats.

While the modifications added over 150 pounds to the C 280 Sport's 3,278-pound (1,487 kg) curb weight, the increase in power enabled the C 36 to accelerate to 60 mph (97 kph) in six seconds, an improvement of nearly three seconds. Top speed was electronically limited to 155 mph (250 kph) as opposed to the C 280's 143-mph (230 kph) top speed. Ungoverned, the C 36 could hit an estimated 163 mph (262 kph).

The last C 36 models were built in 1997 and were fitted with five-speed automatic transmissions. US versions also saw a bump in horsepower to 276 to match the output of all the other markets. About 5,200 were built during its 1993–1997 production run.

In its road test of the C 36, *Car and Driver* concluded: "AMG has imbued the $51,750 C36 with the grunt to see off almost anything with four doors. And it has done so without harming the car's social acceptability. While the aero body kit and big wheels speak of sportiness, they do it without demeaning the car's image. Nor has any of the driveline or suspension work markedly

PREVIOUS Hans Werner Aufrecht with the C 36, the first road-going vehicle developed in conjunction with Mercedes-Benz.

ABOVE Unlike previous AMG models that relied heavily on a monochromatic look, the C 36 retained much of the same appearance as the production C-Class. The lower rocker extensions and deeper front and rear fascias, however, were cues that this wasn't an ordinary C-Class. *John Lamm photo*

ABOVE While the cosmetic changes from stock were minimal, the C 36 benefited from upgrades to the suspension, brakes, and wheel and tire packages. The monoblock wheel design on the C 36 was an evolution of AMG's signature five-spoke wheel look. In keeping with the understated exterior design, the C 36 and AMG badging is discreet.

OPPOSITE, TOP The 3.6-liter engine featured a high compression ratio that helped push output to 280 hp. Note that there's no "one man, one engine" badge; AMG wouldn't begin to label engines as such until 2002.

OPPOSITE, BOTTOM The interior differed more from the standard C-Class than the exterior. In addition to a checkered-flag motif to the seat inserts, the C 36 also had a two-tone sport wheel and a white background surrounding the black-faced instruments. *John Lamm photo*

compromised its versatility for everyday use. In that respect, the C 36 is even better than a BMW M3. Perhaps because of that, it has less of the M3's exuberance, expressiveness, and communication. But for the kind of driver Mercedes is courting, it has about all it needs."

But AMG was far from finished with the Baby Benz. In 1998 it introduced the Mercedes-Benz C 43 AMG, returning yet again to work its V-8 magic, this time in a compact-class car. The donor motor came from the newly launched E 430, which was powered by the M113 4.3-liter V-8. Despite having two additional cylinders, the V-8's aluminum block contributed to a 44-pound (20-kg) weight savings over the C 36's iron block inline-six.

AMG massaged the M113 with a freer flowing magnesium intake manifold, new twin-tube air intakes, revised cams with more overlap, beefier valve springs, and high-pressure lubrication with additional jets to cool the piston skirts. Keeping the stock twin-spark configuration, the AMG modifications boosted horsepower from 275 to 302 and torque from 295 to 302 lb-ft.

The increase in output also represents similar gains over the C 36's 276 hp and 284 lb-ft of torque, allowing the C 43 to crack the six-second mark in 0–60 mph (0–97-kph) acceleration. Like its predecessor, top speed was electronically limited to 155 mph (250 kph).

The V-8 mated to a five-speed automatic transmission from SL to drive the rear wheels. Unlike the five-speed fitted to the last run of C 36 models, this new transmission featured an adaptive shift programming that would learn from the driver's input and adjust the aggressiveness of its gear-change strategy accordingly.

AMG also chose to go sportier with its suspension settings over the previous C 36. The double-wishbone front and five-link rear independent suspension employed coil springs with a 24-percent front and 12-percent rear gain in stiffness. The gas-filled shocks also had greater damping force, with a respective 20- and 8-percent increase in rebound front and rear. The 17-inch (43-cm) wheels were shod with Michelin Pilot SX MXX3 rubber.

3.6
AMG

TOP The 5.0-liter V8 E 50 AMG would succeed the E 500/500 E built with Porsche. U.S. buyers would have to wait until the 5.5-liter E 55 bowed in 1998.

ABOVE In 1997 the C 43 debuted as the first C-Class production model fitted with a V-8 engine. The 4.3-liter M113 had three valves per cylinder and produced 302 hp.

From a styling perspective, there was little to distinguish the new C 43 from the C 36, which received some minor tweaks in the C-Class mid-cycle refresh for the 1997 model year. The look was subtle, with the only AMG cues coming from the more aggressive lower front fascia, the body-colored side cladding and lower aerodynamic sill, and the carbon-fiber accented upper B-pillar. Inside, the C 43 featured white-faced instruments with AMG logos and two-tone leather treatments on the steering wheel and the AMG sport seats. Like the C 36, North American models were equipped with burled wood accents instead of the faux carbon fiber.

Pricing didn't increase dramatically despite the switch to V-8 power. According to *Road & Track*, the 1998 C 43 stickered at $55,880 versus the 1997 C 36 MSRP of $55,815. Over its three-year run, AMG produced 3,857 C 43 models, including 772 station wagons. Limited to only sedans, the US saw 1,150 shipped against the 1,500 (500 per year) originally promised by Mercedes.

The introduction of the all-new W210 E-Class marked the next chapter in the in-house development of AMG models with Mercedes. Recognizable for its round-headlamp theme, the Bruno Sacco–designed E-Class also spawned a wagon version as well as the CLK Coupe.

AMG first installed the 3.6-liter inline-six from the C 36 to create the E 36. This rare model, offered in 1996 and 1997, saw only forty-nine units produced, none of which were available in North America. Likewise, the V-8-powered E 50, introduced at the 1995 Frankfurt Motor Show, was intended primarily for European markets as a successor to the W124 E 500/500 E, which was produced in cooperation with Mercedes' Stuttgart neighbor, Porsche. Just under 3,000 E 50 models were built, each producing 347 horsepower.

TOP AMG offered its take on the SL in 1994, replacing the SL 600's V-12 engine with V-8 power. The striking color scheme was pure AMG: monochromatic yellow right down to the the monoblock wheels. *John Lamm photo*

MIDDLE The exterior color scheme carried over into the interior with yellow leather covering the seats, dash, and center console. *John Lamm photo*

BOTTOM The 6.0-liter M119 V-8 made 410 hp and enabled the car to sprint to 60 mph (97 kph) in about five seconds. *John Lamm photo*

US buyers would have to wait for the E 55, which was manufactured from 1998 to 2002. As the name implies, the V-8 engine displaced 5.5 liters, up a half-liter from the E 50's M113 V-8. Output was rated at 349 hp and 391 lb-ft of torque. About 2,000 of the 12,000 unit run came to the United States—approximately 500 per year. A wagon version also was sold in Europe, including some rare 4Matic all-wheel-drive units.

Like the C 36 and C 43 models that preceded it, the E 55's exterior design was restrained. Everything above the bumpers and side rub strips was stock E Class, from the chromed grille to the stand-up hood ornament. The only telltale cue on the upper body was the use of dark rather than chrome surrounds on the greenhouse and door handles.

But on the lower part, the E 55 had a pronounced chin spoiler, aerodynamic rocker panels, and body-colored cladding. The five-spoke monoblock wheels were also an AMG exclusive. In its road test of the E 55, *Car and Driver* reported, "So suave is this E-Class muscle car that its real potential will not be recognized by many passengers. . . . Yes, the latest 'Hammer' from Mercedes and its in-house speed wizards is a Q-ship."

Despite the car's understated looks, the magazine recorded a 0–60 mph (0–97 kph) time of 4.9 seconds and a 13.5-second sprint through the quarter mile at 105 mph (169 kph). Handling also was sharpened more than a notch by the use of stiffer springs and shocks and the use of sticky Michelin Pilot Sport tires. While the E 55 retailed for over $70,000, it offered better performance than the Porsche-built E 500, which cost over $15,000 more.

The 1990s also saw a wide range of interesting AMG variants, including SL models with 7.0- and 7.3-liter V-12 engines (the SL 70 and SL 73), of which a respective 150 and 85 units were built. There was also a V-8 SL 50 using the same M119 engine of the E 50 between 1993 and 1998.

Then there were eleven 300 SL models (eight Gullwing coupes and three roadsters) that were restomods commissioned mostly by the Sultan of Brunei, who would take six of them. According to *Supercars.net*, the project entailed shoehorning the M113 6.0-liter V-8 into the space formerly occupied by the original 3.0-liter inline-six. The 380-hp engine was mated to a four-speed automatic transmission and the swing-arm independent rear swapped out in favor of a five-link setup from the C 36.

A custom carbon-fiber-clad dashboard sported modern instruments. Nappa leather and Alcantara upholstery along with air-conditioning also were part of the modifications. The reworked cars sported modern five-spoke alloy wheels, a tip-off to the conversion. They were sold for over $1 million each.

Ever since its founding, AMG has sat directly at the intersection of race cars and performance street vehicles. The ultimate example

TOP LEFT Even more displacement was available in the SL 73, which had its 6.0-liter V-12 bored out to 7.3 liters.

TOP RIGHT The M120 V-12 engine was tuned to produce 525 hp, delivered to the rear axle through a five-speed automatic transmission.

OPPOSITE, TOP Drawn back into the top class of sports car racing, Mercedes teamed with AMG and HWA to produce the CLK GTR, show here driven by Bernd Schneider.

OPPOSITE, BOTTOM The CLK GTR AMG is a road-going race car that retains the look and functionality of the competition version. Two distinctive features stand out in this front view: the air scoop on the roof for the mid-mounted engine and the stand-up three-pointed star hood ornament.

of this would be the AMG CLK GTR racer and the subsequent road-going versions offered in both coupe and roadster form.

Following its successes with AMG in German Touring Car (DTM) and the first year of the International Touring Car (ITC) series, Mercedes looked to step up to the new FIA GT Championship in 1997, the year after the DTM and ITC collapsed in 1996.

McLaren, which had introduced its F1 supercar in 1992, had taken the overall Le Mans win with its GT1 category F1 GTR, beating out faster cars in the WSC and LMP2 classes. While Le Mans was a big draw for manufacturers, the global FIA GT Championship for the GT1 class also provided impetus for factory involvement.

Unlike McLaren, which had converted its road-going F1 to GT1 specs, Porsche created its 911 GT1 by grafting the front appearance of the 993 generation 911 to a mid-engine 962 racer and then built the required twenty-five street versions to meet homologation requirements.

Mercedes took a similar tack with AMG to produce the CLK GTR. Using the grille and round headlamp treatment from the E-Class-based front-engine/rear-drive coupe, it fashioned a similar front clip on a mid-engine sports car with a chassis developed by Lola. The mid-mounted V-12 would be a variant of the M120 engine found in the R129 SL and W140 S-Class that was tweaked by Ilmor to produce 592 hp. Called alternatively the LS600 or GT112, this engine had a 12:1 compression ratio compared to the standard 10:1 setup and employed lightweight titanium connecting rods. The CLK GTR could hit a top speed of 205 mph (330 kph).

The CLK GTR was developed in 128 days thanks to the use of a McLaren F1 that Mercedes purchased and converted into a test mule for the powerplant. The car made its debut at the 1997 FIA GT four-hour race at Hockenheim with Bernd Schneider at the wheel. He put it on the pole and recorded the fastest lap, but the car eventually retired with brake issues.

However, things turned around at the Nürburgring four-hour where Schneider and Klaus Ludwig teamed up to take the overall win. Mercedes went on to win five more races and the manufacturers' championship. While the V-12 was fast, it did not have the sustained pace required to win a twenty-four-hour endurance race, so Mercedes skipped Le Mans.

In 1998 Mercedes returned to Le Mans with the CLK LM in the GT1 class. Similar to the GTR, the LM used a more robust V-8 engine. While the cars qualified 1–3, both dropped out after completing just nineteen and thirty-one laps respectively.

However, in contesting the FIA GT World Championship, Mercedes won the other ten rounds, the first two with the CLK GTR and the remaining eight after Le Mans with the V-8-powered LM. McLaren and Porsche dropped out of the class for 1999, leaving only Mercedes, so the FIA decided to eliminate the category altogether.

The program's legacy included more than two dozen homologation Strassenversion or "Street Version" coupes and roadsters, which are among some of the most desirable collector cars today. Virtually all of them are CLK GTR models, although two CLK LM homologation prototypes were built, both coupes. One was destroyed in testing; the other is in the hands of a collector.

Built by AMG with assistance from the newly formed HWA AG (the racing shop established by Hans Werner Aufrecht after Daimler took over AMG), the CLK GTR used the same monocoque as the racing cars. The roof retained its air scoop, but the stanchion-mounted rear racing wing

was replaced by a more elegant hoop-style spoiler that flowed from the bodywork. The small doors opened dihedral style, providing access to a more conventional road car interior.

The airbag-equipped wheel looked like it could have come from a stock CLK, but it was detachable to help the driver ease into a highly bolstered sport seat. Both buckets were upholstered in a plaid in honor of the 300 SLR models of the 1950s. In addition to the conventional dash and center stack, the CLK GTR also was equipped with air-conditioning and a sound system.

The CLK GTR Strassenversion models were not hindered by the FIA GT rules limiting power. A longer stroke boosted displacement from the 6.0 liters of the race engine to 6.9 liters. The V-12 now made 622 hp and 539 lb-ft of torque, according to an HWA spec sheet. The unrestricted motor delivered 0–60 mph (0–97 kph) acceleration of 3.8 seconds on the way to a top speed of 214 mph (344 kph).

Equipped with paddle shifters, all gear changes had to be made using the clutch pedal. Despite its race car underpinnings, Paul Frère, writing in *Road & Track*, was impressed by its tractability in spite of its extreme power. He wrote, "On the exit from a 35-mph [65-kph] corner in 6th gear, the car pulled not only smoothly, but quite vigorously as well, from around 1300 rpm. And, in the correct gear, its immediate response was astonishing. As parts of the track were damp that day, there is little I can report about the car's ultimate handling. However, its available urge is such that power oversteer is almost always on command—even on a dry surface."

"Most people not familiar with such cars would judge the CLK GTR very noisy," he continued. "Mechanical noises from the engine's intake

Mercedes-Benz

Mobil 1
Mobil 1
WARSTEINER
WARSTEINER
2
BRIDGESTONE
Mobil 1

and exhaust mix with those from its straight-cut gears. But, by racing standards, the CLK GTR is quite a silent car, much more so than the Porsche GT1 road version I drove. Obviously, considerable weight has gone into the CLK GTR's soundproofing materials."

AMG relied on HWA to build the six roadster versions. Eliminating the roof and its scoop necessitated opening up two new air ducts behind the twin roll hoops. The front end featured a new grille incorporating the three-pointed star, replacing the grille and stand-up hood ornament of the coupe. A strut-mounted rear wing replaced the coupe's hoop spoiler. The small front doors still opened in a dihedral fashion.

HWA also converted two coupes to a SuperSport configuration that used a larger E73 M297 7.3-liter V-12. This is the same engine that was used in the R129 Mercedes-Benz SL and the Pagani Zonda. Output was bumped to 655 hp and 580 lb-ft of torque. The 0–60 mph (0–97 kph) time dropped to fewer than 3.5 seconds. HWA also retrofitted three other chassis with the same engine tuned for even greater output of 711 hp. The *Guinness Book of World Records* declared at the time that the Strassenversion CLK GTR, which retailed for over $1.5 million each, was the most expensive production car in the world.

In addition to the CLK GTR project, the decade saw a rapid expansion in the AMG model count to over a dozen versions of Mercedes-Benz vehicles, including SUVs such as the ML- and G-Class. After the acquisition of a 51-percent stake in 1999 by Daimler AG, the newly formed Mercedes-AMG division was now responsible for the engine, transmission, chassis, brakes, aerodynamics, interior, design, and sales and marketing of all AMG-badged vehicles. The headquarters in Affalterbach were expanded. A new engine factory, showroom, and two engineering buildings were built in 2003, more than doubling the site from 199,000 to 426,000 square feet. AMG personnel would grow by another 50 percent to 600 employees.

With these additional responsibilities and resources, AMG moved into the first decade of the new century with an ever-growing model portfolio. In addition to the expected sport sedans, coupes, and roadsters, the AMG badge would be used on such unlikely variants as the 2001 Mercedes-Benz S 600 Pullman AMG limousine, the 2002 A32K AMG city car, and the 2006 Mercedes Benz R 63 AMG people mover. A new era had begun.

OPPOSITE, TOP The V-12 engine used in the CLK GTR was developed from the M120 used in the SL. While the displacement remained the same, AMG tuned the engine, now known as the GT112, to produce over 600 hp.

OPPOSITE, BOTTOM Concerned that the V-12 engine, while dominant in the shorter FIA GT championship races, wouldn't hold up over 24 hours at Le Mans, AMG developed the GTR LM that used a GT108B 5.0-liter V-8 engine also tuned to produce 600 hp. With the new engine, CLK LM as it was known, could be distinguished by the front fender louvers.

TOP HWA built this range of vehicles for AMG starting from left, the SL Black Series, CLK DTM convertible, CLK DTM coupe, CLK GTR roadster, and CLK GTR coupe. *HWA photo*

ABOVE The CLK GTR's successor in DTM, which hewed more closely to the production CLK coupes, spawned a limited-edition street version, also coveted by collectors. Only 100 CLK DTM AMG coupes and 80 convertibles were built between 2004 and 2006. None were exported to the United States.

Creating the AMG Crest

FOR TWO DECADES, THE THREE LETTERS A, M, AND G were all that was needed to define the performance brand. A simple badge with just those letters represented both Aufrecht and Melcher as well as Aufrecht's German hometown of Großaspach. Later the logo would sport a single line to underscore the letters. It would morph yet again with a new slanted typeface and hash marks adapted from the Mercedes Sportline badge.

In the late 1980s Aufrecht felt there needed to be a much stronger statement about AMG, one that incorporated the changes in the company, particularly in its relocation to Affalterbach.

But the first crude attempts, which primarily emphasized the company's engine work, were less than satisfying. Two particular samples stand out, the first a representation of an engine valve with a large square in the middle with AMG lettering. Aufrecht's handwritten note across the bottom criticized it for looking too much like an airplane. The second, with a cam lobe as its dominant element, came across as looking more like an egg.

The return to the drawing board was more successful as the logo took shape in a round form with a laurel, not unlike that used some of Mercedes' three-pointed star badging. Across the top of the crest is the hometown Affalterbach lettering. On the left side is an apple tree, which is *affalter* in old German and beneath it waters or *bach*, German for stream. The depiction is taken from Affalterbach's city coat of arms, which reflects the surrounding orchards and streams. In the fall you can find baskets of apples to snack on in lobbies around the AMG campus, reinforcing the company's close ties with the community.

The right side of the badge addresses the company's engine heritage with a much clearer depiction of a valve with its spring and the lobe of a cam. The imagery brings to mind Erhard Melcher's approach of designing engine upgrades one cylinder at a time. Across the bottom is the AMG lettering that appears on all the company's products. Introduced in 1989 at the Geneva Motor Show, the AMG crest is now one of the central elements in promoting the Mercedes-AMG brand.

OPPOSITE The badging on AMG vehicles changed slightly over the years, from the underlined AMG capital letters to the today's AMG lettering preceded by slashes.

ABOVE The AMG crest incorporates elements from the Affalterbach city coat of arms, namely the apple tree and stream, while the right side uses a valve and cam for the company's engineering prowess. The badge was introduced in 1989.

LB MA 4508
LB MA 5500
LB MA 645

9

THE BLACK SERIES

Following the complete integration of AMG into Mercedes-Benz in 2005, a new generation had taken over. While there were plenty of employees with careers dating back to the Affalterbach move, Hans Werner Aufrecht and Erhard Melcher were gone. But to say the passion for performance had waned with the old guard's departure would be wrong.

Just as Mercedes' legendary factory racing effort of the 1950s inspired Aufrecht in his quest to join the team and later strike out on his own, AMG has had a similar effect on this new wave of engineers, product planners, and engine builders.

The German language has many words to describe complex concepts. Taking pleasure at a foe's misfortune is *schadenfreude*. Running into someone who looks exactly like you is finding your *doppelgänger*. While in America we may call a very fast German car a bahnburner or in the case of AMG, a Hammer, Germans, when describing extreme performance, really don't have a word. They use a gesture instead. It involves making a fist perpendicular to the heart. With pursed lips and exhaling two small puffs, you stroke your fist forward twice, no more, no less. Postmerger AMG was filled with and continued to attract the kind of talent that intimately knew the gesture's meaning.

The vision for the new Mercedes-AMG business unit extended beyond the ambitious goal of building its own vehicle from the ground up, which would have to wait until later. In the meantime, there would be a complete range of AMG products available on just about every model in the Mercedes portfolio. Sitting at the pinnacle, there would be halo cars incorporating AMG's racing DNA. These limited-edition specials became known as the Black Series. Further distinguishing these higher output models from the standard AMG fare would be the black background on the engine plates signed by the top technicians who assembled these special motors.

Ralf Sporr, who oversees AMG's historic vehicles, describes the Black Series "as the flagship vehicles or a particularly sporty version of an AMG model range. They represent the performance limit of a model range, where everything possible is drawn out of that model. This creates a new quality standard. Black Series brings together everything that can be achieved in terms of driving technology at a certain point in time and puts it on the road."

The genesis of the Black Series, true to AMG form, traces back to a project to develop an SLK model for a one-make racing series in Asia. The starting point came from Formula 1, where the SLK had been modified and used for safety car duties for two seasons on the grand prix circuit.

Backed by an Asian investor, the plan called for building a run of specially tuned SLKs to compete in a series across China, Thailand, and Indonesia. Known as the SLK 55 AMG Ultimate Experience Asia or alternatively, the Tracksport, this run of thirty-five vehicles involved extensive revisions. The car was lightened by dispensing with the standard SLK retractable hardtop and mechanism, replacing it with a fixed carbon-fiber matte-black roof. Meant for track-only use, this modified SLK featured additional weight-saving measures that included the removal of

insulation, the use of fiberglass reinforced composite bucket seats, and thinner door linings. It also boasted upgraded brakes, a recalibrated transmission for quicker paddle shifts, and stiffer suspension settings.

While the 5.5-liter V-8 engine, which was rated at 360 hp and 376 lb-ft, remained the same as the production model, it benefited from a lightweight titanium exhaust system and additional oil and transmission cooling. The cars were fitted with roll cages, fire extinguishers, and safety harnesses.

Rumors in the press of roadgoing Tracksports were realized in the form of the first Black Series, which debuted in late 2006. It also featured a fixed carbon-fiber roof, while the M113 5.5-liter V-8 engine featured a bump in output to 400 hp. The car retained its seven-speed automatic transmission but added an adjustable suspension, upgraded brakes, a stiffer chassis, and Pirelli performance rubber. Mercedes said the upgrades knocked nearly a half-second off 0–62 mph (0–100 kph) acceleration of the standard SLK 55 AMG, the time dropping from 4.9 to 4.5 seconds.

Intended for road use, the Black Series SLK eliminated the roll cage and upgraded the racing seats to more comfortable sport buckets that still were more aggressively bolstered than those found on the stock SLK. Also, unlike the competition model, the Black Series came with the standard infotainment and audio systems used in regular production cars.

The SLK 55 AMG Coupe Black Series also set parameters of what could be expected in future iterations. All would be coupes with just two seats. The drivetrains would feature additional output, the suspension and brakes upgraded to allow for track-day outings and the vehicles made lighter by using carbon fiber in the structure and body panels.

Although AMG set no fixed number on the production run of the SLK Black Series, only about 120 were sold. The low numbers were due to the high sticker of $125,000 and the fact that none were available in North America.

The second installment in this limited-edition sport coupe series came along quickly after the SLK in the form of the 2008 CLK 63 AMG Black Series. The C209-based CLK was somewhat of a tweener between the C- and E-Class, drawing on chassis and suspension bits from both. The CLK 63 AMG Black Series also had a serious pedigree drawing on both the previous CLK DTM coupe and cabrio models produced between 2004 and 2006 as well as the then current F1 safety car, which was also CLK-based.

Beneath the hood sat AMG's M156 6.2-liter normally aspirated V-8, which produced 500 horsepower and 465 lb-ft of torque. While the latter figure is unchanged from the standard CLK 63

PREVIOUS AMG has produced six Black Series models, starting with the SLK 55 that debuted in late 2006.

ABOVE Based on a model called the Tracksport, which was initially built for a racing series in Asia, the SLK 55 Black Series sported a fixed carbon-fiber roof. Priced at $125,000, it wasn't available in the US market.

BELOW To differentiate the Black Series models from standard AMG fare, the engines feature black badges signed by the select master technicians who assemble them.

AMG, the Black Series benefited from an extra 25 horses. The seven-speed dual-clutch transmission of the standard AMG model also was retained. Mercedes said the setup was good for 0–62 mph (0–100 kph) acceleration of 4.1 seconds. Top speed was electronically limited to 186 mph (300 kph).

Keeping true to the Black Series spirit, the CLK had its rear bench seat removed. While the steel roof was retained, carbon fiber was employed in the exterior aero kit. Additional stiffening of the front shock towers and in the rear end, along with wider front and rear tracks, took advantage of the extra grip provided by the Pirelli P Zero Corsa rubber and manually adjustable coil spring suspension.

Depending on the market, the CLK Black Series would be equipped with fixed shell bucket seats while the American models had leather upholstered sport seats that were manually adjusted fore and aft with a power recline and lumbar and bolster support functions.

Mercedes says 700 were built worldwide, with about half coming to the United States priced from about $130,000.

The wildest member of the Black Series family bears only a passing resemblance to the F1 Safety Car that migrated to the newest generation of the SL-Class in 2008–2009. The Mercedes SL 65 AMG Coupe Black Series shared only the door skins and outside rearview mirrors with its regular production counterpart.

Development of this particular Black Series model was outsourced to Hans Werner Aufrecht's HWA AG race shop. The redesigned body, which featured large hood air extractors, side vents, and an aggressive aero kit with a pop-up rear wing, is made of carbon-fiber reinforced plastic. Like the original SLK Black Series, the retractable hardtop has been replaced with a fixed carbon-fiber top with a lower roofline. Ditching the top and mechanism saved over 400 pounds (181 kg). The muscular bodywork also stretches over a track that is widened 4.5 inches (11 cm) in the front and

TOP The first Black Series model to make it to America was the second in the series, the CLK 63. Available with only two-passenger seating, it's fitted with a body kit that gives it a more aggressive look.

SECOND FROM TOP A carbon-fiber rear wing, large diffuser, and four exhaust tips completes the CLK 63 Black Series package.

THIRD FROM TOP The M156 V-8 engine packs 500 hp. Note the black badge atop the intake manifold.

BOTTOM AMG also built safety cars for use in Formula 1, including this SL-based model. It would become the inspiration for another member of the Black Series family.

4.1 inches (10 cm) in the rear. Lightweight forged aluminum wheels measure 19 inches (48 cm) front and 20 inches (51 cm) rear, shod with Dunlop SP Sport Maxx GT rubber.

The M275 6.0-liter V-12 saw an increase of 57 horsepower over the SL 63 AMG to 661 horses, thanks to larger turbochargers. Torque remained unchanged at 738 lb-ft, which was about all that the five-speed automatic could handle. Additional heat exchangers and cooling systems were added to the turbochargers and limited-slip rear differential. According to Mercedes, the SL Black Series could accelerate to 60 mph (97 kph) in 3.8 seconds while top speed was electronically limited to 199 mph (320 kph).

Other enhancements included larger brakes and an adjustable coil-over shock suspension. While European models were again fitted with shell-back racing seats, US versions were equipped with standard SL sport seats. Even though the body is essentially all new, the interior retained many of the amenities found in the standard SL 63 AMG. Limited to a run of just 350 units, half of the SL 6 AMG Coupe Black Series models were destined for North America. The car quickly sold out despite a sticker of $300,000.

With the introduction of the SLS AMG and its subsequent use as the F1 safety car, the linkage between that program and the Black Series was broken when the C 63 AMG Coupe Black Series arrived for 2011–2012.

Based on the W204 C-Class Coupe, this particular Black Series model employed the M156 6.2-liter V-8, which borrowed reinforced components such as connecting rods, a crankshaft, and other bits from the M159 motor used in the SLS. Horsepower was increased to 510, a bump of 59 over the standard C 63 AMG model. Torque was also tweaked to 457 lb-ft, which was delivered to the rear axle via a seven-speed SpeedShift MCT transmission. Merecedes claimed 0–60-mph (0–97-kph) acceleration of 4.2 seconds, with top speed capped at 186 mph (300 kph). At the time, it was touted as the fastest C-Class ever.

Even as it stayed true to form with its coupe bodywork and two-passenger seating, buyers could opt to have the four-passenger seating arrangement from the standard C63 AMG installed. The interior also featured the first use of Dinamica microfiber on the seat inserts, while Nappa leather covered the side bolsters.

The exterior was aggressive, but perhaps not as extroverted as the preceding SL Black Series. Most of the differentiation comes from the larger front inlets as well as the flared and vented wheel arches that help to accommodate the wider track that grew 1.57 inches (4 cm)

TOP The most extreme Black Series model produced was the SL 65. Virtually all the body panels were replaced, most with carbon-fiber pieces. The wildly flared fenders accommodate a wider track and larger wheels. Like the SLK Black Series, the retractable hardtop was replaced with a fixed carbon-fiber lid.

ABOVE Production of the AMG SL 65 Black Series was outsourced to HWA. Here the vehicles are being assembled in the company's shop adjacent to the AMG complex in Affalterbach.

in the front and 3.11 inches (8 cm) in the rear. A stepped lower sill connects the two flares, while the tail sports additional vents and a large diffuser.

Buyers could opt for an AMG Aerodynamics package that added winglets on the front carbon-fiber splitter and an adjustable rear wing on the decklid. An AMG Track pack featured specially designed Dunlop sport tires measuring 255/35 front and 285/30 rear fitted to the forged alloy 19-inch (48-cm) wheels. An 800-unit worldwide production run was planned, with US versions priced from $105,000.

In a turnaround from previous models, which took their inspiration from DTM racers and F1 safety cars, the C 63 AMG Coupe Black Series influenced the last run of standard C 65 AMG coupes and sedans. In 2014, to mark the end of production of that model, AMG introduced the Edition 507 built around an increase in output from the 6.2-liter engine, which grew from 451 to 507 hp, nearly matching that of the 510-hp Black Series. Again, the M156 V-8 used forged pistons, lightweight connecting rods, and a forged crankshaft from the V-8 found in the SLS. Mercedes

TOP In 2012 Mercedes-AMG introduced its next Black Series, this one based on the C-Class Coupe. Like the CLK it has a much more aggressive body kit and a hunkered-down look. A larger rear wing was part of an optional aerodynamic package.

LEFT Adding to the C 63's sporty looks were black, thin-spoked, lightweight alloy wheels.

ABOVE Not really an official Black Series model, the 2014 C 63 Edition 507 Coupe used some of the same components, including the M156 V-8. As name implies, the modifications netted 507 horsepower..

ABOVE The AMG SLS also benefited from the Black Series treatment. This photo shows five of the color combinations available in 2014.

said the improvements were good for a 0–60 mph (0–97 kph) time of 4.1 seconds, while top speed was electronically limited top speed at 174 mph (280 kph).

Unlike the Black Series, the Edition 507 was an option that replaced a previous AMG Performance Package that bumped engine output to 481 hp. The Edition 507 cost $10,000 above the base price of the $60,000 C63 AMG sedan and the $62,500 C63 AMG coupe.

The fifth installment in the family, the SLS AMG Black Series Coupe, was introduced in 2013 with a production run said to number about 350 units. Not nearly as radical as the SL 65 Black Series, the SLS had an increase in output from 583 to 622 hp on its resume. Torque would drop slightly, to 468 lb-ft, but thanks to a shorter final drive ratio and lighter weight, the 0–60 mph (0–97 kph) performance improved to 3.5 seconds. When *Car and Driver* tested the car, it proved even quicker, posting a time of 3.2 seconds.

The horsepower boost came from a revised intake and modified valvetrain, with revised cam timing and lift that helped to bump the redline to 8,000 rpm. At the time, it was the industry's most powerful normally aspirated engine fitted to a production model.

In addition to a more muscular powerplant, the SLS AMG Black Series Coupe leveraged the weight-saving techniques used in the GT3 competition program. Under the AMG Lightweight Performance banner, the SLS Coupe benefited from the use of carbon fiber in both the space-frame components and the body panels. Other weight-saving efforts included the use of a titanium

instead of a steel exhaust system and even going as far as replacing the lead acid battery with a lithium-ion unit. Total weight savings were 154 pounds (70 kg).

Other race-proven technology included standard carbon-ceramic brakes, a fixed rear wing, a front aerodynamic splitter, a large rear diffuser, and an interior fitted with lightweight carbon-fiber-backed sport bucket seats upholstered in Alcantara. The Black Series also was equipped with fully adjustable coil-over shocks, a faster shifting transmission, and an electronically controlled differential in place of the standard mechanical setup. Price of admission? A cool $275,000.

Nearly six years would pass before another Black Series model was released, this most recent iteration based on the AMG GT successor to the SLS. While still a two-seat coupe, the 2021 Mercedes-AMG GT Black Series featured a new biturbo flat-plane crank 4.0-liter V-8 for power. Carrying the designation M178 LS2, it replaced the venerable 5.5- and 6.2-liter V-8s that saw service in all Black Series models, except for the SL. Like the SL Black Series, the GT relied on forced induction to make 720 hp and 590 lb-ft of torque. Larger turbochargers that deliver up to 24.6 psi of boost are largely responsible for the increased output. Power is delivered to the rear seven-speed SpeedShift dual-clutch transaxle, which has been specifically modified to handle the high level of torque.

With a top speed of 202 mph (325 kph) and the ability to hit 60 mph (97 kph) in only 3.1 seconds, the Mercedes-AMG GT Black Series certainly was quick. But it also handled exceptionally well. For proof, Mercedes took to the Nordschleife (North Loop) of the famed Nürburgring in 2020 and came away with a time of six minutes and forty-eight seconds to cover the nearly 13-mile-long (21-km) circuit. It was a new production car record.

Taking a page from earlier models, Mercedes again looked to both the F1 Safety Car program and its successful AMG GT3/GT4 privateer racing program for inspiration. Among these cues are larger cooling ducts in the front fascia, along with a carbon-fiber hood with exhaust air vents for better cooling and enhanced aerodynamics. Further weight reduction comes from the carbon fiber used on the fenders and the low-profile roof. Even the glass used in the rear window is thinner to reduce mass.

Aerodynamic improvements include a front splitter with adjustable elements and a two-piece adjustable rear wing. The front aero device has two settings, street and race, the latter designed specifically for track use. It can be extended to create venturi ground effects

TOP Not as radical as the SL 65 Black Series, the SLS variant still employed a lot of the weight-saving measures and performance upgrades found in the GT3 racing machines. A fixed rear wing replaced the deployable airfoil found on standard production SLS models.

MIDDLE The V-8 engine in the SLS Black Series was boosted from 583 to 622 hp.

ABOVE Lightweight sport bucket seats clad in Alcantara were among the changes to the SLS Black Series interior.

S MB 2016

S MB 2019

S MB 1103

S MB 1103

on the underbody, providing more downforce on the front axle to enhance steering and vehicle turn-in. Meanwhile, the top element of the rear wing moves electronically through a range of 20 degrees. For instance, when the top "Master" driving mode is engaged (the other settings include Basic, Advanced, and Pro), the wing will flatten above 155 mph (250 km), reducing drag to allow the vehicle to reach top speed more quickly.

In addition to the electronic adaptive coil-over shocks, manually adjustable suspension settings include camber and roll bar stiffness front and rear. Front 19-inch (48-cm) and rear 20-inch (51-cm) forged alloy rims can be equipped with the standard soft-compound Michelin Pilot Sport Cup 2 R MO tires or an optional harder compound tire designed for high temperatures generated in track use.

As has been the case with previous Black Series models, European versions use fixed-back racing seats with harnesses, while the US models feature an adjustable sport bucket seat. Lighter-weight door panels use straps instead of traditional door pulls, while the upholstery is a blend of Nappa leather and Dinamica microfiber with orange contrast stitching.

Besides being one of the fastest production cars of its time, this particular Black Series also has the distinction of the first one identified as a Mercedes-AMG rather than a Mercedes-Benz model. Around 1,700 were built over the two-year production run with nearly half coming to North America at a starting price of $326,000.

Though not a regularly recurring element in the Mercedes-AMG product portfolio, the Black Series remains a potent reminder of the brand's engineering excellence. With new hybrid and electric vehicles in the pipeline, in all likelihood, there will be future models joining this exclusive lineup.

OPPOSITE, TOP Like the 507 Edition, AMG used much of the Black Series equipment when it came time to say good-bye to the SLS. The SLS Final Edition Coupe and Roadster were distinguished by their contrasting carbon-fiber hoods.

OPPOSITE, MIDDLE LEFT The sixth Black Series model debuted in 2021. The Mercedes-AMG GT is striking in appearance with its wider body kit, additional hood and fender vents, and a large rear wing.

OPPOSITE, MIDDLE RIGHT The black carbon-fiber roof, heavily tinted rear window, and a black diffuser offers contrast to the body color. The high, multi-element rear wing is an adaptation of the airfoil used on the GT3 race car.

OPPOSITE, BOTTOM This cockpit view is framed by the roll cage. The front buckets are Euro-spec fixed back carbon-fiber shells. US models have conventional sport buckets adjustable for rake.

ABOVE Marking ten years of offering GT3 models for customer racing, Mercedes-AMG created a commemorative model (left) that shows racing's influence on the road-going Black Series.

AMG Performance Studio: More Options and Exclusivity

MOVING BEYOND AMG'S ORIGINS of boosting performance levels of Mercedes' standard models, the now completely in-house Mercedes-AMG operation set its sights on offering a wider range of exclusive and bespoke product offerings. To appeal to this more discriminating set of buyers, Mercedes-AMG created the Performance Studio.

While the Black Series is a product of this department, the Performance Studio was also responsible for Signature Series and Editions models and well as providing the ability to cater to the individual customer desires. While not as extensive as some of the modifications that AMG performed in catering to its client's tastes in the late 1970s and throughout the 1980s, where it would add TVs, coolers, and car phone handsets, the studio was very much involved in the *Optik* and the *Technik* when it came to paint, interior materials, and performance enhancements.

When the studio was created in 2006, AMG chief Volker Mornhinweg said in a press release that it was a response to "more and more requests from AMG fans and sports car enthusiasts from around the world for even more dynamic vehicles, special equipment features and specific components. And the new Performance Studio makes it possible for us to meet these requests."

Upon its inauguration, the Performance Studio demonstrated its wide-ranging approach by showcasing two other models alongside the first SLK 55 AMG Black Series. The Signature Series spawned the CLK DTM AMG Cabriolet, of which only eighty were built. An evolution of the coupe version introduced in 2004, the cabrio featured the same 582-hp supercharged 5.4-liter V-8. Mercedes-AMG boasted that its 0–62 mph (0–100 kph) acceleration of 4.0 seconds and electronically limited top speed of 186 mph (300 kph) made it the fastest open-top four-seater in the world. Priced around $300,000, it was sold primarily in Europe—neither the coupe nor the cabriolet DTM models was offered in the US.

The Editions models would focus more on appearance and tie-ins with other luxury brands as well as AMG-specific performance upgrades. Mercedes-AMG cited the CLS 55 AMG IWC Ingenieur, which bowed in 2005, as an example of this approach. In a joint product and marketing effort that continues to this day, AMG worked with Swiss watchmaker IWC Schaffhausen to develop a car that would incorporate design cues of the Ingenieur series of watches. Chief among these was the instrument panel, which resembled the jeweled look of an IWC watch face. The production run was limited to 165 of the four-door coupes.

The Performance Studio followed up that model in 2008 with the SL 63 AMG Edition IWC. This 200-unit run of SL models, all in Kashmir white matte finish, featured exterior body kit in carbon-fiber plus an AMG suspension upgrade package. Again the analog gauges reflected the look of the IWC Grosser Ingenieur (Great Engineer) watch, one of which would be given to each buyer.

AMG later teamed up with Nick Hart, creative director of noted London tailor Spencer Hart in 2013 to create a special edition of the CLS 63 AMG Shooting Brake. Painted in "Nick Hart Midnight Blue" (a favorite color of the designer), the car's understated look is enhanced by darkened wheels and chrome exterior accents. The appearance package included a chocolate brown leather interior inspired by the "Vault," the walnut-paneled personal shopping area inside Spencer Hart. The headrests featured the tailor's logo, along with Midnight Blue contrast stitching on the hides and Hart's signature on the center console.

The Production Studio was eventually incorporated in Mercedes' broader Manufaktur program that has since taken over requests for custom exterior paint schemes and individualized interior treatments. Meanwhile, customers can also access the full AMG catalog of performance and appearance items. Buyers can order specific wheel/tire packages, high-performance carbon-ceramic brakes, tauter suspension pieces (which include springs and dampers), electronic limited-slip differentials, and additional cooling packages.

Mercedes-AMG also will continue to create limited-run special editions from the CLA-Class up through the G-Wagen. Giving Mercedes-AMG customers such a wide range of options rings true to one of Hans Werner Aufrecht's sayings: "You can't really improve a Mercedes . . . but you can make it different."

TOP The many color offerings of the Performance Studio. Eventually the Performance Studio offerings became part of Mercedes' bespoke Manufaktur program catering to the specific needs of its customers.

ABOVE This white on piano black customer interior is an example of the customization possible on AMG vehicles. Note the Manufaktur script on the center console.

10

PARTNERS IN PERFORMANCE

WHEN AMG MOVED FROM outside supplier to greater integration within Mercedes-Benz, its new parent found plenty of new projects on which Affalterbach's expertise would be put to good use. Chief among them was a supercar born from the expanded Mercedes-McLaren Formula 1 tie-up that saw the German company assuming a new 40-percent share of its British partner.

This car would take its inspiration from the Uhlenhaut Mercedes 300 SLR Coupe from 1955. The SLR designation, a combination of the German Sport, Leicht, and Rennsport, essentially means lightweight sport racer. Others have stated it means Super-Leicht Rennsport or super-light racer.

The new car debuted as the Vision SLR concept at the 1999 North American International Auto Show in Detroit. It was referred to as "Tomorrow's Silver Arrow," a callback to the silver cars that dominated grand prix racing in the 1930s and 1950s. A roadster version rolled out later that year at the IAA Frankfurt Motor Show. The show cars featured a 5.0-liter supercharged V-8 prepared by AMG.

The Vision SLR derived its looks from a number of influences, including some proportions from the range-topping SL and the 1955 SLR's upward swinging doors and side exhaust. From the McLaren-Mercedes F1 entry, the SLR derived its prominent nose with the three-pointed star and curved aerodynamic wings in the front intake.

While the Vision SLR and the production models that followed didn't have the gullwing doors of the 300 SLR (and '50s SL coupes), it did use a dihedral butterfly arrangement on the coupe and subsequent roadster models. Also, a pop-up airbrake on the rear deck can be traced directly back to the '50s-era cars.

Internally called Project 9 at McLaren, the final product became known as the Mercedes-Benz SLR McLaren. Much of the design engineering fell to Gordon Murray, who had overseen the company's previous exotic road car effort, the McLaren F1.

While styling would remain under Mercedes control, Murray was responsible for shepherding the concept to production. The British firm would supply the monocoque carbon-fiber body and chassis and would build the cars at its new McLaren Technology Center in Woking, England, using the skills of many who had worked on the race team. McLaren's experience in building the SLR set the table for its later solo efforts in bringing the MP4-12C road car to the market in 2011.

Even though it bore the pedigree of the Mercedes-McLaren F1 efforts, the Mercedes-Benz SLR McLaren was more of a front mid-engine GT than a purpose-built track car like McLaren's earlier mid-engine F1, which boasted BMW V-12 power.

Mercedes, which provided the mechanical bits in addition to the final exterior look, relied heavily on the expertise of AMG in developing the engine and supplying the five-speed dual-clutch automatic transmission.

In the period between the concept's debut and the launch of the production car in 2003, AMG boosted the output of the concept's 5.0-liter engine by modifying a larger 5.4-liter M113 K

PREVIOUS Taking shape on a designer's sketch pad, the Vision SLR concept would evolve into the Mercedes-Benz SLR McLaren.

TOP The design brief called for a front mid-engined sports grand tourer. McLaren's Gordon Murray wanted a car with a more performance bent.

ABOVE Another early sketch reflects the design intent from Mercedes as a luxury coupe.

V-8. While this engine was used in AMG 55 models and utilized the same aluminum construction with three valves per cylinder, it was strengthened and had its compression reduced to 8.8:1 from 9.0:1, while its rev limit was upped from 6,500 to 7,000 rpm.

Other improvements included a freer flowing exhaust, a more aggressive cam lift, an improved intake with larger throttle body, and a Lysholm-type twin-screw supercharger producing 13 psi of boost. A race-inspired dry-sump lubrication system resulted in a more compact package that allowed the engine to be mounted lower and aft of the front axle, greatly improving the car's front/rear weight distribution and lowering its center of gravity. This move to a front mid-engine layout also lengthened the nose of the production model considerably, changing the original and tidier SL proportions of the concept.

AMG's efforts resulted in an engine that produced 617 hp and 575 lb-ft of torque. All these changes earned the V-8's own designation as the M155. Its output drives the rear wheels through an AMG SpeedShift five-speed automatic transmission. While Mercedes had a seven-speed gearbox available, it opted for the simpler and more robust five cog option to handle the high levels of torque. According to *Car and Driver*, the SLR was capable of 0–60 mph (0–97 kph) in 3.4 seconds and 11.2 seconds in the quarter mile at 130 mph (209 kph). Mercedes said the car could hit a top speed of 207 mph (333 kph).

Mercedes planned on selling 500 SLRs per year over a seven-year model run, priced at upward of $450,000. That estimate proved to

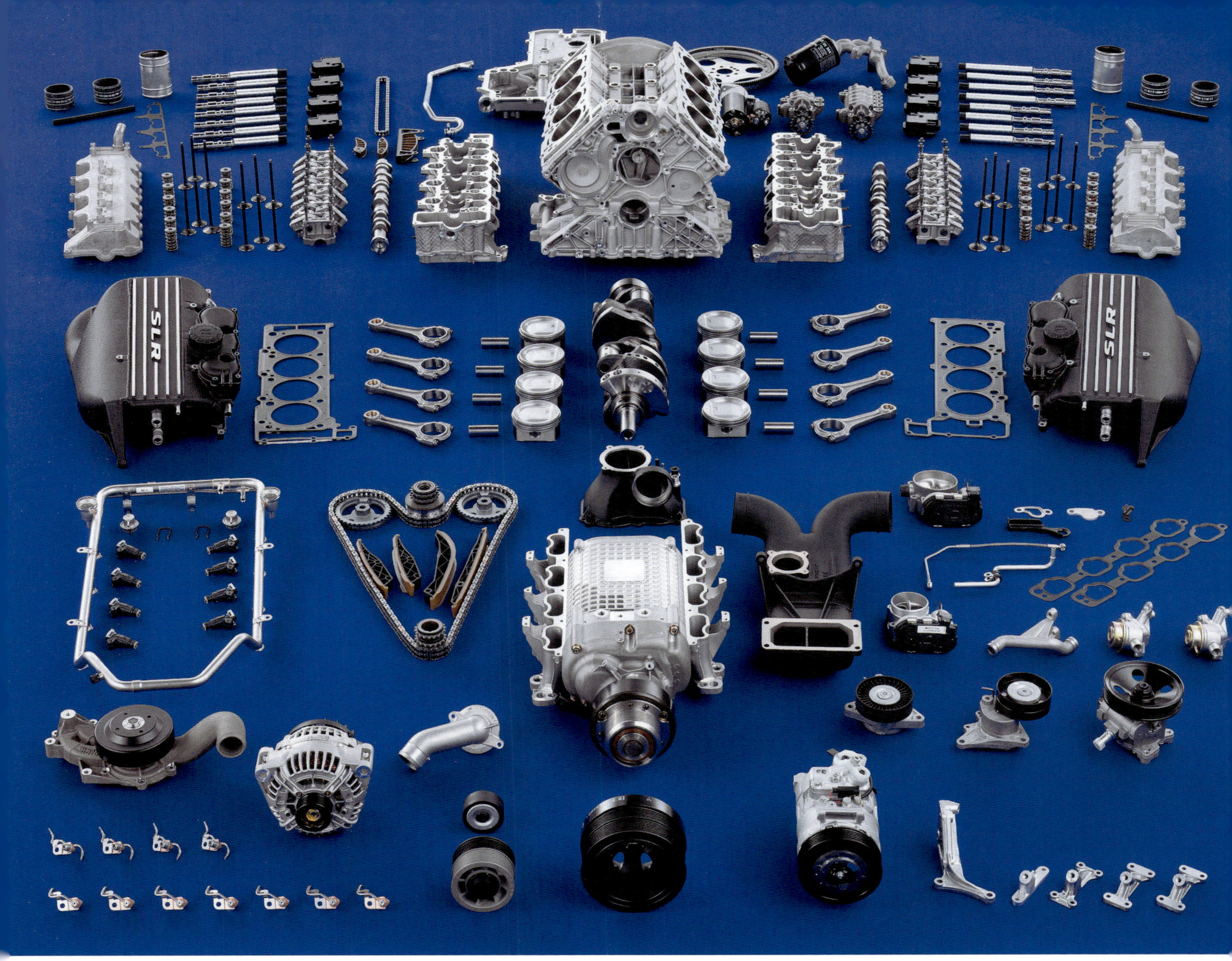

be optimistic. It took three years to sell the first 1,000 units, and with interest seemingly peaked, the sales figures declined. As a result, Mercedes turned again to AMG to increase performance and to create a new limited-run variation called the 722 Edition.

This new model linked the Mercedes SLR McLaren with the 1955 Mille Miglia–winning 300 SLR piloted by Sir Stirling Moss with Denis Jenkinson navigating. Cars were numbered by their departure time from Brescia, in this case 7:22 a.m. Moss and Jenkinson covered the nearly 1,000-mile (1609-km) course to Rome and back in a record-setting ten hours, seven minutes, and forty-eight seconds at a phenomenal average speed of 97.96 mph (158 kph).

For the modern SLR, dubbed the 722, AMG reprogrammed the engine to increase boost while lowering the redline to 6,500 rpm. As a result, the 5.4-liter supercharged V-8 now made 641 horsepower and 605 lb-ft of torque. Top speed increased to 209 mph (336 kph). Other modifications included the use of lightweight alloy 19-inch (48-cm) wheels to reduce unsprung weight, the ride height was lowered, the suspension stiffened, and the front brake rotors enlarged.

OPPOSITE, TOP The SLR looked to tie together the heritage of the 300 SL Gullwing with Mercedes' Formula 1 effort.

OPPOSITE, MIDDLE In profile the SLR McLaren had an extremely long nose with the cockpit pushed back to almost the rear axle. The generous space beneath the hood allowed the engine to be positioned behind the centerline of the front axle. Instead of the 300SL's gullwing doors, the SLR used scissor-style butterfly doors.

OPPOSITE, BOTTOM The rear three-quarter view reveals a look similar to the early design sketch. Massive side grilles helped channel air out of the engine bay. The SLR's wide stance enhanced the car's roadholding capabilities.

ABOVE A new engine, the M155, was developed from the supercharged 5.4-liter M113 K V-8 used in AMG 55 series vehicles. This expanded detailed view shows all the components.

TOP In 2006 Mercedes-Benz chairman Dr. Dieter Zetsche introduces the 722 trim level that offered more horsepower and paid tribute to Stirling Moss's 1955 Mille Miglia victory in an SLR.

ABOVE Producing 641 hp, the 722 saw its top speed rise to 209 mph (336 kph).

OPPOSITE, TOP The 722 badging, outlined in red, is similar to the red number worn by Moss's car.

OPPOSITE, MIDDLE LEFT The red accents used in the engine bay further distinguished this limited-edition model.

OPPOSITE, MIDDLE RIGHT The interior of the 722, upholstered in red, provided contrast to the black Alcantara dash and exterior silver paint scheme.

OPPOSITE, BOTTOM A roadster version was added in 2007. It featured a semiautomatic cloth roof instead of the retractable hardtop found on Mercedes' SL and SLK models.

The 722 was also distinguished by the use of a new front air dam and rear diffuser, blackened tail lamp lenses, and darker headlamp bezels. The car was also fitted with carbon-fiber accents and a black leather/Alcantara interior and red "722" badging. Only 150 were built, priced from $480,000.

To further rekindle interest in the series, Mercedes introduced a roadster version in 2007. The fixed roof was replaced by a semiautomatic cloth top that required the occupants to release latches on the header before powering the top down. The Mercedes SLR McLaren roadster was equipped with the same engine as the coupe with 617 hp and 575 lb-ft of torque. Because of the less slippery shape from the convertible roof, top speed was 1 mph less, at 208 (335 kph). The base price increased to $500,000.

A year later Mercedes brought the 722 Edition treatment to the roadster. Also limited to a run of 150 units like the coupe, it benefited from the more powerful engine and incorporated the larger brakes, stiffer suspension, and other improvements that comprised the 722 Edition package.

In the interim some 722 GT Coupes were built by Ray Mallock Ltd. for the SLR Club, a one-make racing series. The body was modified to accommodate wider racing rubber; a large fixed rear wing was attached, and the upper grille vents were opened for better airflow. Other changes included adding an adjustable Eibach racing suspension, and the ceramic discs replaced by an FIA-compliant system with steel rotors. In true race car fashion, the luxury interior was stripped out and replaced by Recaro racing seats, with six-point harnesses, new carbon-fiber door panels, and a full roll cage. Only twenty-one were built.

Another ten Mercedes SLR McLaren coupes were built in 2008 at the behest of Bahrain's king as gifts for other Arab emirates. All were built to 722 specification and are identified as the Crown Edition.

The program began to wind down in 2009 as Mercedes and McLaren prepared to go their separate ways. Coupe production would officially end, and in the last two years, only roadsters were sold.

722

TOP For the final run of the SLR series, Mercedes planned a special model paying homage to racing great Sterling Moss. Unlike the 722, this special model would be an open-top roadster much like his racing SLR.

ABOVE Thanks to its roofless design, the Stirling Moss models were the lightest and fastest SLR yet with a top speed of 217 mph (350 kph). Only seventy-five models were built, priced at $1.5 million each. The Stirling Moss Edition is highly prized by collectors to this day.

As part of this sendoff, Mercedes introduced the SLR Stirling Moss Edition, a roofless speedster that paid homage to the original 722 race car he campaigned in the Mille Miglia. The striking look, penned by designer Yoon Il-hun, featured all-new bodywork starting with a more aggressive shark-nose front end with much larger lower inlets. A single air scoop was offset to the right side of the hood. Tiny wind deflectors on the cowl directed airflow up and over the occupants.

Other changes included redesigned headlamp and taillight modules for a cleaner look. The side vents had been opened to house the exhaust tips, which previously exited at the base of the body behind the rear wheels. To add further stiffness to the monocoque, the side sills were much higher, resulting in much smaller, butterfly-opening doors than the roadster. A pair of aerodynamic roll hoops were perched atop the faired-in headrests, completing the look that recalls the original 722.

While it uses the same 641-hp engine from the 722 Edition, the Stirling Moss model is faster with a top speed of 217 mph (349 kph) thanks to its lighter bodywork and other tweaks that dropped 441 pounds (200 kg) from the standard roadster's curb weight.

Priced at over $1 million, only seventy-five Mercedes SLR Stirling Moss models were built and were available only to those who owned an SLR. Throughout the entire production run from 2003 to 2009, approximately 2,150 SLR models were made.

The significance of this project cannot be understated. There certainly were differences on what the two partners expected from the SLR—Mercedes wanted a high-performance GT with an emphasis on luxury, while McLaren was pushing for a lighter, more track-oriented performance car.

Both partners, however, took away knowledge that would become invaluable in the days ahead. McLaren got a taste of what it would

TOP As part of the DaimlerChrysler tie-up, AMG supplied 3.2-liter supercharged V-6 engines for the Chrysler Crossfire SRT-6 Coupe (shown) and Convertible in 2005. *DaimlerChrysler press photo*

MIDDLE AMG has been the source of V-12 engines for Italian supercar maker Pagani. One of the vehicles currently using the engine is the Utopia. *Pagani press photo*

BOTTOM The M158 biturbo 6.0-liter V-12 makes 852 hp in the Utopia. Just like all hand-built engines from AMG, the V-12 in the Utopia carries a badge at the front of the engine signed by its builder, Michael Kübler in this case. *Pagani press photo*

need to build series production cars for the road (it's previous road car foray, the exotic F1 saw only 106 produced). Meanwhile, Mercedes-Benz, as a volume manufacturer, got a feel for building limited-run, high-dollar exotics that could go toe-to-toe with cars such as the Ferrari Enzo and Porsche Carrera GT.

But even more importantly, Mercedes took what it learned from McLaren to transform AMG from a producer of high-output performance drivetrains into a manufacturer in its own right.

The McLaren connection is part of a longer history of collaboration with other makers in developing performance upgrades. AMG has provided its hand-built engines to partners, including Italian supercar maker Pagani, Aston Martin (in which Daimler AG holds a stake), and Lotus, as well as some lesser-known arrangements with mass market brands.

Among the latter, AMG worked with both Mitsubishi and Honda. The 1987 Mitsubishi Debonair V300 Royal AMG was a styling exercise with a body kit, wheels, and steering wheel with AMG badging. Also, for the Japanese Domestic Market (JDM) was the 1989–1991 Galant AMG, which had an AMG engine and body kits. About 500 were built.

The project with Mitsubishi, however, almost became AMG's undoing. In the book, *AMG Reaching for the Stars*, Aufrecht relates this story: "Suddenly a Japanese guy turned up and claimed he held the name rights for AMG. We just laughed to begin with. But the worst of it was that he was right. In 1978, when no one could have suspected what would become of AMG and few people knew anything about the existence of so-called name rights, he secured the rights to the acronym. He had the right nose for business and waited seven years for his time to come. We spent three weeks negotiating in Japan before we finally got the name back." In 1993 the German patent office designated AMG as a trademark establishing a worldwide copyright.

Honda also teamed up with AMG to do a special edition of its Ballade (known as the Civic in the United States) for the South African market. This model, which appeared in the late 1980s and early 1990s, included Eibach springs, alloy wheels, and larger rear spoilers.

Another little-known application of AMG V-8 power was in about thirty units of the Isdera Imperator 108i built between 1984 and 2000. Originally conceived as a futuristic successor to the Mercedes 300 SL Gullwing by Porsche developer Eberhard Schulz, the car first appeared as the CW 311 concept. Built by Rainer Buchmann's bb-Auto Exclusive, it got the blessing of Mercedes and appeared with a three-pointed star on its nose. When it went into production as the Isdera Imperator 108i, it was equipped with a 375-hp M100 V-8 prepared by AMG. A later model boasted 410 hp from an AMG M119 V-8.

HII ADN

During the DaimlerChrysler days, the 3.2-liter supercharged V-6 from the SLK 32 AMG was transplanted in the 2005 Chrysler Crossfire SRT-6. The M112 V-6 was tuned to produce 335 hp, giving the Crossfire a top speed of 158 mph (254 kph), 3 miles per hour (5 kph) more than its SLK counterpart, which was limited to 155 mph (250 kph).

Better known in performance circles is the use of AMG V-12's in Pagani supercars, AMG V-8 engines in Aston Martins, and Lotus' sourcing of an AMG four-cylinder powerplant.

When Argentinian native Horacio Pagani decided to build his own supercar after helping Lamborghini set up its carbon-fiber processes, one of his supporters was fellow countryman Juan Manuel Fangio. Pagani had hoped to call his car the Fangio F1 but decided not to in respect after the driver's death. Still he wanted to use a Mercedes engine and struck a deal with AMG to provide V-12 powerplants that he uses to this day.

His first, the Pagani Zonda, which debuted in 1999, was powered by an AMG-prepared normally aspirated M120 V-12 making up to 444 hp. It was followed closely thereafter by the Zonda C12-S, which was bumped up to 7.0 liters and 542 hp. The Zonda S 7.3 coupe and roadster with its 7.3-liter V-12 supplanted it in 2002 with a slight increase to 547 hp. The 2003 Pagani Zonda GR dropped back down to 7.0-liters but made 592 hp.

Pagani Zonda R track models and the Cinque road car saw a return to 6.0 liters of displacement for the M120, but a higher compression ratio and further tuning by AMG lifted output to 740 hp. Pagani also began to source the new M297 V-12. Displacing 7.3 liters, it was used until 2017 in a wide range of Pagani models with output ranging from just under 600 to nearly 800 hp.

With the debut of the C9 Huayra (which replaced the C8 Zonda series), Pagani adopted AMG's M158 biturbo 6.0-liter V-12. This engine appeared in a succession of Huayra models with output ranging from 730 to nearly 900 hp. The C10 Utopia series, which was introduced in 2023 as a run of ninety-nine coupes, also uses the M158 tuned to 852 hp.

Through a technology tie-up with Daimler AG dating back to 2013, Aston Martin began working with Mercedes-AMG to use V-8 engines and electrical architectures developed specifically for the British brand. The relationship resulted in Daimler taking a 5-percent nonvoting stake in the company.

The first Aston Martin to receive an AMG engine was the DB11 in 2018. It was equipped with a 503-hp M177 4.0-liter biturbo V-8 built in Affalterbach. The engine, upgraded to produce over 670 hp, continues to be used in the DB12 replacement, which bowed in 2023.

Also switching to AMG power was the Vantage, which received its M177 4.0-liter biturbo V-8 at about the same time. In a 2024 refresh, the Vantage benefitted from a huge increase in power from the engine, which was boosted from 503 to 656 hp.

The Aston Martin DBX SUV uses two AMG engines, the 4.0-liter biturbo V-8 for most of the world, while Chinese market versions are equipped with M256 3.0-liter turbo inline-six, which makes 429 hp.

AMG also will supply a V-8 to Aston Martin for use in its Valhalla mid-engine hybrid supercar. While the original concept was shown with a 3.0-liter turbo V-6 developed by Aston, the production car is slated to have a Mercedes-AMG M178 LS2 biturbo V-8. Aided by a pair of electric motors, total system output of 937 hp is expected.

A deal struck in 2020 with Mercedes-AMG ensures the supply of internal combustion engines to Aston Martin through 2030. In addition, rather than being built to standard Mercedes-AMG specification, they will be adapted to meet the British company's needs. At the time, Aston Martin chairman Lawrence Stroll said, "Our current AMG engines are just that—AMG engines in an Aston. With this new deal, we will have bespoke AMG engines for Aston with different outputs, torque characteristics, etc. They'll still be AMG components but bespoke manufactured in Germany."

In addition to a Toyota-sourced V-6 for its Emira sports car, Lotus offers two versions of the 2.0-liter M139 Mercedes-AMG turbocharged inline-four. In base four-cylinder trim, the engine produces 360 hp and 317 lb-ft of torque compared to the 400 hp and 310 lb-ft of torque from the Toyota engine. A more powerful version of the M139 engine is being offered in global markets outside the US that now matches the V-6 on horsepower, but outclasses it in torque with 354 lb-ft.

This long string of partnerships helped prepare AMG for its next big step—developing their first in-house vehicle that would be new from the ground up.

OPPOSITE, TOP AMG provides the biturbo 4.0-liter V-8 engines that first appeared in the Aston Martin DB11. Both the coupe and convertible Volante use AMG power. *Aston Martin press photo*

OPPOSITE, BOTTOM Lotus is another AMG partner. The M139 2.0-liter turbocharged inline-four is the alternative powerplant to a Toyota-produced V-6 in the Emira sports car. *Lotus press photo*

Mercedes-AMG's Future: The Mythos Series

Having built its iconic reputation over the past half century, AMG is well-positioned to draw inspiration from legendary Mercedes-Benz racing cars and create a new range of models, just as it did with the SLR 722 models.

This time around, it will be doing it without external partners, although it is part of a larger effort in creating limited edition models for Mercedes-AMG, Mercedes-Maybach, and G-Class nameplates. This new category is called the Mythos Series.

AMG's contribution to the new Mythos Series seeks to connect the past to the present through expressive design and leading-edge technology. The inaugural vehicle of the series is the Concept Mercedes-AMG PureSpeed. The public was given its first glimpse of what will be a limited run of 250 cars when the concept was floated on a platform in the harbor during the Monaco Grand Prix in May 2024.

This first Mythos project is an important milestone for Mercedes-AMG, as it signals its ability to develop special models that cater to loyal customers, much like Ferrari has done with its Monza SP1/2, Aston Martin with the V-12 Speedster, and McLaren's Elva. These specials burnish their maker's performance credentials while providing virtually one-of-a-kind limited editions that appeal to driving enthusiasts and collectors alike.

This open roadster blends styling cues and technology from both Formula 1 and the Mercedes AMG ONE hypercar. Chief among the elements borrowed from F1 is the halo system, a three-pronged structure that protects the occupants, in place of a traditional windshield.

"The Concept Mercedes-AMG PureSpeed offers a glimpse of what is probably the most direct way to experience performance and driving pleasure," explained Michael Schiebe, head of Mercedes-AMG. "Radically open, neither a roof nor the windscreen separates the two passengers from the elements. You can experience light, air, and passion unfiltered with all your senses."

That unfiltered experience comes from the open cockpit where the two passengers sit on either side of the halo's front post, giving both unobstructed forward and side views. A pair of specially crafted wind-cheating helmets are provided for the PureSpeed's occupants.

The lack of a roof and low profile of the halo system gives the PureSpeed a hunkered-down appearance. Based on the body shell of the Mercedes-AMG SL, the concept dispenses with the signature vertical bar grille treatment inspired by the 1952 Mercedes SL Panamericana race car. Instead, it has a shark-like nose and a horizontal mesh grille with the white AMG logo emblazoned on it.

Taking cue from the Mercedes-AMG ONE, the soft nose features an embedded three-pointed Star in dark chrome. An additional air outlet in the hood and a pair of lower air inlets framed by a carbon-fiber splitter flow into vanes positioned ahead of and behind the front and rear wheel arches. The wheels are fitted with carbon-fiber cladding with the rear rims closed off from the airflow, while the fronts remain open to create downforce and improve brake cooling.

The car is equipped with a carbon-fiber sill that runs between the axles, plus a larger rear diffuser flanked by dual rear exhaust tips. Atop the front cowl are transparent deflectors (similar to a cut-down windshield) that channel air up and over the cockpit.

In addition to using the SL sports car architecture, PureSpeed is equipped with AMG's hand-built biturbo 4.0-liter V-8, which produces 578 hp and 590 lb-ft of torque. Output is delivered through an AMG SpeedShift nine-speed MCT transmission to the 4Matic all-wheel-drive system. PureSpeed accelerates to 62 mph (100 kph) in 3.6 seconds on its way to a top speed of 197 mph (315 kph).

While the PureSpeed is contemporary in its styling and application of technology, there are aspects that recall the past. One such detail is the analog chronometer mounted high on the dash. Other cues include the rear flying buttresses encasing protective roll hoops behind the two seats. This look pays homage to the 300 SLR driven by Sir Stirling Moss.

Even the paint job, which fades from Le Mans red in the front to graphite gray and black with a unique AMG pattern in the rear, has a connection to another Italian race win for the marque. In 1924, Mercedes entered the Targa Florio with a 2.0-liter supercharged race car using the chassis from the previous year's effort at Indianapolis and fitted with the new engine developed by Ferdinand Porsche. It was painted red, the national racing color of Italy instead of the traditional white reserved for German makers. This was done so that the cars wouldn't stand out and possibly be interfered with by overenthusiastic local fans.

The No. 10 car, driven by Christian Werner, won the classic Sicilian road race in six hours, thirty-two minutes and thirty-seven seconds. Using the No. 10 on the PureSpeed and its Targa Florio red paint scheme pay tribute to that historic victory of 100 years ago.

TOP Much like the limited-edition Sterling Moss Edition of the SLR, Mercedes-AMG has created another open-top sports car in the PureSpeed Concept. The 250-unit run Mercedes-AMG PureSpeed is part of the new Mythos project at Mercedes to create special vehicles for a select clientele.

ABOVE Like a Formula 1 car, the PureSpeed uses a halo to protect its passengers in the event of a rollover. Retro touches such as the IWC analog clock set high on the dash recall chronometers from Mercedes' rich motorsports heritage.

11

DAWN OF A NEW ERA: THE MERCEDES-AMG SLS

AFTER MERCEDES GAINED a controlling share in 1999, expansion came rapidly with Wolfgang Bernhard taking over chief executive duties. Sales more than doubled from 5,000 vehicles to over 11,500 in just one year, the most popular being the ML 55 AMG, which accounted for 4,500 of the total. Ulrich Bruhnke became CEO in 2001 as sales climbed to 18,700 units.

An ambitious expansion of the product program in 2002 saw the introduction of five new AMG models, while the workforce grew to 580. Hubertus Troska took over as CEO in 2003 with four more models added to the AMG line. By 2004 AMG offered sixteen vehicles ranging from C- to G-Class with thirteen powered by V-8 engines and three with V-12s. Sales topped the 20,000 mark and the division now had 650 employees.

With the experience gained from engineering this wide range of products and working with McLaren to create the SLR, the next step in the company's evolution was to build Mercedes-AMG into a standalone performance car brand in its own right.

Volker Mornhinweg was put in charge of the unit and set about creating a business plan that would expand beyond AMG's origins of tuning existing Mercedes product. "In 2005, we developed a strategy here at AMG. The highlight of this new strategy was that we wanted to build our own car," he said. That car would be the Mercedes-Benz SLS, a modern interpretation of the legendary 300 SL Gullwing.

The SLS, which stands for Super Leicht Sport (Super Light Sport), served two purposes. First it would pay homage to that legendary 1950s coupe. The second, according to Mercedes-Benz chairman Dr. Dieter Zetsche, it would be a halo car that "bolsters both the Mercedes-Benz and AMG brands equally."

One of the requirements was a front-engine layout, which is more in line with the company's core product. In an April 2010 interview with *Car* magazine, Mornhinweg admitted, "We don't have a heritage of a mid-engine supercar. So, I think you will see a range of cars based around the SLS," and its front mid-engine layout.

A preliminary sketch by designer Mark Fetherston of the gullwing SLS was the inspiration for the production model. "This is what—for me—is so special and unique about the SLS," Fetherston told *Top Gear* in 2011. "I have worked on many cars, but never has a final design looked so similar to the chosen sketch."

Building a modern car with gullwing doors proved to be a challenge. The automotive landscape had changed dramatically since the 1950s, with many new safety regulations. The weight of doors was also a concern, given the structural reinforcements that would be needed to support such a system.

Mornhinweg, in the same *Car* interview, observed that work was begun on a convertible, which was part of the original plan. "We engineered it to be stiff enough without a roof because we were planning a roadster version of the car," he said. "Then I was looking at a model of the gullwing

and noticed how similar the cars were in mechanical layout and how far back the driver sat. So, we tried a few different designs, and it just worked as a gullwing. It was luck, good fortune and coincidence all in one. Amazing."

Manual doors assisted by gas struts were developed to save weight and complexity. Rollover concerns were addressed via explosive bolts that would detach the doors if the SLS tipped over and was resting on its roof.

Just as the SLS would use the latest in modern safety technology, Fetherston wanted to give the SLS a contemporary look that also paid homage to the 300 SL.

"Of course, I looked at the original 300 SL to understand where we were coming from, but I also needed new influences," Fetherston told *Top Gear*. "I didn't want to make 'just' a retro car, or 'just' a modern supercar. No, it had to appeal to existing Mercedes customers, and also new customers. The priority for me was that it should be simple and timeless, that the design should age well and not be fashionable. So, I looked at the simplicity of aircraft, their volumes, the fuselage, and how the cockpit of jets can sit on the main body—something the SLS does."

Mornhinweg echoed that sentiment: "We want not only to live up to the legend, we wanted to create our own legend."

The proportions are not unlike those of the Mercedes-Benz SLR McLaren. The hood is just under 6 feet (2 m) long with the cabin pushed back nearly to the rear wheels, allowing for the engine to be positioned behind the centerline of the front axle.

PREVIOUS AMG SLS. *John Lamm photo*

TOP Sketches by designer Mark Fetherston show the heavy influence of aircraft design elements. The body is curved like a fuselage and the Mercedes logo is encased in what looks like a jet engine nacelle. From the rear, the low roofline resembles a jet fighter canopy.

ABOVE A sketch of the cabin by interior designer Andreas Frank carries on the aeronautical themes with the jet engine–style vents.

ABOVE In early testing, camouflaged prototypes were sometimes mistaken for Dodge Vipers. AMG did use the American sports car to test drivetrain layouts.

Besides the gullwing doors, other cues from the original SL include the wide grille opening with a single wing element sporting a prominent three-pointed star. The hood features a pair of small power domes and straked vents near the cowl. On the side, air extractors also feature similar chrome strakes, which serve two purposes. One recalls the 300 SL, while the other functions as an aerodynamic styling cue.

The other aircraft-inspired elements add a contemporary touch. For instance, the star in the grille is housed in a piece that resembles the nacelle of a jet engine. Gentle sculpting of the hood and side panels suggests the subtle contouring of an aircraft fuselage. The high beltline contributes to the hunkered-down look of the cockpit-inspired cabin.

Unlike the first gullwing, which had a gently tapered rear that fell away, the SLS has a tall deck defined by a sharp character line in the interests of reducing drag. At 75 mph (121 kph) a rear wing deploys with a shape that looks like the air brakes so popular in racing Mercedes in the 1950s. Projector beam LED headlamp units and LED taillights also add modern flair to the design. Overall the look is muscular, purposeful, and, above all, clean. The Mercedes pedigree comes through loud and clear.

The aircraft theme is echoed in the interior. The width of the car is emphasized by the winglike dashboard that sports air vents also shaped like jet engine nacelles. The aeronautical cockpit theme is further reinforced by the large matte-finish metal console with a shifter that looks like a jet's thruster lever.

Under the guiding hand of project leader Christoph Jung, the SLS took shape in just thirty-seven months, from its approval in 2006 to the reveal of the production car at the Frankfurt Motor Show in 2009. During that compressed period, a significant organizational change occurred when the DaimlerChrysler partnership created in 1998 dissolved after nine years. Chrysler was spun off under the control of the Cerberus venture-capital concern.

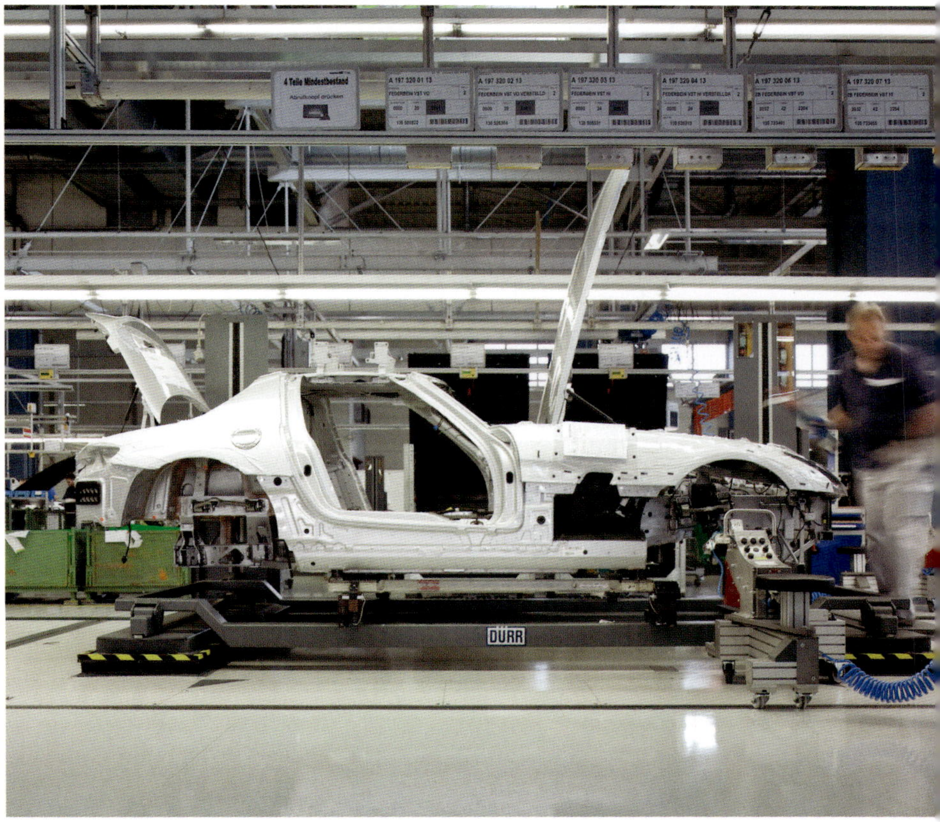

Until then, ties between Mercedes and Chrysler led to speculation that the SLS and the next generation Dodge Viper were being jointly developed. In fact, the engineering team at AMG discovered that the American sports car was the perfect test bed for the engine and drivetrain and it had purchased about a dozen of them to use in SLS development. Test mules wearing some of the cobbled-up bodywork of the Vipers caught hot testing in Death Valley, California, did little to tamp down the rumors that the vehicles were being jointly developed. The Viper, for the record, received a freshening in 2008, and a redesign in 2012 before going out of production in 2017, retaining its original approach of using a tube-frame chassis.

The truth of the matter is that AMG used the cars to speed product development, taking a page from its own history when it acquired a McLaren F1 to develop the CLK GTR and a couple of TVRs when it was working on the Mercedes-McLaren SLR.

Beneath the skin, the Mercedes-AMG SLS would be very different from a Viper. It would employ space-frame construction fitted with body panels made of lightweight aluminum. The material would be used for structural supports, suspension components, sheet metal, and die-cut pieces assembled using glue, rivets, bolts, and welded joints to create a stiff body. This structure was not only lightweight (the body shell tipped the scales at just 531 pounds [241 kg]), but it also met exacting crash standards. Only 4 percent of the structure was steel, which was hot rolled and used primarily in the A-pillars. The final curb weight of the SLS came in at 3,573 pounds (1,621 kg), around 400 pounds (181 kg) less than the Mercedes-McLaren SLR.

The body shells of the SLS were fabricated at Magna-Steyr in Graz, Austria, and shipped to Mercedes' factory in Sindelfingen, outside of Stuttgart, Germany, where it was assembled. AMG sent the hand-assembled drivetrain over from its Affalterbach facility.

Unlike the SLR's butterfly door arrangement, the SLS coupe's use of gullwing openings was its unique calling card. The doors swung upward through an arc of 70 degrees and provided a 5-foot (1.5-m) opening between the bottom of the door and the ground and 42 inches (107 cm) from the door to the sill. That higher sill means a step-in height of 17.7 inches (45 cm), while the seat bottom's H-point is 14.5 inches (37 cm) off the ground.

Dimensionally the SLS is tidier while offering more cabin space than the Mercedes-McLaren. The SLS rides on a 105.5-inch (268-cm) wheelbase, which is almost an inch shorter than the SLR's 106.3 (270 cm). Likewise, the newer car is 182.6 inches (464 cm) in overall length, down 0.8 inches (2 cm) from its predecessor. It's over an inch wider at 75.3 inches (191 cm), and inside the SLS offers 38.9 inches (99 cm) of headroom, 41.6 inches (106 cm) of legroom, and 58.4 inches

TOP LEFT Power came from the M159 6.2-liter V-8, a reworked version of the M156 employed in the E 63 sedan and ML 63 SUV.

TOP RIGHT While the engines would be built in Affalterbach, the Mercedes-AMG SLS would be hand-crafted at the parent company's Sindelfingen assembly plant.

ABOVE The gullwing doors and front styling of the SLS pays clear homage to its inspiration, the legendary 300 SL.

(148 cm) of shoulder room. The SLR is much tighter with only 34.4 inches (87 cm) of headroom, 39.6 inches (101 cm) of legroom, and 54.0 inches (137 cm) of shoulder room.

AMG decided on an all-new normally aspirated V-8 engine developed from the M156 used in the E 63 sedan and ML 63 SUV. While it's called the 6.3, it actually displaces 6.2 liters. Mercedes kept the 6.3 designation to commemorate the 6.3-liter M100, Mercedes' first V-8. AMG further developed the 451-hp M155 by reworking the intake system, upgrading the valvetrain and camshafts, and optimizing the flow of the headers while freeing up the exhaust.

The reworked engine, known as the M159, produces 563 hp and 479 lb-ft of torque. Like the SLR, AMG added dry-sump lubrication, which eliminates the oil pan and allows for the engine to be mounted lower and further back in the engine bay. Weighing just 452 pounds (205 kg), the engine also contributes to the reduced mass of the SLS.

A slick feature developed for the powertrain was a smart alternator that recharged the battery on deceleration or engine overrun. The alternator also could switch to a no-load setting (essentially disengaging) on acceleration. This level of attention underscores AMG's engineering prowess in sweating the smallest detail to boost performance and fuel efficiency.

Though less powerful than the SLR, the SLS had the highest output of any Mercedes model on the market at the time. The lower torque also meant that the SLS could be equipped with AMG's SpeedShift seven-speed dual-clutch automatic, which was incorporated into a rear transaxle. Power was delivered by the engine via a carbon-fiber driveshaft and torque tube that weighed just 64 pounds (29 kg). With the engine behind the front axle centerline and the rear-mounted transmission, the SLS boasted a front/rear weight distribution of 48/52 percent.

With gear changes of 100 milliseconds, the DCT gearbox featured a choice of four driving modes: C for Controlled Efficiency (a polite way of saying supercar Eco mode), Sport (S), Sport Plus (S+), and a Manual (M) mode. There is also a Race Start setting for launch control. When

engaged in Sport Plus or Manual (which allows sequential paddle or gear lever shifting), the car's automatic rev matching engaged.

In addition to tailoring the drivetrain to the SLS, AMG developed the braking system to offer a choice of standard composite or optional ceramic packages. The advantages of the carbon-ceramic setup included higher heat tolerance, discs with a larger swept area, and less unsprung weight. AMG also employed an innovative flow-forming process for the lightweight front 19-inch (48-cm) and rear 20-inch (51-cm) alloy wheels to further reduce unsprung weight. Further, AMG had a hand in developing the specific compound and design of the 265/35R-19 front and 295/30R-20 rear Michelin tires to maximize grip and performance.

Mercedes-AMG claimed an electronically limited top speed of 196 mph (315 kph) along with a 0–60 mph (0–97 kph) time of 3.6 seconds. *Car and Driver* recorded a 0–60 mph (0–97 kph) time of 3.5 seconds along with quarter mile performance of 11.6 seconds at 126 mph (203 kph). The magazine also reported that the SLS generated 0.98g on a 200-foot (61-m) skidpad. Its test results for the 2005 Mercedes-Benz SLR McLaren showed a 0–60 mph (0–97 kph) of 3.6 seconds, a similar quarter mile time of 11.6 seconds at 125 mph (201 kph), and a skidpad number of 0.97g.

SLS deliveries began in early 2010 as 2011 models, which hit the United States priced from $183,000. As part of the global launch of the coupe, a couple of custom packages showcased the high level of

TOP Developed from the F1 safety car (above), the SLS GT3 racer won its first race in 2010 at the Nürburgring. Thomas Jäger and Christopher Haase teamed up for the victory for the Black Falcon privateer team.

ABOVE A special model of SLS called Desert Gold, after its unique paint scheme, was presented at the Dubai Motor Show.

LEFT The SLS had a long nose in order for the engine to be mounted behind the centerline of the front axle for better weight distribution. *John Lamm photo*

BOTTOM The deployable rear wing is shaped like the pop-up air brake used on 1950s 300 SLR racers. With the rear wing stowed, the AMG SLS still sported a slight ducktail look to the rear end for aerodynamic efficiency. *John Lamm photo*

personalization possible through AMG. The first was a Desert Gold model at the 2010 Dubai Motor Show. In addition to blacked-out rims with gold edging on the wheel flange, this one-off model featured a matte-gold paint scheme that inspired the name.

Meanwhile, at the Australian Motor Show, the local Mercedes distributor had commissioned the Blackbird, which like the Dubai car featured a custom matte-black body with red accents.

With both coupe and roadster versions being developed in parallel, it was just a year later that the open-top SLS debuted, again at the IAA in Frankfurt. At a time when retractable hardtops seemed ubiquitous, Mercedes-AMG decided that a fabric roof would be lighter and less complex. The triple-layer automatic top (which could be raised or lowered in eleven seconds at speeds up to 31 mph (50 kph) required additional stiffening of the body and the addition of pop-up rollover protection for the occupants.

Two braces were added to the body to make it more rigid. These supports were fitted to the crossmember that carried the dashboard and were joined to the windshield frame and the center tunnel. Behind the seats, a structure that tied the soft-top assembly and fuel tank to

TOP The gullwing doors are a showstopper. In case of a rollover, explosive bolts would release the doors, providing escape for the occupants. *John Lamm photo*

MIDDLE A roadster version soon followed the coupe. The car was developed with the open-top version in mind. The stiffer body required for the drop-top made adapting the gullwing doors easier. *John Lamm photo*

BOTTOM The tagline in this German print ad states "A cockpit. An engine. Two wings. Is it still a car?" in an allusion to the aircraft-inspired styling.

the rear axle along with another crossmember carrying the pop-up roll bars reinforced the car's rear end. While these bits, along with the top and roll bars, added weight, removing the gullwing doors in favor of smaller conventional opening portals resulted in minimal weight gain. The roadster's body weighed a scant 5 pounds (2 kg) more than the coupe's 531-pound (241-kg) mass. All told, the roadster's curb weight exceeded the coupe by only 88 pounds (40 kg).

Using the same M159 V-8 engine and seven-speed DCT transmission, the SLS Roadster had performance on par with that of the coupe, the factory claiming similar 0–60 mph (0–97 kph) acceleration of 3.6 seconds for both variants. The Mercedes-AMG SLS Roadster went on sale as a 2012 model with a list price of just under $200,000.

Even though production of the SLS was limited, Mercedes-AMG continued to offer new versions, including a one-off "ambulance," official F1 safety cars, GT3 racers, and even a pure electric. But, more importantly, the SLS saw improvements with each model year in the form of the SLS GT, a Black Series variant, and the Final Edition that closed out the production run.

From 2013 onward, both the coupe and roadster would be called the Mercedes-Benz SLS AMG GT. The new GT designation signaled a major upgrade to the M159 engine, which was tweaked to deliver 20 additional horsepower. While output now hit 583 hp, torque would remain at 479 lb-ft, which meant that despite the bump, the factory claimed 0–60 mph (0–97 kph) time remained at 3.6 seconds. Top speed also continued to be electronically limited to 196 mph (315 kph).

Besides the engine upgrade, AMG also recalibrated the seven-speed dual-clutch transmission for quicker shifts and more pronounced rev-matching throttle blips. The Comfort setting on the adjustable suspension was removed in favor of just a Sport and Sport+ mode, while the base spring and shock settings stiffened for a tauter ride. These improvements resulted in sharper handling and quicker midrange response.

The GT is distinguished from previous SLS models by its darker head- and taillamp bezels along with piano black replacing the chrome exterior accents. Other upgrades included standard leather/Alcantara seating with red stitching and piano black interior accents, ten-spoke matte-black wheels, adaptive suspension, and red brake calipers. The base price was raised to $199,000 for the coupe and $206,000 for the roadster.

To close out the SLS run, Mercedes-AMG introduced the Final Edition in 2013 at both the Los Angeles Auto Show and Tokyo Motor Show. A total of 350 were built for the 2014 model year and incorporated many of the features found on the Black Series, and the Final Edition was available in both coupe and roadster body styles.

The use of carbon-fiber body panels carried over from the Black Series and the GT3 race car included a carbon-fiber hood with a single center air extractor rather than the dual outlets positioned near the cowl as found on the original SLS and SLS GT versions. In addition to the exposed carbon-fiber hood, the Final Edition sported a carbon-fiber rear wing, a front spoiler, and a rear diffuser.

Also migrating from the Black Series to the Final Edition were the upgraded 583-hp engine, a quicker-shifting seven-speed dual-clutch transmission, carbon-ceramic brakes, and a carbon-fiber engine cover and interior accents. Instead of the Alcantra upholstery in the Black Series, the Final Edition seats and door trim were covered with diamond-pattern stitched leather. While most limited-edition models are numbered, each Final Edition model carries a commemorative plate indicating that it is just one of 350. It was also priced lower than the harder-core Black Series, with an MSRP of $221,000.

Throughout the SLS AMG production run, a series of 86 GT3 competition cars were produced from 2011 to 2014. Built to Fédération Internationale de l'Automobile (FIA) specs, the GT3 employed a six-speed sequential shift racing gearbox with column rather than steering wheel–mounted paddles. Other racing gear included a fully adjustable suspension, a fixed wing, a larger front splitter and rear diffuser, steel racing brakes, 18-inch (46-cm) lightweight alloy wheels, and a single racing seat shell with integral Head and Neck Support (HANS) anchor system.

The race-tuned engine put out about 550 hp in keeping with the GT3 classification. They were considerably lighter than the road cars, weighing just under 3,000 pounds (1,361 kg). The SLS GT3 scored over 100 victories in international racing, including long-distance events at Spa Francorchamps, the Nürburgring, Dubai, and Australia's Bathurst. Privateers could purchase them for $450,000.

During its five-year production run, the Mercedes SLS AMG saw about 12,000 units built with 2,721 coming to the United States. The split between coupes and roadsters favored the gullwing, which accounted for about two-thirds of the output. For its first in-house effort at building a road car from the ground up, the SLS AMG nailed Volker Mornhinweg's goal of not just living up to the legend of the 300 SL, but also in creating a legend in its own right.

More importantly, the experience in producing the SLS paved the way for Mercedes-AMG to build the next generation of sports cars for the brand, the AMG GT family.

OPPOSITE, TOP LEFT These aero influences can be seen in the use of strakes on the side vents. *John Lamm photo*

OPPOSITE, TOP RIGHT The nose, as well as the cone surrounding the three-pointed star, bear resemblance to jet aircraft intakes and engine nacelles. *John Lamm photo*

OPPOSITE, MIDDLE ROW, LEFT The gas cap looks like it could be used on an airplane. *John Lamm photo*

OPPOSITE, MIDDLE ROW, MIDDLE The fuselage shape of the body is seen in the tapering of the rear end. *John Lamm photo*

OPPOSITE, MIDDLE ROW, RIGHT More strakes appear on the hood, further echoing the 300 SL. *John Lamm photo*

OPPOSITE, BOTTOM The cockpit is a faithful re-creation of the design sketches. The dash itself resembles a wing. The shifter is designed to resemble a jet thruster, while the buttons flanking it on the center console reinforce the aircraft theme. *John Lamm photo*

TOP The engine cover is a work of art with the badge signed by the technician who built the engine taking center stage. *John Lamm photo*

ABOVE With more than 560 horses on tap, the SLS has little trouble in lighting up the rear wheels. *John Lamm photo*

Mercedes-AMG's Electric Avenue

CONCURRENT WITH THE REVEAL of the Mercedes-Benz SLS AMG at the 2009 Frankfurt Motor Show, the company revealed plans for an electrified version of its new supercar. "With the SLS AMG with electric drive, we wanted to redefine the super sports car. For us, it is not just about responsibility. We attach just as much importance to excitement and classic AMG performance," said AMG CEO Volker Mornhinweg.

In less than a year, Ola Källenius, who succeeded Mornhinweg as head of Mercedes-AMG, took the wraps off the SLS AMG E-Cell prototype in July at a program in Norway, one of the world's leading EV markets.

Powered by four electric motors, two on each axle to provide all-wheel drive, the E-Cell promised to deliver 525 hp and 649 lb-ft of torque. "With the SLS AMG E-Cell, we are demonstrating a further milestone in our 'AMG Performance 2015' strategy," Källenius said. "It is our goal to continually reduce the fuel consumption and emissions of new models in the coming years, while at the same time enhancing the core brand value of performance."

The four motors drew power from 48 kWh lithium-ion polymer battery producing 400 volts. Preliminary performance figures put the 0–60 mph (0–97 kph) acceleration at about four seconds, still not quite as quick as the gas-powered SLS, which could turn the trick in 3.6 seconds.

At the North American International Auto Show in January 2011, Mercedes-AMG announced that it would take the E-Cell into production with further development resulting in the 2013 Mercedes-Benz SLS AMG Electric Drive Coupe. The production model, shown at the Paris Salon in 2012, featured a larger 60-kWh battery pack and greater output from the four electric motors, which would make 740 hp and 738 lb-ft of torque.

The car was not light. The battery alone weighed over 1,200 pounds (5,443 kg), pushing the curb weight to about 4,700 pounds (2,132 kg). But with that massive power on tap, Mercedes estimated a 0–60 mph (0–97 kph) time of 3.7 seconds and a quarter mile in 12. 5 seconds. Top speed was electrically limited to 155 mph (250 kph). Range was estimated at just 128 miles (206 km), which translates to 160 miles (247 km) on the more generous European test cycle. This figure drops precipitously the harder the car is pushed.

Unlike the internal combustion SLS models, the coupe electric drive units were assembled in-house at the Affalterbach headquarters. This production line featured seven stations for the process. In addition to hand-assembly of the axles, cooling systems, transmissions, and electric motors, highly skilled craftsmen also handled the delicate tasks of putting together the high-voltage components including the liquid-cooled lithium-ion battery packs, inverters, powertrain control units, and on-board chargers, as well as their associated cables.

Much of the development work to extract the highest levels of performance from the drivetrain came from Mercedes High Performance Powertrains, the unit charged with building the hybrid power units for the Formula 1 racing effort. Those systems, which use Kinetic Energy Recovery Systems (KERS), enabled HPP to maximize the output of the battery not only for acceleration, but also for handling. With one electric motor for each wheel, the software can use torque vectoring to rotate the car more quickly on turn-in and give an extra boost on exit to the corners with the most grip.

As part of the car's introduction, Mercedes took the car to the famed Nordschleife (north loop) of the Nürburgring to set a record for the fastest lap by an electric vehicle. The previous mark of 8:09.09 minutes was held by the Audi R8 e-tron, of which nine prototypes were built, but none were sold to the public. The Mercedes SLS AMG Coupe Electric Drive, which would go on to be sold publicly in Europe, for nearly $550,000 each, lapped the circuit in 7:56.234, a new record. In comparison, the SLS AMG GT, which cost half as much, lapped in just over 7:44.

Only nine SLS AMG Coupe Electric Drive models were sold worldwide. Aside from the price and exclusivity, the downside to owning one was its woefully slow charging time for not much range. While direct current (DC) charging takes about three hours, it takes about twenty hours to charge the car using Level 2 alternating current (AC) at home. Still, the experience in building even a limited number of electric SLS coupes would pay huge dividends in future AMG concepts and road cars.

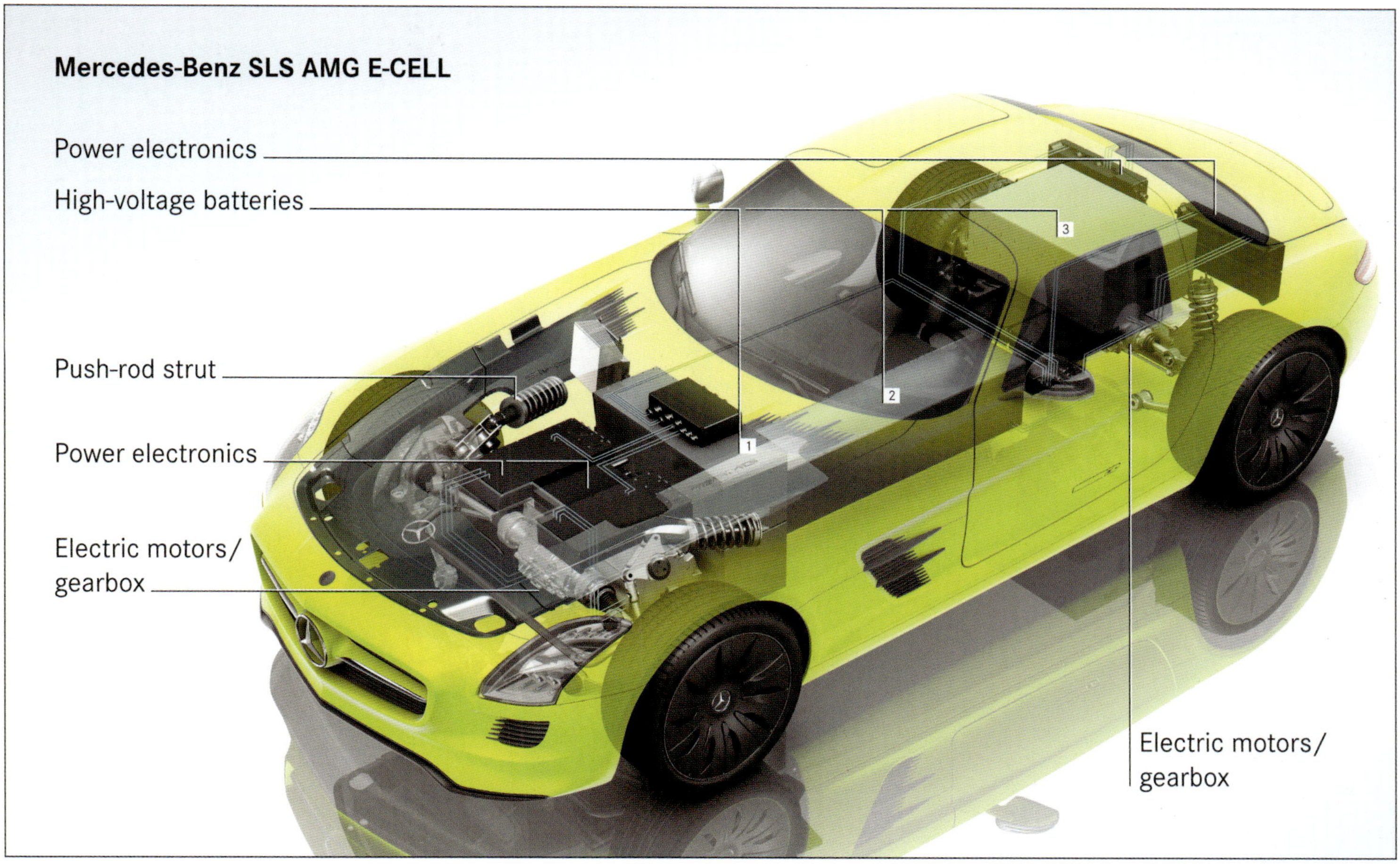

TOP LEFT The SLS E-Cell was introduced as a concept, which later became the SLS Electric Drive. It retained the signature gullwing doors.

TOP RIGHT The SLS E-Cell interior was much simpler due to the large center touchscreen and a lack of a traditional shifter.

ABOVE A diagram shows the layout of the battery, electronic controls, and electric motors.

LEFT Production SLS Electric Drive models came in a bright blue paint scheme. Though slower around the Nürburgring than its gas-powered counterpart, the SLS Electric Drive set the fastest lap for a pure electric production vehicle.

12

MERCEDES-AMG GT: FOUNDATION FOR THE FUTURE

FOLLOWING THE SUCCESSFUL RUN of the SLS, it was time for Mercedes-AMG to prepare a replacement. This successor would play a critical role in the brand's direction. Developing the SLS in-house was a big step for AMG, although the car's high price and low production limited its reach.

The GT model that would replace it would not be a big-buck exotic, but a more mainstream sports car that would spawn a new range of AMG-exclusive vehicles designed to grow the business.

The first decade of the twenty-first century saw substantial changes in the industry. Legacy brands such as Ferrari faced increased competition from McLaren. Porsche, in what would be considered by purists as heresy in the 1980s, was now building SUVs and four-door sedans. Bentley and Rolls-Royce would soon have SUVs of their own. With the market in a state of flux, Mercedes-Benz needed to change with it. Having two sub-brands in Mercedes-AMG and Mercedes-Maybach positioned the parent company to respectively address the growing high performance and ultra luxury segments.

Mercedes-Benz continued as the mainstay of the group, serving the broadest customer base in the luxury segment. Mercedes-Maybach would focus on pure luxury, as Stuttgart's answer to Rolls-Royce and Bentley. Its models would primarily leverage the S-Class and G-Wagen by producing its own bespoke versions for a highly discriminating clientele.

Mercedes-AMG, as it had always been, would focus on road-going performance models and motorsports. Nearly every model in the Mercedes-Benz portfolio would have an AMG variant. But beyond that, the division would develop its own family of vehicles. The target was not necessarily Mercedes' traditional Bavarian archrival BMW, but rather, Porsche, which was becoming a powerhouse in its own right with its expanded product offerings.

"Our goal [for AMG] is to bring it to a level of Porsche, so it is independent," Gorden Wagener, chief design officer of Daimler AG told *Kelley Blue Book* in 2016. "It is still Mercedes, so it follows our rules, but we are giving them more and more unique profiles."

While there would be AMG versions of Mercedes-Benz SUVs, coupes, and sedans to counter what its German rival produced, there still needed to be a core family of vehicles that represented the essence of Mercedes-AMG. That core would be built around the GT.

Unveiled at the 2014 Paris Motor Show, the Mercedes-AMG GT shared the same long-hood, short rear deck proportions of the SLS with the engine mounted behind the centerline of the front axle. Its dimensions were tidier, riding on a 103.5-inch (265-cm) wheelbase and measuring 179.0 inches (455 cm) in overall length, down by 2.0 and 3.5 inches (5 and 9 cm) respectively. The biggest change was the use of conventional doors instead of the SLS gullwing arrangement. Power would come from an all-new biturbo 4.0-liter V-8, each assembled by one technician in Affalterbach. Final assembly would be on a line at Mercedes' Sindelfingen plant near Stuttgart.

Mark Fetherston, who had penned the SLS, was again lead exterior designer on the GT. He told *Car Advice*, "The design brief for the GT was to design a more compact sports car to compete directly with the 911, Aston Martin Vantage and the Jaguar F-Type, and make it something special.

PREVIOUS By 2014 the Mercedes-AMG lineup had grown to fourteen models. With the SLS series (lower left) ending production, it was time to expand the volume of in-house-developed replacements.

ABOVE The 2016 AMG GT S replaced the SLS. Although it shared similar proportions, it dispensed with the eye-catching gullwing doors in favor of more conventional portals. Built to have a lower price point, the AMG GT S was positioned as a direct competitor to the Porsche 911.

"If people see similarities among these cars, then that's fine, but we've made sure that this new design has a Mercedes DNA, and falls in line with our new design language, which emphasizes purity and softer edges." He added that "[t]he surfacing of the AMG GT highlights the new direction we're taking with our coupes and sports cars, where we are saying the cars that have stunning proportions don't need as much entertainment, or as many features in the design."

In addition to the familiar proportions of the SLS, the AMG GT incorporated a similar front-end design theme with the three-pointed star anchoring a wing in the grille opening. The lines were softer with the lower inlet framed by a flowing airfoil that wrapped into the two large inlets on the front corners. LED running lights framed the faired-in headlights, while the sides had rounded contours that avoid the use of sharp creases. Small, rounded air vents were positioned behind the front wheels, while the greenhouse sported a low, fastback design that tapered into the rear end. The flowing nature of the back end of the GT evoked some comparisons to Porsche's 911.

The interior featured an evolution of the SLS cabin that muted the previous jet aircraft theme. The dash still dominated with a wing-inspired shape, but the jet engine nacelles on the vents disappeared in favor of four central spotlight vents. The center display screen was propped on top in an opening that looked like a NACA duct. The high center console and twin binnacle instrument panel added to the cockpit feel of the passenger cabin.

At the car's launch, Professor Dr. Thomas Weber, head of Mercedes' car development, explained, "With the new Mercedes-AMG GT, we are venturing out into a challenging sports car segment with its top-class competitive field. This is an incentive and motivation for us at the same time to prove to sports car enthusiasts around the world the kind of performance that AMG is capable of."

Tobias Moers, CEO of Mercedes-AMG, echoed these sentiments: "With the new GT we are positioning Mercedes-AMG even more aggressively than to date as a dynamic sports car brand. With its technological substance, the Mercedes-AMG GT fulfills our high aspirations with regard to driving dynamics, agility, and sportiness. The new GT is the second sports car developed fully independently by Mercedes-AMG. The car is manufactured according to the motto 'Handcrafted By Racers'—which perfectly encapsulates our heritage and our spirit."

ABOVE AMG developed an all-new 4.0-liter biturbo V-8 for the new GT series. One of the unique features of the new V-8 was "hot Vee" placement of the turbos in the center of the engine. This location allows for quicker spool-up for boost, increasing efficiency and lowering emissions.

The Mercedes-AMG GT was a direct challenge to that other Stuttgart-based maker, Porsche, and its iconic 911. There would be detractors who wouldn't buy the comparison between the hotrod front-engine V-8 Merc versus that flat-six rear-engine 911. However, closer scrutiny of the current 911 reveals a roadgoing car that is hardly the lithe sports car on which its reputation was built. Even more important was AMG's commitment to a GT3/GT4 customer racing program that would prove the car's mettle on the track against its erstwhile rival.

In its 2014 head-to-head test of the Mercedes-AMG GT and a 911 GTS, *AutoExpress* concluded that "AMG now has a sports car to rival the very best in the business. The GT's stunning looks, upmarket cabin, and powerful V-8 engine are all highlights. However, it's the handling that sets it apart. A truly athletic car, with a dynamism not seen before in a Mercedes sports car, the new GT S is a great looking, beautifully engineered, and accomplished rival for the 911."

While the car's design is engaging, it is engine technology that built the AMG brand. The all-new M178 4.0-liter biturbo contributed much to the GT's appeal thanks to its innovative approach with forced induction. Instead of positioning the turbos on either side of the engine near the exhaust manifolds, they are now mounted inside the Vee of the block.

Called a "hot inside Vee" arrangement, the design results in more compact dimensions, quicker turbo spool up and power delivery, and lower exhaust emissions. Further adding to the engine's smaller size is the use of dry-sump lubrication. Mercedes said the V-8's dry weight of 460 pounds (209 kg) made it the lightest in its competitive set. The engine came in two states of tune: a base version making 456 hp and 443 lb-ft of torque, while the GT S boasted 503 hp and 479 lb-ft of torque. All models featured a seven-speed SpeedShift dual-clutch automatic transmission. Like the SLS, it was located in the rear as a transaxle. Mercedes said the top performance numbers included a 0–60 mph (0–97) time of 3.7 seconds, with a top speed limited to 193 mph (311 kph).

Built on a shorter version of the aluminum space frame used by the SLS, the GT's body shell weighed 509 pounds (231 kg). It was made of more than 90 percent aluminum and utilized

lighter-weight magnesium in the front section. Forged aluminum used in the double wishbone front and rear suspension and hub carriers reduced unsprung mass. The GT models came with 19-inch (48-cm) alloy wheels, while the GT S sported 20-inch (51-cm) rims, the latter available with optional Michelin Pilot Sport Cup 2 performance rubber.

Mercedes-AMG brought the GT S to the market first in the United States in the spring of 2014 as a 2015 model, priced from $132,400. The standard GT didn't arrive until a year later with a sticker of $112,400. New variations started coming fast and furious. The AMG GT R bowed in 2016 with a fresh look, more power, and additional innovations that would have an effect on subsequent GTs as well as the AMG overall lineup.

Introduced in a green metallic paint scheme known as Green Hell Magno (a tribute to the Green Hell nickname given to the Nürburgring's famed Nordschleife), the GT R featured the M178 engine, which produced 577 hp and 516 lb-ft of torque. It retained the seven-speed DCT rear transaxle and was capable of 0–60 mph (0 97 kph) in 3.5 seconds and had a limited top speed of 198 mph (319 kph). *Sport Auto* took it to the Nürburgring where it lapped in 7:10.9, which at the time was the fastest lap for a production sports car in the magazine's history.

Other changes that came with the GT R included a 2-inch-wider (5-cm) body to accommodate 20-inch (51-cm) wheels and a wider rear track. In Race mode at above 50 mph (80 kph), an active aerodynamic panel added to the car's underside of the car's nose would drop 1.6 inches (4 cm), delivering additional ground-effect downforce. Other active air management included the use of temperature-controlled louvers in the lower intake that open or close within a second.

The suspension was stiffened thanks to larger diameter rear anti-roll bar, while a new AMG coil-over suspension allowed for manual adjustment of the spring rates. The electronically controlled shocks offered the driver a choice of three damping rates, while active rear steering enhanced handling. The GT R would retail in the US for $157,000.

The GT R also spawned the GT C Coupe. While it retained the wider track and bodywork of the GT R, as well as technology such as active rear steering, the M178 engine put out slightly less power: 550 hp and 502 lb-ft of torque. It also was priced about $12,000 less than the GT R.

Mercedes-AMG quickly added convertibles to the lineup, returning to the Paris salon in 2016 with the GT and GT C Roadsters. The open-top cars retained the performance and price differences between the standard GT and GT C coupe models.

The GT Roadster produced 469 hp and 465 lb-ft of torque, and it was capable of 0–60 mph (0–97 kph) acceleration of 3.9 seconds and a limited top speed of 188 mph (303 kph). The GT C Roadster benefited from the wider track and body and had the more powerful 550-hp M178 V-8. It could accelerate to 60 mph (97 kph) in 3.7 seconds and had a top speed of 196 mph (315 kph). Both models were fitted with triple-layer automatic cloth tops that could be raised or lowered in eleven seconds at speeds up to 31 mph (50 kph). The convertibles sold for about $12,000 more than their coupe counterparts—$124,000 for the base roadster and $157,000 for the GT C version.

To mark the fiftieth anniversary of AMG, a run of 500 GT C Edition 50 coupes and roadsters were built for the 2017 model year, of which fifty were sent to the United States. These models could be distinguished by their Matte Gray Magno paint offset by black chrome accents on the grille, air outlet strakes, tailpipe, and front splitter. The mechanical package, with the 550

TOP LEFT Like the SLS, the GT lineup quickly expanded to include a roadster version, introducing the GT and GT C versions at the 2016 Paris Auto Salon. The C boasted a wider track and more power from its M178 V-8.

TOP RIGHT The AMG GT interior differed from the SLS by being less inspired by aircraft themes. Still there was a cockpit feel to the interior thanks to a large center console fitted with an array of switches and buttons.

TOP The AMG GT R stepped up the performance quotient by extracting 577 hp from the 4.0-liter V-8 and fitting the car with a 2-inch (5-cm) wider body and 20-inch (51-cm) wheels.

SECOND FROM TOP While it wasn't the first time the Panamericana grille was seen on an AMG vehicle, the GT R would be the first model sold to the public with the signature styling cue.

THIRD FROM TOP In celebrating AMG's fiftieth anniversary in 2017, the AMG GT Vision concept, which would be the first four-door developed in-house by the brand, debuted at the Geneva Motor Show. Alongside the Panamericana grille, the large twin intakes on the car's nose became another signature cue for the brand.

BOTTOM In profile the GT Vision reveals itself as a four-door sports car with coupe-like styling. The sleek fastback look was a tip-off to its liftback body style.

horsepower V-8, remained unchanged. Because of the limited run, the asking price was an eye-watering $335,000, more than twice the base price of the standard model.

A more hardcore track-focused version of the AMG GT R debuted in 2018 at the Los Angeles Auto Show. While using the same 577-hp powertrain as the GT R and retaining the same 3.9-second 0–60 mph (0–97 kph) capability, the new GT R Pro focused primarily on the suspension, brakes, and extensive use of carbon-fiber aerodynamic elements. Options from the GT R, such as a carbon-fiber roof and carbon-ceramic brakes, were now standard. The coil-over suspension featured manual adjustments, and GT R Pro sported specific lightweight forged 19-inch (48-cm) front and 20-inch (51-cm) rear wheels. Buyers could opt for a track package that included a steel roll cage, four-point harnesses for the racing buckets, and a fire extinguisher. Priced at $200,000, 750 of the track specials sold worldwide.

With a complete range of AMG GT models, which now included coupes and convertibles and varying levels of performance up through the track-oriented GT R Pro, plus a burgeoning customer racing program, Mercedes-AMG felt it had the Porsche 911 lineup covered.

Even though there were compelling examples of AMG performance across the Mercedes lineup, from compact sedans up through the mightiest of SUVs, the G-Class, there was still one piece missing in the matrix. That would be a four-door model that could compete with the Porsche Panamera and the Aston Martin Rapide. It would manifest itself in the form of the Mercedes-AMG GT 4-Door Coupe.

As part of its celebration of AMG's fiftieth anniversary at the 2017 Geneva Motor Show, the company revealed the Mercedes-AMG GT Concept. This vehicle would not only foreshadow the first four-door model developed in-house at Affalterbach, but it would mark a big departure in engine philosophy. The concept bore EQ Power+ badging signifying the debut of gas/electric hybrid technology for the brand.

"With the Mercedes-AMG GT Concept, we are giving a preview of our third completely independently developed sports car and are extending the attractive AMG GT family to include a four-door variant," said Moers. "The AMG GT Concept . . . illustrates how we are defining performance of the future at AMG. Impressive driving dynamics, coupled with high efficiency, resulting from an innovative drive system tailored specifically to the vehicle segment—that is 'Future Performance' made by AMG."

"With our AMG GT Concept, that means a combination of an ultra-modern V-8 gasoline engine and a high-performance electric motor, both intelligently networked with an extremely powerful yet lightweight battery concept," he announced. "This performance hybrid powertrain offers an impressive electric range and the opportunity to generate a system output of up to 805 horsepower in its last level of development and covers the sprint from 0–60 mph [0–97 kph] in less than three seconds—which corresponds to the performance of a super sports car."

As Daimler chief of design Wagener promised, the GT Concept introduced a new form that was unique to Mercedes-AMG. It was also the first appearance of the GT3 racer's Panamericana grille on an AMG road car even though it was just a concept. The grille would appear first in series production on the GT R street version and eventually migrate across the entire AMG product portfolio.

While AMG shares Mercedes-Benz' iconic three-pointed star, and developed its own logo, the use of the toothy grille was another way to further distinguish its products as well as tie all the AMG models together as a family. Design chief Wagener explained that "the new face, what we call the Panamericana grille, comes from the 1952 300SL Panamericana racer, which really came from the prewar racing cigars, the Silver Arrows."

The multiple vertical-bar grille treatment was a common sight on Mercedes Grand Prix cars of the 1930s, starting with the W25 in 1934 and perhaps most elegantly executed on the W154 raced in 1939. The look was again picked up in 1952 with the W194 300 SL in both gullwing and roadster configurations. The 300 SL raced successfully, finishing second in that year's Mille Miglia in Italy, a team 1–2–3 in Bern, Switzerland, and a 1–2 sweep at Le Mans that summer.

The cars closed out the season in November, contesting the grueling 2,000-mile (3219-km) Carrera Panamericana open road race in Mexico. That's where the winning car, copiloted by Karl Kling and Hans Klenk, won the race despite hitting a buzzard at speed. The bird went through the windshield, resulting in a head injury for Klenk. Overnight, mechanics fitted eight "buzzard" bars to the windshield as a preventive measure. With that bird strike, the 300 SL gullwing took on mythical status, birthing the Panamericana grille nomenclature.

This striking grille design speaks to the essence of AMG, which was born of motorsports. The debut of the grille on both the roadgoing AMG GT R and the racing GT3 model reinforced the connection. From there, it began to roll out across the AMG range.

ABOVE The AMG GT 63 4-Door Coupe in production trim remained faithful to the Geneva GT Vision concept.

S MB 641

On the GT Coupe four-door, the Panamericana grille signals that this is no ordinary sedan. Wagener describes the look as a "hot cool" design. The aggressive grille pattern and muscular wheel arches bring the heat in a nod to the powerful engine lurking beneath the hood. The flowing body work, with its sensuous lines, lack of sharp defining character lines, and steeply raked liftback, is simply cool to look at.

The Verge website described it thusly, "In spite of all its glistening sheen and modern technology, the Mercedes-AMG GT Concept unveiled at the Geneva Motor Show today feels almost primal. Its exaggerated, dominant front end is like a neanderthal's oversized jaw, grinning a toothy radiator smile. The designers aimed for and indeed accomplished 'extremely muscular proportions.'"

While the design was warmly received, the hybrid powertrain offered plenty of intrigue. Taking the EQ Power+ name from the Mercedes-AMG Petronas Motorsport Formula 1 car, the 4Matic all-wheel-drive GT Concept combined the 4.0-liter biturbo V-8 engine with an electric motor and a small battery to store energy. With a total system output of 805 horsepower, the car had a claimed 0–60 mph (0–97 kph) performance of fewer than three seconds. The system also allows the vehicle to be operated in pure electric, hybrid gas/electric, or just gas-only modes.

Making its way into production, the AMG GT Coupe four-door shared little with the two-seat coupes beyond the GT moniker. Using a modified version of the Mercedes MRA platform underpinning the C- and E-Class model ranges, AMG engineers worked to put their own stamp on the GT. Using data gathered from its racing activities, the development team reinforced the body structure in key areas using the latest carbon-fiber-reinforced plastics for increased stiffness and reduced weight.

The GT 4-Door Coupe launched with the M177 biturbo 4.0-liter V-8 engine, but it lacked the hybrid setup of the concept. That technology was initially reserved for a new turbocharged inline-six. The V-8s were handcrafted in Affalterbach, with final assembly in Hall 36

To broaden the appeal of Mercedes-AMG flagship models, the brand introduced the GT 53 4-Door Coupe powered by an in-line-six engine.

ABOVE By 2018 the AMG GT family had grown to eight, a lineup that included coupes, roadsters, and GT 3 competition models.

OPPOSITE, TOP A second generation of the GT was introduced in 2025, sharing the platform with the R232 Mercedes-AMG SL. Retaining similar proportions, the new AMG GT continues its role as the brand's answer to the Porsche 911. A larger grille opening is one of the distinguishing features of the second-gen GT.

OPPOSITE, BOTTOM A major change is the addition of 2+2 seating to the previous two-place cockpit layout.

at the Sindelfingen factory. Designated the X290, it was built alongside the W213/S213 E-Class sedan and wagon as well as the C257 CLS four-door coupe.

The car that debuted a year after the concept was shown in Geneva looked virtually identical with little lost in the transition to production. The GT 4-door Coupe featured the shark nose, the Panamericana grille, smooth and flowing body sides, and a coupe-inspired fastback that functioned as a rear hatch.

In breaking with the tradition of offering V-8 and V-12 engines, the new M256 inline-six with its mild hybrid technology would be assembled by Mercedes-Benz rather than the technicians in Affalterbach. Also, all models would be equipped with a new nine-speed SpeedShift TCT torque-converter automatic mated to AMG Performance 4Matic+ all-wheel drive.

The V-8 came in two states of tune. The AMG GT 63 4-Door Coupe would have 577 hp and 590 lb-ft of torque. The range-topping AMG GT 63 S model would deliver 630 hp and 664 lb-ft of torque. It would be capable of 0–60 mph (0–97 kph) acceleration of 3.1 seconds, two-tenths quicker than the standard model. It would have a limited top speed of 195 mph (314 kph), again 2 mph (3 kph) more than the GT. The GT 63 4-Door Coupe started at $136,500 while the S model retailed for $159,000.

The AMG 53 GT 4-Door Coupe's turbocharged inline-six displaced 3.0 liters with a rating of 429 hp and 384 lb-ft of torque. The transmission also incorporated an electric motor that provided 21 hp and 184 lb-ft of torque as an extra boost. Mercedes said the AMG 53 GT could accelerate to 60 mph (90 kph) in 4.4 seconds on its way to a top speed of 175 mph (282 kph).

The hybrid setup of the AMG 53 GT introduced a new 48-volt architecture to support the 48-volt battery that energized the starter/generator electric motor positioned between the engine and transmission.

LB GT 633

BELOW The switch to the R232 platform and designation of all SLs as Mercedes-AMG models meant the GT Roadster is no more, making for a simpler lineup.

OPPOSITE, TOP Introduced in 2024, the GT 63 S Performance indicates the future of Mercedes-AMG performance, where many of the internal combustion offerings will be electrified. It adopts the hybrid powertrain first seen on the GT Vision concept. With more than 800 horsepower on tap, the car can accelerate to 60 mph (97 kph) in 2.7 seconds.

OPPOSITE, BOTTOM The plug-in hybrid features a 6.1-kWh lithium-ion battery pack. While it's good for 9 miles (14 kph) of pure electric operation, the hybrid technology is geared more toward bursts of performance than outright fuel economy.

The GT four-door coupe line opened up a wider market for Mercedes-AMG thanks to the four-passenger cabin configuration and much friendlier price tags than the GT Coupe and Roadster. The four-door GT 53 models started at $99,000, while the V-8 models came in at a respective $136,500 and $159,000 for the GT 63 and GT 63 S.

After the 2019 model year introduction of the 53 GT, a fourth model, the AMG 43 GT, joined the lineup as a 2021 model. As the badge implies, the 43 lowered the inline-six's output to 362 hp and 369 lb-ft of torque. Like the 53, the hybrid system is capable of delivering an additional boost of 21 hp and 184 lb-ft. Pricing started at $90,000.

Big changes by Mercedes-Benz at its Sindelfingen plant to retool Hall 39 for its new range of electric vehicles based on its EA platform impacted production of the X290 four-door coupe. The solution was to outsource assembly to Valmet, a supplier based in Finland, which had been building A-Class sedans and GLC SUVs for the German automaker.

Meanwhile the GT Roadster and Coupe would see a second generation, this time based on an improved platform that would be shared with the SL Roadster. In order to eliminate confusion and overlap in the marketplace between the SL and GT Roadster, Mercedes used the new R232 platform for the seventh-generation SL and introduced the car in 2021 as an AMG-only model. It eliminated the retractable hardtop in favor of a fabric roof similar to the GT Roadster's. The new AMG SL, which would come with two states of tune from the 4.0-liter biturbo, also would feature 4Matic all-wheel drive and 2+2 seating in standard configuration. The roadster series would add the SL 43, an entry-level model that used a turbocharged 2.0-liter four-cylinder engine and an electric hybrid drivetrain.

The AMG GT would continue solely as a coupe using the C232 architecture. Now offered with optional 2+2 seating for the first time, the all-wheel-drive GT would see its wheelbase grow by 2.8 inches (7 cm), to 106.3 (270 cm). Overall length would grow by 7.1 inches (18 cm), to 186.1

S MB 2288

GT 63 S

ABOVE The four-cylinder Mercedes-AMG GT 43 offers 416 hp and 4.5-second 0–60 mph (0–97 kph) acceleration. This least-expensive model costs $110,000.

(473 cm). It would be about a half inch narrower at 78.1 inches (198 cm). Offered in the GT 55 and GT 63 variants, the V-8 engine produced a respective 469 and 577 hp and 516 and 590 lb-ft of torque. The GT 55 was capable of 0–60 mph (0–97 kph) in about 3.8 seconds with a limited top speed of 183 mph (295 kph). The GT 63 was much quicker to 60 (97 kph) at 3.1 seconds with a 196-mph (315 kph) top speed. Pricing ranged from $134,900 and $179,000. Production of the GT Coupe shifted to Mercedes' Bremen plant, to be built alongside the SL.

More powerful versions soon followed. Next up was the Mercedes-AMG GT 63 S E Performance, which combined a 603-hp V-8 engine (with 627 lb-ft of torque) with a 201-hp electric motor capable of producing 236 lb-ft of torque. Mercedes-AMG says total system output is similar to that of the 805-hp hybrid system first seen on the GT Concept. Torque of 1,047 lb-ft is claimed, the firm saying that the nine-speed automatic gearbox, plus the electric motor's built in two-speed transmission, multiplies the combined 863 lb-ft of output from the drivetrain combo. The car sprints to 60 (97 kph) in just 2.7 seconds and reaches a 199-mph (320 kph) top speed.

With a usable 4.8 kWh from the 6.1-kWh lithium-ion battery, this plug-in hybrid can go about 9 miles (14 km) on a charge. And like an F1 KERS (Kinetic Energy Recovery System), the small battery can recoup juice from the regenerative braking system. Despite its nearly 5,000-pound (2,268-kg) curb weight, the AMG GT 63 S E Performance was the fastest AMG model to hit the road. The price started at $200,000.

In addition to the GT 63 S E Performance flagship, Mercedes-AMG added two new variants to bring the model count to five. Joining the GT 55 and GT 63 were the GT 63 Pro 4Matic+ and an entry-level GT 43. The Pro model is essentially the S E Performance without the hybrid setup. As a result, the 4.0-liter biturbo V-8 makes 603 hp and 627 lb-ft of torque. To handle track-day duties, the GT 63 Pro has a larger cooling package, carbon-ceramic brakes, and a front splitter, a rear diffuser, a decklid spoiler, and side sills made of carbon fiber. The interior is fitted with more aggressively bolstered sport seats and a sport steering wheel. The car is priced at $187,000.

At the other end of the line is the new AMG GT 43 Coupe powered by a 2.0-liter turbocharged four-cylinder engine making 416 hp and 369 lb-ft of torque. The rear-drive coupe is equipped with a nine-speed MCT automatic transmission. Capable of 0–60 mph (0–97 kph) acceleration in 4.5 seconds, GT43 has a top speed limited to 174 mph (280 kph). This least expensive GT Coupe is priced from $110,000.

With a core of exclusive product-embracing internal combustion and hybrid technology, Mercedes-AMG has proven that it can adapt its race-bred performance to meet stringent emission and fuel economy standards and still meet the expectations of driving enthusiasts.

ABOVE While the GT S E Performance is the flagship, MercedesAMG offers a track-oriented GT 63 Pro 4Matic+ without the hybrid assist. A larger cooling package and carbon ceramic brakes are among the performance upgrades.

Mercedes-AMG GT: The Racer's Edge

MOTORSPORT IS AMG'S UNDERLYING REASON for existence. With a long history of building Mercedes racing cars and winning, the focus on track success sharpened once the brand began building its own cars, the SLS and GT. Capitalizing on the modest success of the SLS, it was the GT, which through a customer-oriented (rather than a factory-run) program, has turned Mercedes-AMG into a global sports car racing powerhouse.

All the GT competition cars use body shells pulled off the Mercedes' assembly line and shipped to HWA in Affalterbach for the final build, which includes the installation of their hand-built racing engines as well as roll cages, racing seats, and other competition components.

The program dates back to 2016, when the first AMG GT3 debuted at the 24 Hours of the Nürburgring. The newly minted competition model finished 1-2-3-4, led by the Black Falcon racing team. The four drivers taking the overall win were Adam Christodoulou, Maro Engel, Manuel Metzger, and Bernd Schneider. In 2021 Maximillian Götz won the first title in the DTM German touring car series that had changed over to the GT3 classification.

In all, more than 700 GT race cars (built to GT3, GT4, and GT2 specifications) have been built in Affalterbach by HWA. These cars have participated in more than 12,000 starts in 150 series around the world. Mercedes-AMG GT models have more than 750 overall victories, 1,000 class wins, and 300 championship titles as of April 2024. What's more, the AMG GT3 has taken the last six manufacturer titles in the GT World Challenge.

The top GT3 model, soon to be retired, is powered by the M159 6.2-liter V-8 making 542 hp, which is in line with GT3 homologation calling for output between 500 and 600 hp, depending on a balance of performance formula that takes into consideration the vehicle's weight. The GT3 comes in at 2,833 pounds (1,285 kg), some 800 pounds (363 kg) less than its production counterpart. Other changes from the production models include the use of a six-speed sequential-shift racing gearbox.

The GT4 model more closely reflects the current roadgoing GT by using the M178 4.0-liter biturbo V-8. Also equipped with the six-speed racing gearbox, the GT4 makes 536 hp, again in line with the class specification. Like the GT3, both models are equipped with steel rather than carbon-ceramic brakes, as required by the rules.

The third member of the racing family is the GT2. Introduced in 2018, this new category slots between the GT4 and top GT3 class. While the GT2 has considerably more power than GT3 (the 4.0-liter biturbo engine produces 697 hp), it lacks the downforce that ultimately makes the GT3 cars quicker on track. While the GT3 is for professional drivers, the GT4 is aimed at a mix of pros and seasoned amateurs, while the GT2 caters to "gentlemen racers."

Mercedes-AMG also offers a GT2 Pro version with a unique push-to-pass mode that temporarily boosts turbo pressure to produce up to 740 hp. However, these models are ineligible for GT2 competition and are best suited for track days and AMG-specific drive programs.

continued

OPPOSITE, TOP The development of the SLS and the GT allows Mercedes-AMG to broaden the brand's racing efforts, including hosting a robust program for privateers. Among them are (from right) the SLS GT3, CLA 45 Racing Series, and the current lineup of GT2/3/4 racers.

OPPOSITE, MIDDLE Mercedes-AMG efforts in IMSA go back to this 2017 GT3 entry. The AMG GT3 has won its class in the Daytona twenty-four-hour race twice, in 2021 and 2023.

OPPOSITE, BOTTOM In addition to the GT3 cars, which race in the top categories around the world, Mercedes-AMG also has developed a GT4, which is not as heavily modified, for amateur racers.

AMG

AMG
33
WeatherTech
PATRON

AMG
4
EDGAR CHU

TOP LEFT As a fitting end to first-generation AMG GT race car production, a limited run of GT 130Y models was produced to commemorate Mercedes-Benz' 130-year racing history. The paint scheme recalls the 300 SL Gullwing of the early 1950s. The GT 130Y is built to GT3 specification but isn't limited in horsepower and is equipped with carbon ceramic rather than the steel brake package required in competition. The 130Y is meant for private track use and for collectors.

TOP RIGHT The interior features such throwback cues as the wood-rimmed yoke steering wheel and plaid seat coverings.

ABOVE At the end of 2024, Mercedes-AMG captured its sixth straight European Fantec GT World Challenge sports cars title, winning a six-hour race in Jeddah, Saudi Arabia.

LEFT On the Jeddah podium are, from left, drivers Lucas Auer, Maro Engel, and Daniel Morad.

OPPOSITE Where it all started in Macau. Maro Engel celebrates his sixth straight win and ninth for the AMG GT3 at the same Guia circuit that Waxenberger won with a 300 SEL 6.3 in 1969.

And unlike a purebred competition car, the GT2 Pro can be ordered with air-conditioning. It also comes in a variety of colors and has a plusher interior than the standard racing machines. Buyers also get a car cover, a helmet, and a full racing suit including shoes. If a customer wants to enter a GT2 Pro in an official GT2 event, Mercedes-AMG will convert the car back to competition trim.

With the increased use of electrified powertrains, Mercedes-AMG decided to mark the end of its use of the M178 normally aspirated 6.2-liter V-8 engine by building a limited-run model called the GT3 Edition 130Y Motorsport. More of a collector car with mad racetrack skills than a homologated GT3 racer, this special commemorates 130 years of racing activities by Mercedes. The car was unveiled at Pebble Beach during Monterey Car Week to mark the 130th anniversary of the first race won by a vehicle using a Daimler engine. That event was the Paris to Rouen Race on July 22, 1894. Just thirteen GT3 Edition 130Y models were built, priced at $1.1 million each.

Because the GT3 130Y is not built for competition, output was increased to 671 hp by dispensing with the race-required air restrictor and installing a freer flowing exhaust system. The rear-drive coupe is also equipped with a six-speed sequential-shift racing gearbox. A new front air splitter, vents, and a wider rear wing help increase downforce by 15 percent.

Among the other GT3 homologation bits that were ditched include the steel rotor braking system, which has been upgraded to a carbon-ceramic setup. The interior includes a steel roll cage, window safety nets, five-point racing harnesses, a fire-suppression system, a safety escape hatch, and a racing fuel cell.

The car's blue and silver paint scheme recalls the original Silver Arrows grand prix cars as well as the 1952 Le Mans– and Carrera Panamericana–winning 300 SL. The interior takes a page from Juan Manuel Fangio's 1955 grand prix–winning SLR with blue-checkered upholstery, brown leather headrests, wood-trimmed steering yoke, and leather door pulls.

The GT3 Edition 130Y Motorsport is a fitting end to AMG's long history of building performance V-8s going back to the M100 of 1967 for both road and track. It also opens the door to a new chapter as Mercedes-AMG begins work on a successor to the M159-powered GT3 category cars. These new models will be adapted from the current C192 GT family, which shares its underpinnings with the R232 Mercedes-AMG SL.

As part of this transition, Mercedes-AMG reorganized its motorsports operations and transferred it to a new company, Affalterbach Racing, GmbH, which will take charge of the development for the next-gen GT3 racer. In addition the new entity also will be responsible for supporting the customer car racing program.

13

GOING BEYOND THE END OF THE ROAD

AMG'S PASSION FOR performance isn't limited to public roads or racing circuits as evidenced by its association with Mercedes' premier SUV, the G-Class, nearly since its inception as the Geländewagen in the late 1970s. As legend has it, this versatile utility vehicle was suggested to Mercedes-Benz by Shah Mohammad Reza Pahlavi of Iran, who wanted it for his military.

Development began in the early 1970s through a joint agreement between Daimler-Benz and Steyr-Daimler-Puch, based in Graz, Austria. Strictly utilitarian in nature, the original scale model had its boxy shape carved out of wood rather than being a more traditional clay prototype. Early models were hand-assembled from 1975 with volume production beginning in earnest in 1979 at a new factory in Graz.

The W460 featured body-on-frame construction, which it maintains to this day. It has been available in a variety of body styles, including a short wheelbase three-door and convertible configurations, and long wheelbase three- and five-door wagons and panel vans.

By 1981 Mercedes had upgraded the G-Wagen with features such as air-conditioning, an automatic transmission, more comfortable seats, and central door locks, in order to widen its appeal in the retail market. It wasn't long after the W460 hit the market that AMG began to offer performance and accessory upgrades to the vehicle. An AMG catalog at the time said, "the G Model is the best example of the way that AMG finds a solution to improve on every Mercedes model. Even a cross-country vehicle can be individualized by means of AMG modifications."

AMG offered an engine kit for the stock M110 2.8-liter inline-six, boosting it from 156 to 196 hp. *Optik* or appearance package options for the G-Wagen included brush guards, off-road lights, wheel and tire packages and interior amenities including custom seats, premium sound systems, steering wheels, and wood shift knobs. The list extended to such esoterica as telephone handsets, TVs, and even iceboxes.

As utility vehicles like the G-Wagen became more mainstream, Mercedes moved with the times. It updated the original work-oriented model, renaming it the W461 and maintained a more spartan approach to the engine choices and interiors.

Mercedes then created a second-generation W463 model that catered to the consumer luxury market that had emerged for big SUVs. As a result of this shift, the panel van versions in short and long wheelbases were dropped. The new G models, which debuted at the 1989 Frankfurt Auto Show, would still come in short wheelbase three-door wagons and cabriolets as well as the long wheelbase five-door wagons.

Meeting the demands of its luxury segment positioning, the new G-Wagen moved beyond its strictly functional form by offering plusher seats, wood trim, and leather upholstery. Mechanical upgrades included anti-lock brakes, full-time four-wheel drive, and electronic locking differentials.

AMG would have a hand in the first V-8-equipped G-Wagen that debuted at the 1993 Geneva Motor Show. Offered for just one year, this special edition was equipped with an M117 5.0-liter

V-8 installed in Affalterbach. The 237-hp engine with 277 lb-ft of torque could propel the hulking G to 62 mph (100 kph) in 11.4 seconds with a top speed of 112 mph (180 kph). It was also the first G to carry a sticker price of over $100,000. Only 446 of these 500 GE V-8s were built since that was the number of two-valve M117 engines that Mercedes allocated for the project. The four-valve M119 units in series production were too wide for the engine bay. Despite Affalterbach's involvement, the 500 GE V-8 did not carry AMG badging.

Still the 500 GE V-8 set the bar for what buyers could come to expect from Mercedes' luxury SUV. In addition to its monochromatic amethyst metallic-blue paint scheme, the interior sported two-tone black/gray leather upholstery, a walnut-trimmed shift knob, and a handbrake lever and center console. Other standard features included a sliding sunroof, a leather steering wheel, heated seats, and air-conditioning.

At the same time, AMG began offering its own upgrade of the M117 E 50 engine. Bored out from 5.0 to 6.0 liters, the V-8 would make 326 hp and 387 lb-ft of torque. Despite the bump in power, the 500 GE 6.0 AMG knocked only a half second off the 0–62 mph (0–97 kph) acceleration. From 1993 to 1995, AMG built only one short-wheelbase and thirteen long-wheelbase models.

In 1994 the Geländewagen was rechristened the G-Class. At the same time, AMG introduced its C 36 and E 36 models under the new cooperative development arrangement and used the same M104 inline-six in the G 36 AMG. With 276 hp and 284 lb-ft of torque, the new engine propelled the vehicle to 62 mph (100 kph) in 9.6 seconds.

PREVIOUS Originally designed as an all-purpose utility vehicle, the Mercedes-Benz Geländewagen developed from its relatively modest off-road application to a highly coveted luxury vehicle.

ABOVE Introduced in 1979, the G-Wagen family included an open-top short-wheelbase model and longer wheelbase models that included a five-door wagon and three-door panel van and wagon models.

ABOVE AMG was quick to offer a lineup of engine, suspension, and interior upgrades for the new off-roader. This early 1980s catalog highlights some of the exterior enhancements, including wheels, a brush guard, and a custom paint scheme.

OPPOSITE, TOP LEFT While not specifically branded an AMG product, the 1993 500 GE V-8 was a breakthrough model for the G-Wagen, where performance and luxury boosted the utility vehicle's profile thanks in part to is Euro-look monochromatic paint scheme.

OPPOSITE, TOP RIGHT The 500 GE V-8 featured Mercedes' M117 5.0-liter V-8; however, its limited availability resulted in only 446 units being produced. AMG would upgrade fourteen of them using a bored-out 6.0-liter engine like the one found in the E 50 AMG sedan.

OPPOSITE, BOTTOM A lavish interior upholstered in two-tone leather announced that the G-Wagen was not just another SUV, but a luxury vehicle worthy of Mercedes' three-pointed star. Extensive use of walnut on the dash, center console, brake lever, and shifter added to the luxury vibe.

Even though AMG models were being sold through Mercedes dealerships throughout the world, Mercedes still hadn't officially launched the G-Class in the United States. Among those pre-U.S. distribution models were the G 43 AMG, of which thirty-eight were built between 1997–1998 using the M113 4.3-liter V-8 and five G 63 AMG V-12 units in 2002. The G 63 could accelerate to 62 mph (100 kph) in 6.5 seconds thanks to its 437-hp V-12.

For the 2002 model year, the G-Class finally came to America, and included in the portfolio was the G 55 AMG, which was equipped with the M 113 5.4-liter normally aspirated V-8. It made 349 hp and 387 lb-ft of torque. The AMG models were fairly indistinguishable from the standard G 500 except for the wider tires mounted on five-spoke wheels, chrome side exhaust tips, chrome running boards, and, of course, the AMG badging.

For the extra $16,000, which pushed the price up to nearly $90,000, the 2002 G 55 AMG boasted 57 additional horses and 51 lb-ft more torque. Mercedes estimated the 0–60 mph (0–97 kph) sprint at 7.2 seconds, about two seconds quicker than a stock G 500. In 2006 AMG introduced supercharging to the engine, pushing horsepower to 493 and torque to 516 lb-ft. The 0–60 mph (0–97 kph) time dropped below six seconds. AMG turned up the wick on the 2008–2012 models to an even 500 hp. These models, bearing Kompressor badging indicating the forced-induction engine, adopted a new three-bar grille and sold for more than $120,000.

In 2012 the W463 received a major update including a new interior adapted from the smaller ML-Class SUVs. This included a new center console, revised infotainment screen placement, as well as the adoption of a host of driver aids such as adaptive cruise control and blind-spot monitoring. Exterior changes included LED running lights and new outside rearview mirrors while AMG versions sported a new front bumper with a trio of large air intakes.

The G 55 AMG was replaced by two new models, the G 63 and G 65 AMG. The former would see the supercharged V-8 replaced by a new biturbo 5.5-liter V-8 initially making 536 hp and 590 lb-ft of torque. A year later, output was bumped to 563 hp. The G 65 came with the M279 6.0-liter biturbo V-12, which made 603 hp and a massive 738 lb-ft of torque. That engine was uprated to 621 hp in 2015.

The most audacious variant of the G-Wagen cooked up by AMG was the G 63 AMG 6×6 in 2013. Never sold in the United States, this limited-edition model was based on the W461 pickup version of the G-Wagen. Power came from the 5.5-liter biturbo V-8, which made 536 hp and 561 lb-ft of torque. It propelled this behemoth, which measures over 19 feet (6 m) in length and 7 feet (2 m) in height, to 60 mph (97 kph) in just over seven seconds.

Derived from a vehicle Mercedes had made for the Australian military in 2007, this extra-long-wheelbase G-Wagen featured six-wheel drive that incorporated five locking differentials. It also marked the first appearance of portal axles. Instead of having the axles connected directly to the wheel hub, the half shafts are mounted higher and are connected to the hub center through gears. This allows for greater ground clearance (more than 18 inches [46 cm]), further enhancing the vehicle's off-road capability. The technology would later appear on other G-Class models.

Another bit of kit to enhance the off-road chops of the G 63 6×6 was a system that allowed for on-the-fly air-pressure adjustment of the 37-inch (94-cm) tires. At the push of a button, the pressure could

S LM 9401

S LP 7685

OPPOSITE, TOP An AMG-prepared G-Wagen made its first official appearance in the US market as the G 55. Subtle cues such as its signature monochromatic paint scheme, custom five-spoke wheels, and chrome exhaust tips peeking from beneath the running boards distinguished it from stock models.

OPPOSITE, BOTTOM The G 63 succeeded the G 55 and offered a biturbo 5.5-liter V-8 in place of the previously supercharged engine. A V-12 variant also would be sold as the G 65.

TOP The full-size SUV offerings by AMG expanded in 2013 when the second-generation Mercedes-Benz GL was introduced. With three rows of seating for seven passengers, the GL 63 also would employ the biturbo 5.5-liter V-8 used by the G 63.

MIDDLE The wildest G-Class model sporting an AMG badge was the G 63 6×6. This six-wheel-drive variant of a G-Wagen pickup is based on a vehicle developed for the Australian military.The power from the AMG-tuned engine made the G 63 6×6 capable of running at high speeds over rough terrain. Exceptional off-road capability came from the vehicle's tall ride height and high ground clearance. An onboard compressor enabled the vehicle to raise or lower tire pressure to handle transitions from sandy to firm surfaces.

BOTTOM Introduced as the Extreme-G concept, the G 500 4×4^2 employed the same ground-clearance enhancing portal axle as the 6×6. This technology would be adapted later in the G 63 4×4^2.

be lowered to increase traction in loose sand or raised quickly for higher speeds on firmer terrain.

While it's certainly a beast, there is beauty to be found inside. The cabin rivals that of a Mercedes' flagship S-Class sedan. Tufted diamond-pattern leather upholstery is used on the door panels and power-adjustable seating for four. Bamboo is used to line the load area in the pickup bed. Mercedes-AMG had produced only two prototypes and didn't know how big the market would be for this vehicle that retailed for about a half-million dollars. In the end, 100 were built.

Increased competition in the full-size luxury SUV space contributed to a quickening of the product cycles for the G-Class. In the past, a decade could easily pass before there would be any major changes. Now the makeovers were every six years. In 2018 even though the model designation W463 remained the same, the G-Wagen redesign resulted in a slightly larger vehicle with smoother exterior styling.

The biggest change was the switch to the M177 4.0-liter biturbo V-8, now backed by a nine-speed automatic transmission. Still called the Mercedes-AMG G 63, the revamped SUV now produced 577 hp and 627 lb-ft of torque, which knocked down 0–60 mph (0–97 kph) acceleration to just 4.4 seconds. A top speed of 149 mph (240 kph) could be achieved when equipped with the AMG Driver's Package.

The AMG versions, which now started at nearly $150,000, adopted the vertical-bar Panamericana grille introduced across the Mercedes-AMG line with each new vehicle launch or major model change. And despite the boxy exterior profile, the new G continued to be more like a luxury car in its interior cabin appointments and—especially in the case of the AMG models—its handling.

To ensure that the G 63 performed as well on paved surfaces as it did off-road, AMG designed new adaptive dampers to go with the coil spring suspension that featured a front independent double-wishbone

S MB 9072

setup for the first time to go along with the rear five-link solid axle. Reflecting this focus on improved roadholding, the full-time all-wheel-drive system biased power delivery to the rear axle. The selectable driving modes offered five on-road settings versus only three for off-road use.

That doesn't mean AMG couldn't get down and dirty. In 2022 it released its version of the more extreme four-wheel-drive system first introduced on the previous generation G 500 4×4.² The 2022 Mercedes-AMG G 63 4×4² offered the ultimate in off-road capability thanks to its raised ride height and the use of portal axles first seen on the G 63 6×6.

The taller ride height and portal axles resulted in 13.8 inches (35 cm) of ground clearance, an increase of 4.3 inches (11 cm) over the standard G 63. It enabled the vehicle to wade through nearly 3 feet (91 cm) of water, more than 8 inches (20 cm) more than stock. The G 63 4×4² sported 22-inch (56-cm) wheels shod with 47-inch (119-cm) Pirelli all-terrain rubber, larger carbon-fiber fenders, an LED light bar, a roof rack, and a carbon fiber rear spare cover. The 4.0-liter biturbo V-8 saw a slight increase in output to 585 hp (an 8-hp bump). All this capability had a cost, namely an MSRP that topped $350,000.

Keeping to the six-year product cycle, the G-Class again was updated in 2024 with most of the big changes under the skin. The Mercedes-Benz model, while keeping its G 550 designation, no longer has V-8 power, the first time since its US introduction in 2002. Instead output comes from a 3.0-liter inline-six bolstered by a mild hybrid 48-volt starter motor/generator.

The 2025 Mercedes-AMG G 63, which has a sticker approaching $200,000, carried over its 4.0-liter biturbo V-8 engine. The 577 hp and 627 lb-ft of torque remain the same as previous models but now is assisted by that 48-volt starter motor/generator that provides an extra 20 hp and 148 lb-ft of boost from a standing start. This enables a 0–60 mph (0–97 kph) time of just 4.2 seconds.

Further enhancements to the suspension are also part of the changes. Building on the standard Ride Control adaptive damping, the new optional AMG Active Ride Control adds hydraulic roll stabilization to the struts at all four corners. Via lines in and out of the struts, a hydraulic pump regulates both compression and rebound for real-time body control. This feature can also be added to the off-road package, replacing the conventional torsion anti-roll bars. The active ride control system also provides for additional articulation of the wheels, allowing them to remain in better contact with the surface below for greater traction in extreme off-road environments.

In early reviews the improvements to the G 63 have been well-received, with several reports calling the Mercedes-AMG G 63 the best model in the lineup. As demonstrated over its long history, the Mercedes-AMG brand is about performance and its ability to adapt its expertise on the road, at the track, off the beaten trail, and beyond.

OPPOSITE, TOP As the high-end luxury SUV segment became increasingly competitive, updates became more frequent. The 2018 G 63 featured a new, smoother body and adapted the Panamericana grille theme for the first time.

OPPOSITE, BOTTOM LEFT The G 63 also featured a significant overhaul of the interior, a contemporary design that incorporates a large center infotainment display.

OPPOSITE, BOTTOM RIGHT True to its performance roots, the G 63 sports lightweight multispoke alloy wheels and large red brake calibers emblazoned with the AMG logo.

TOP LEFT In a throwback to some of the first AMG-tuned G-Wagens, the 2023 Grand Edition sports a two-tone gold and black scheme that includes gold 22-inch (56-cm) wheels and gold accents on the spare tire carrier. Only 1,000 of these models were built.

TOP RIGHT For the 2025 model year, the G 63 received a freshening and some changes under the hood where the Mercedes-AMG 4.0-liter biturbo V-8 mild hybrid appears. Meanwhile, the standard G-Class models use only inline-six engines. Minor tweaks to the exterior give the new G 63 a more aggressive look.

AMG at Sea

AS MERCEDES-AMG CONTINUES TO PUSH the performance boundaries of SUVs with the G-Wagen, it also discovered that its branding is an asset in the world of offshore powerboats—thanks to its relationship with Cigarette Racing.

Originally AMG teamed up with the boat builder in 2007 in a joint marketing effort to reach potential clients for both through the AMG Private Lounge, which offered exclusive experiences for owners and prospects. Virtually all this effort revolved around the Miami International Boat Show, the largest boat and yacht show in the world.

With the launch of AMG's first in-house product, the 2011 SLS, Cigarette developed a 46-foot (14-m) *Rider* powered by a pair of 9.0-liter Mercury Marine V-8s producing a combined 2,700 hp, which propelled the craft to a top speed of 130 mph (209 kph). The Cigarette *Rider "Inspired by AMG"* featured a paint scheme using the Alubeam silver and Designo Mystic White metallic treatments available as exterior colors on the SLS, along with bold AMG lettering on the hull.

It would be the first of thirteen boats to be commissioned by the partnership through 2021, each keyed to a specific AMG vehicle. Mercedes' design team, headed by Gorden Wagener, provided input in colors and interior design elements.

AMG's C 63 Black Series provided the inspiration for the 50-foot (15-m) Cigarette *Marauder* launched at the 2012 installment of the Miami show. Using a black-and-white paint scheme keying off the look of the 510-hp 6.3-liter V-8-powered C 63, the *Marauder* again relied on the twin Mercury Marine Racing engines to make 2,700 hp. Among the innovations found on this boat was the use of corrosion-resistant anodized billet aluminum pieces for various grab handles, seat supports, trim pieces, dash accents, and even the sound system.

The 2013 show saw two AMG/Cigarette projects' debut. The first was a 42-foot (13-m) *Huntress* paired with a G 63 AMG SUV. More experimental in nature, the second was the Cigarette AMG Electric Drive Concept, a 38-foot (12-m) electric boat keyed off the AMG SLS Electric Drive.

The center-console *Huntress* was selected because it's the sea-going equivalent of an SUV, a rugged, open-prow boat that can carry a lot of people. Power would come from five Mercury Racing Verado 350SCi outboard motors featuring inline-six configurations and boasting 350 hp each for a total output of 1,750 horses. Like an SUV, it wasn't as fast as the previous models with a top speed of "only" 78 mph (126 kph).

The bright yellow electric boat concept, paired with an equally eye-catching AMG Electricbeam Magno paint scheme on the corresponding SLS Electric Drive, was billed as the fastest and most powerful electrically driven motorboat of its time. Output was rated at 2,200 hp and 2,213 lb-ft of torque through twelve liquid-cooled permanent-magnet synchronous electric motors powering two drive units. A 240-kWh battery pack with four modules supplied power to the motors. Top speed was estimated at 100 mph (161 kph).

The fifth boat in the series wasn't based on a real car. The 50-foot (15-m) Cigarette *Marauder* was tied to the Sony PlayStation 3 game that featured the Mercedes-AMG Vision Gran Turismo Concept. A 1:1 scale model of the concept made the rounds of the auto show circuit and was pictured with the boat that debuted at the Miami International Boat Show in February 2014.

The *Marauder*, which featured an Alubeam silver and matte-black paint scheme, was powered by twin 1,650-hp Mercury Marine Racing engines. Top speed was estimated at more than 140 mph (225 kph). Cigarette offered the one-of-a-kind boat for $1.5 million.

In 2015, with the launch of the SLS-succeeding Mercedes-AMG GT S, Cigarette built a 50-foot (15-m) *Marauder* painted in AMG Solarbeam Yellow. The *Marauder* GT S Concept showcased a pair of Mercury Racing 1,550-hp V-8s in an engine bay also decked out in Solarbeam Yellow. Cigarette priced this one-off model at $1.2 million.

The seventh boat in the series was a 41-foot (12-m) "open performance" boat that showcased the Mercedes-AMG GT3 race car. The open performance concept blends a center console layout with the hull and engines used in offshore racing. This boat built by Cigarette and called the SD GT3, relied on a pair of Mercury 1,100-hp V-8s to give it a top speed of over 100 mph (161 kph). In addition to upscale touches such as the teak floor, the SD GT3 was the first Cigarette boat to have a full extreme marine-grade leather interior designed by Mercedes.

Breaking with tradition, the next boat to come from the collaboration was not shown at the Miami show but rather made its debut in 2016 on the harbor in Monte Carlo before the 2016 Monaco Grand Prix. Called the Cigarette Racing 50 *Marauder* AMG Monaco Concept, it boasted a top speed of more than 142 mph (229 kph) courtesy of the twin 1,550-hp Mercury Racing V-8s.

continued

TOP Paired with a C 63 Black Series, this 50-foot (15-m) *Marauder* was the second boat in the Cigarette Racing series.

MIDDLE LEFT With the introduction of the all-electric AMG SLS E-Cell, Cigarette commissioned an electric boat billed as the fastest and most powerful electric boat of all time.

MIDDLE RIGHT The electric battery pack and electric motors produced 2,200 horsepower delivered to the twin prop shafts.

LEFT Though the concept was rendered in full-scale, the AMG Gran Turismo wasn't a real car but rather created for the Gran Turismo video game. Nonetheless Cigarette built a real 50-foot (15-m) *Marauder* for the 2014 Miami Boat Show.

AZAMARA QUEST
PETRONAS
EPSON
AMG

AMG

ONE
AMG
CIGARETTE

Drivers Lewis Hamilton and Nico Rosberg helped with the unveiling, taking the boat out for a run on the Mediterranean. The black-and- silver paint scheme with turquoise highlights mirrored the look of the Mercedes AMG Petronas Formula 1 car. The boat was priced at $1.6 million.

The boat prepared for the 2017 Miami International Boat Show marked the tenth anniversary of the tie-up between Cigarette and AMG and paid tribute to AMG's fiftieth anniversary. Fittingly Cigarette chose a 50-foot (15-m) *Marauder* equipped with Mercury Marine's 1550/1350 QC4v (quad cam four-valve) V-8 engines. The boat has a key fob that allows the engines to switch from 1,350 to 1,550 hp (which requires higher octane racing fuel) for a total output of 3,100 hp.

A bow decal uses the number 50 to commemorate the AMG anniversary, while the Green Hell Magno accent paint matches up with the paint scheme on the AMG GT R. The hue is named after the Nürburgring North Loop, where the GT R set a production car lap record.

When the AMG ONE launched, Cigarette Racing undertook the most radical redesign of its boats to create the *515 Project One.* As the name implies, the boat measures 51.5 feet (16 m) long and features a wider beam to accommodate up to six passengers.

While it's 10 feet (3 m) longer than the SD GT3-and has 30-percent more surface area than the standard *Marauder* 50, it weighs less thanks to the use of Kevlar and carbon fiber, tipping the scales at 5,000 pounds (2,268 kg) less than the 41-footer (12 m). Using the same team of Mercury 1550/1350 QC4v engines, at full power, the Cigarette Racing *515 Project One* is capable of 140 mph (225 kph).

Cigarette Racing took some of the techniques employed on the 515 and applied them to a 41-foot (12-m) boat similar to the 2016 SD GT3. Called the 41' AMG Carbon Edition, extensive use of carbon fiber reduced weight by 500 pounds (227 kg), allowing a lower center of gravity that improved the boat's handling.

Power comes from four Mercury Racing 400R outboard inline-six engines that displace 2.6 liters each and produce 400 hp. Together, the 1,600 hp they generated produced a top speed of 83 mph (134 kph).

The boat's design also was inspired in part by the introduction of the Mercedes-AMG GT 63 S 4-door Coupe. The extra doors and seating connected to Cigarette's boast about the Carbon Edition's ability to carry eight passengers at speed, and up to twenty when just cruising around, thanks to its open console design. Both the boat and the car share the Designo graphite gray and bright red paint scheme.

The largest boat built by Cigarette carrying AMG branding was 2020's 59-foot (18-m) *Tirranna AMG Edition*. Befitting a big boat, its on-land counterpart was a G 63. In addition to the bespoke nature of the *Tirranna*, the luxury SUV was sent through AMG's Performance Studio for custom upgrades to create the Mercedes-AMG G 63 Cigarette Edition.

In addition to the black and gold paint scheme shared with the boat, the G 63 Cigarette Edition included 22-inch (56-cm) cross-spoke forged wheels, dark chrome exterior accents, and matte-black running boards. Inside the leather macchiato beige and dark blue Nappa leather interior is the same upholstery used in the *Tirranna*'s cockpit.

With 2,700 horsepower on tap from six Mercury Racing supercharged 4.6-liter V-8 engines, the *Tirranna AMG Edition* has an estimated top speed of 80 mph (129 kph). Its console design allows for up to twenty-six passengers. A cross between a power boat and a yacht, the *Tirranna* is also equipped with a gyrostabilizer to reduce roll by up 80 percent. It also has bow and stern thrusters to aid docking. Below deck, there's a sofa, a refrigerator, a television, a forward sleeping area with a king-size bed, and even a lavatory with a separate shower. The price for all this luxury? Only $3 million.

The last and thirteenth boat in the series is the Cigarette *41' Nighthawk* AMG Black Series. Like the Mercedes-AMG GT Black Series counterpart, the boat places its emphasis on handling and performance. Extensive use of carbon fiber for the deck and hardtop lowers the center of gravity to make the *Nighthawk* even more responsive.

A total of five Mercury Racing 4.6-liter V-8 engines produce 2,200 hp, enabling a top speed of over 90 mph (145 kph). An advanced throttle system allows the driver to control all five engines using just two levers. The open-bow center console provides seating for up to ten.

Both the boat and car are painted in a black and Magmabeam orange scheme. Instead of using decals, the large and small AMG logos are all hand painted. Interiors are a combination of gray and black with orange detailing. Due to COVID, the 2021 Miami International Boat Show was cancelled. It resumed in 2022, but the string of AMG and Cigarette boats had ended.

OPPOSITE, TOP Cigarette built its *Monaco* concept boat in 2016, which it unveiled ahead of the 2016 Monaco Grand Prix with Lewis Hamilton.

OPPOSITE, MIDDLE LEFT As part of AMG's fiftieth anniversary, Cigarette built a 50-foot (15-m) *Marauder* with Green Hell Magno accents to match the paint scheme of the accompanying Mercedes-AMG GT R.

OPPOSITE, MIDDLE RIGHT The AMG ONE inspired the next boat in the series called the *515 Project ONE* by Cigarette. Employing similar lightweight construction techniques to those used on the hypercar, the boat also measured 51.5 feet (16 m) in length, hence the name.

OPPOSITE, BOTTOM The last boat in the AMG/Cigarette tie-up involved the AMG GT Black Series. It was teamed with a 41-foot (12-m) *Nighthawk* capable of a top speed of over 90 mph (145 kph).

14 THE AMG ONE STORY

AS PRODUCTION of the AMG SLS began to wind down in 2014 and plans moved forward to make its GT successor more of a 911 fighter than a limited-run halo car, Mercedes-AMG also embarked on a new direction that would electrify its internal combustion engine expertise.

Its experience with the SLS E-Cell concept and the subsequent Electric Drive production model may have been too far ahead of the curve to find practical application in its lineup. But with the GT Concept, Mercedes-AMG demonstrated that electric hybrid technology to further boost performance, reduce emissions, and raise overall efficiency would be the track it would pursue with its production vehicles.

AMG also needed a new halo car, but rather than reaching into Mercedes' rich history with another 300 SL tribute, it would come up with an idea as audacious as racing a large luxury car at Spa or cramming a big V-8 in a midsize sedan to go 300 kph (186 mph). AMG would go big in bringing its F1 drivetrain—which had been using hybrid energy recovery systems since 2009—to the streets. This new roadgoing flagship would be known as AMG ONE.

Both the hybrid four-door GT and AMG Project ONE concepts debuted as the featured players in festivities marking the fiftieth anniversary of AMG in 2017 at the Geneva Motor Show.

At the concept reveal, Mercedes-Benz CEO Ola Källenius told *Autocar*, "The team at AMG and the [AMG] High Performance Powertrain Formula 1 arm came to us about four years ago and said, 'we've got a great idea, let's put a Formula 1 engine into a road car.' I will have to go back to check the meeting minutes, but I'm sure we were drunk when we said yes."

Just before then, Källenius had turned the reins over as Mercedes-AMG CEO to Tobias Moers, who would oversee AMG ONE development.

Mercedes-AMG Project ONE's specs were impressive. The hypercar promised more than 1,000 horsepower with a top speed in excess of 217 mph (350 kph) and 0–60 mph (0–97 mph) acceleration of fewer than three seconds. It would represent a collaborative effort among Mercedes-AMG in Affalterbach, Mercedes-AMG High Performance Powertrains (HPP) in Brixworth, England, and the Mercedes-AMG Petronas Formula 1 team in Brackley, England.

"The hypercar is the most ambitious project we have ever undertaken," Moers said at the Frankfurt unveiling. "It marks yet another pinnacle of the successful, strategic development of Mercedes-AMG towards a performance and sports car brand. Project ONE raises the bar in terms of what is currently technologically feasible and thanks to its combination of efficiency and performance it represents an absolute benchmark. At the same time, Project ONE provides an outlook on how AMG will define driving performance in the future."

But it wouldn't be an easy road adapting F1 technology to the street. Steffen Jastrow, director of Mercedes-AMG vehicle development, worked closely with HPP to modify the hybrid powertrain to meet these different requirements. Among them, and the most daunting, were tuning the engine to comply with emissions and pass-by noise regulations. This also included a change in the 1.6-liter V-6 engine itself to run on premium gasoline rather than the witches' brew used

in F1. When you add the complexity of all-wheel drive with two additional motors on the front axle, factor in supply chain issues, and also consider the COVID-19 shutdown, it's no wonder the timeline from concept to production for this limited-run vehicle stretched over five years.

While some of this technology is too expensive to apply to other production models in the AMG range, there are other facets in AMG ONE that can be applied on a wider scale. When introducing the concept, Moers said, "Electrified powertrains are the key success factor to the future of performance cars. You can count on that: Electrification of powertrain is going to be the key. We have a lot of components in this car that I see coming to the AMG street cars. We're going to bring bits and pieces out of that car [Project ONE] to life. For example, the electrified turbo."

Any discussion of Project ONE and the production Mercedes-AMG ONE should, in true AMG fashion, center on the drivetrain. It is the sole reason for this hypercar's existence.

Based on the PU106B engine used in the W06 Mercedes-AMG Petronas F1 car from 2016, Project ONE was designed to capitalize on that engine's extreme performance and efficiency thanks to its use of its two-level hybrid technology. The first, known as MGU-K or Motor Generating Unit-Kinetic, is a way of recapturing energy through the vehicle's motion. The heart of this system is a 161-hp electric motor/generator connected to the crankshaft.

When the throttle is lifted and the vehicle is coasting, the main MGU unit sends current to the battery pack. On acceleration, the battery power supplements the engine's horsepower and torque. In the case of the AMG ONE, the two motors on the front axle, which make 161 hp each, draw power from the pack for an instantaneous boost and return current when not driving the front wheels. The two-motor setup also allows for torque vectoring to assist handling.

The second unit, the MGU-H (Motor Generator Unit-Heat), is positioned on a long shaft connecting the impeller or exhaust-driven end of the turbocharger with the compressor, the turbine blades that boost the intake side of the engine. In this case, this 121-hp MGU generates energy recaptured from the turbo, which can spin up to 100,000 rpm and stores that power in the battery pack. When not under load, it draws power to keep the turbo spinning, thereby eliminating lag found in nonelectric turbos.

While the 1.6-liter turbocharged V-6 is similar to the one used in F1, it has undergone significant modification for road use. Adam Allsopp, powertrain director at HPP who worked on Project

PREVIOUS The AMG ONE successfully transplanted Formula 1 technology in a hypercar that can be street driven. Only 275 examples were built.

ABOVE With its dihedral-opening doors and roof-mounted air scoop, AMG ONE looks like it's more ready to take on the 24 Hours of Le Mans than a leisurely Sunday drive.

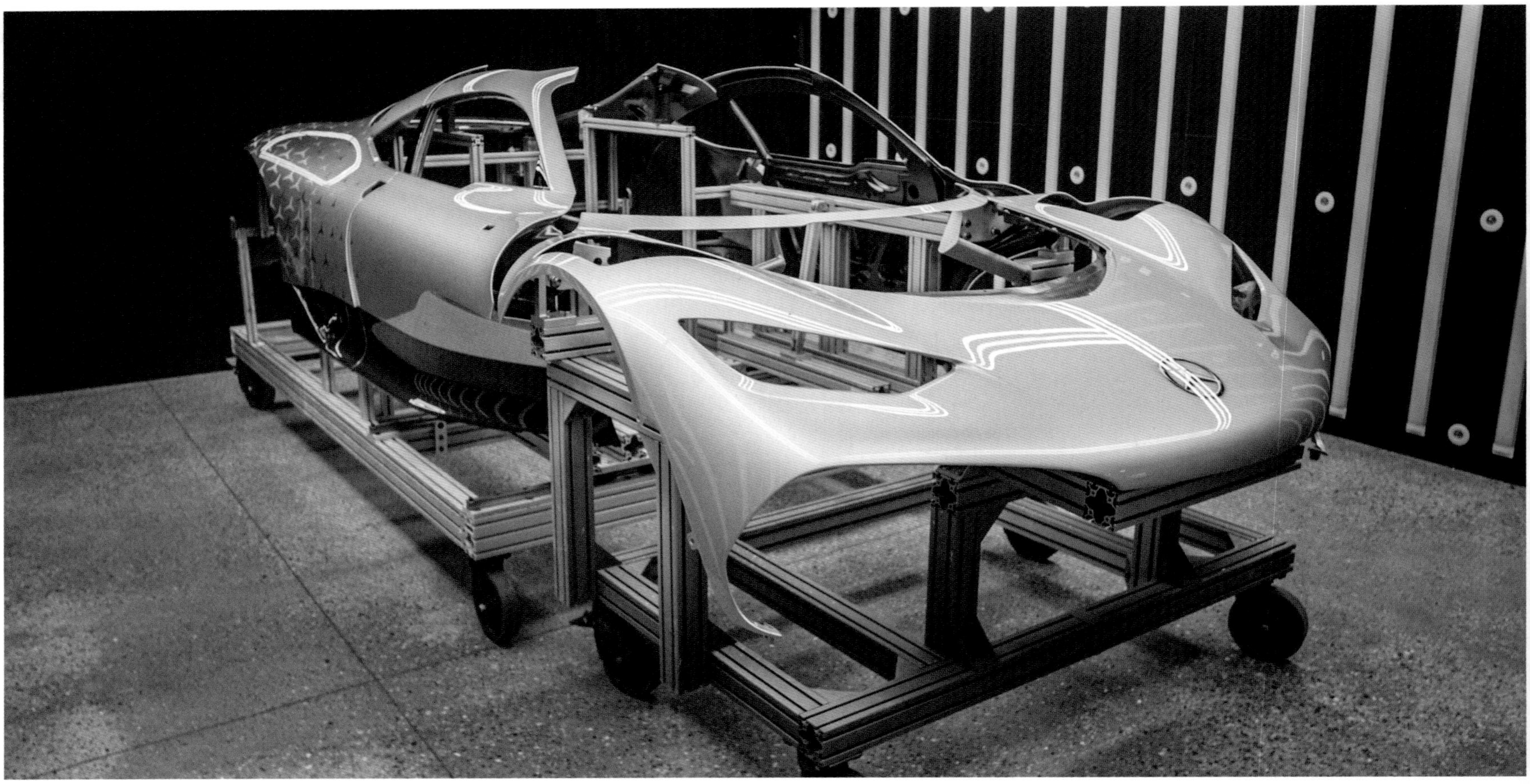

ABOVE Body panels are placed in jigs and hand painted as part of the meticulous attention to detail that goes into its assembly.

OPPOSITE, TOP LEFT The lithium-ion battery pack used to provide an instantaneous boost in performance is a sophisticated design in which the cells are immersed in liquid coolant to maximize their efficiency.

OPPOSITE, TOP RIGHT Assembly of the AMG ONE is completed by Multimatic at a facility in Coventry, England. Here technicians are mating the power unit to the car's monocoque structure.

OPPOSITE, BOTTOM As part of the final assembly process, a completed AMG ONE is put through a high-pressure water bath to check for leaks. It is part of a process that includes sixteen separate assembly and testing modules.

ONE, said that while F1 powertrains are rebuilt after just a few races, the AMG ONE production engine will be configured to go at least 31,000 miles (50,000 km) between overhauls. Engine compression was reduced and the crankcase stiffened. With the V-6 engine making 566 hp and the four electric motors in the AMG ONE contributing an effective combined 483 horses, the total output of the drivetrain is 1,049 hp.

While there were many modifications to adapt the drivetrain, some unique features were retained, like the pneumatic valvetrain, a first for a road car in the AMG ONE. But that's where the commonality ends.

Jastrow noted, "When a Formula 1 car is started and idles, it idles between 4,000 and 5,000 rpm. One of our biggest challenges was getting that idle down, which is not easy because this engine is made for high revs. At the end, we reached [an idle speed of] about 1,200 rpm, nothing is possible below that." He added that while an F1 car can rev to about 14,000 rpm, "redline on the AMG ONE is limited to 11,000 rpm."

According to Allsopp, "Our next hurdle was particulate emissions. A Formula 1 engine produces high emissions without a catalyst and filter, and gaseous emissions play a role here as well. We optimized combustion with high charge motion in-cylinder, along with in-cylinder vaporization; added a second, port fuel injection system; and the latest in filter and catalyst technology in order to reach the correct levels.

"It was a tough road to get to where we are, but I think we're in very good shape at this point. Distribution and mixture preparation were improved by putting a large amount of fuel into the combustion chamber via the GDI system and then applying the second, port fuel injection on the other side of the cylinder head. This, along with optimized airflow, slightly smaller ports, and the use of the latest in after-treatment, really made the difference," he said.

Jastrow also pointed out that the four metallic catalysts used on the AMG ONE must be preheated before the engine even starts. "We need to get them to 500 degrees [Celsius / 932 degrees Fahrenheit] before they will work," he explained. Because it has a pure electric mode, when the driver starts the car and begins to drive, the AMG ONE remains in EV mode for about 50 to 60 seconds before the catalysts reach the desired temperature and the engine can fire. The AMG ONE is also equipped with two ceramic catalytic converters and two particulate traps.

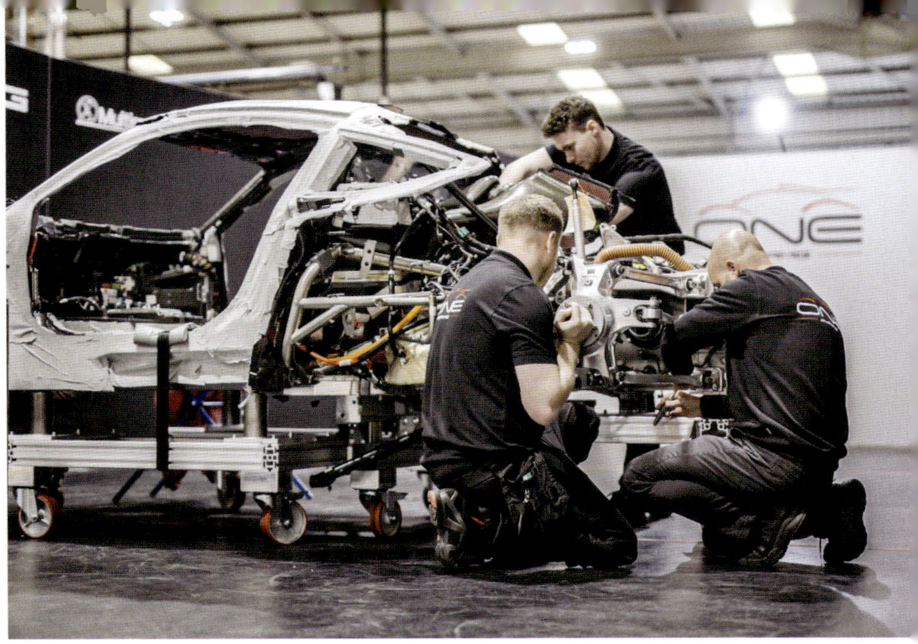
ONE

AMG

LB ON 175

The Mercedes-AMG ONE shares the same type of batteries as the F1 car, a lithium-ion array storing 8.4 kWh of energy. In addition to having four times the capacity of the race car's, the battery is connected to a 3.7-kW onboard charger allowing the AMG ONE to be plugged in for replenishment. But unlike other PHEV models, the pure electric range is somewhat limited, about 11 miles (17 km). The primary function of the battery pack allows it to be quickly charged by the MGU-K, MGU-H, and MGu-F (the front motor) units, which then in turn will provide the bursts of power that provide the AMG ONE with its stellar performance.

As Allsopp explains, "In EV mode, it does not have the range of a standard EV, which is typically a couple of hundred kilometers. This vehicle has the advantage that it's geared for speed and efficiency, recuperating energy as the battery is drained and charged during driving. It is not dependent on a plug somewhere to recharge the battery, but it can still be plugged in to achieve a charge or be recharged. The battery is smaller compared to standard hybrids. This is a totally different concept with only one target: maximum driving dynamics, maximum fun while driving, and reaching the next level of performance."

Because the battery pack is quickly charged and discharged in multiple cycles during the driving experience, heat becomes an issue. To ensure maximum performance and prolong the pack's life, the batteries employ direct liquid cooling that bathes the cells in coolant. An electric pump circulates fluid, which passes through an external cooler to keep the temperature at a constant 50 degrees Celsius (113 degrees Fahrenheit).

Adapting the F1 engine to a road car meant a raft of software that needed to be written to enable the vehicle to be started by the push of a button. As Jochen Hermann, Mercedes-AMG chief technical officer, told *Autoweek* in a 2021 interview, the scope of these issues became apparent on a visit to the F1 team. Hermann was "standing next to Lewis [Hamilton's] car, and when he is coming out, there were like 10 or 12 people coming out who all ran to the car, everybody's opening something, puts a screwdriver in, puts a laptop to the car, before you can actually start the car. With Project One, you turn the key and people expect the car to start. So we had to put software for

Large front inlets manage the airflow for used for cooling the brakes and providing the necessary downforce to give the AMG ONE exceptional road-holding capability.

BELOW, LEFT As part of the airflow management, deployable louvers atop the front fenders can be opened to help reduce lift. The wheels also are fitted with carbon-fiber inserts that reduce drag.

BELOW, RIGHT The AMG ONE sports a multifunction steering yoke that would look at home in the cockpit of a Formula 1 car.

BOTTOM Air is channeled from behind the front wheels over the rocker sills, where it enters the body again ahead of the rear wheels for brake cooling.

(the equivalent of) 10 or 12 race engineers into the coding. I think that was something that was really underestimated."

While the AMG ONE has the heart of an F1 car, the body in which it is wrapped is closer to a Le Mans prototype. The engine is mid-mounted, and along with the seven-speed sequential shift transmission are load-bearing components in the carbon-fiber monocoque body and chassis. The seven-speed transmission, which features a four-disc clutch, was originally specified as an eight-speed on the Project One concept.

As in a race car, the suspension uses pushrods connected to the inboard-mounted springs and dampers. The car is equipped with a wide range of movable aerodynamic devices, including deployable front fender louvers and rear wing. A unique feature adapted from the F1 car is a DRS (drag reduction system) that allows the wings and louvers to retract at the push of a button for less drag and more straight-line speed.

The aggressive and purposeful design starts with large front intakes that flank a trapezoid-shaped mesh grille emblazoned with a white AMG logo. The flat hood ends in a large air vent

TOP With the rear engine covers removed, you can see the power unit sits well forward of the rear axle in the middle of the body. The engine is fed air by the roof-mounted scoop that morphs into the car's dorsal fin.

MIDDLE In true race car fashion, the suspension is a pushrod setup with coil springs over the shocks.

BOTTOM The movable rear wing has multiple elements that can be positioned for maximum downforce or opened up like an F1 car's drag reduction system (DRS) for top straight-line speed.

ahead of the cowl, while a large roof-mounted scoop feeds air into the drivetrain. The engine cover is also equipped with large NACA ducts to feed the rear-mounted radiators.

In profile, the AMG ONE sports a large dorsal fin, winglets at all four corners, and deep rocker sills that channel air from the wheel arches. Forged aluminum ten-spoke center-lock wheels (19-inch [48-cm] front and 20-inch [51-cm] rear) wearing Michelin Pilot Sport Cup 2R M01 tires. The tires are embossed with an outline of the car and the number 1. To further enhance aerodynamics, the rims are fitted with partial carbon-fiber covers. Even lighter magnesium forged nine-spoke wheels are an option.

The rear of the Mercedes-AMG ONE has a ducktail spoiler that extends out to a full wing, while an F1-style single, large rear exhaust incorporating two smaller tips is framed by twin rear diffusers. The fuel filler is located on the right rear fender, while the left rear houses the port for electric charging.

As befits the exotic nature of the car, the front-hinged doors swing upward butterfly-style to provide access to the rather spartan cockpit. There is a pair of shell-style racing seats with two levels of adjustment on the backrests. The F1-style steering wheel with multiple buttons surrounding a center airbag features power adjustment, while the pedals and passenger side footrest can be manually set. Two screens, one ahead of the driver and a larger center display, provide information on and access to the various vehicle systems, including climate control, navigation, and infotainment. The center console, which has a small storage bin, is dominated by a red illuminated start button.

When that button is pushed, the vehicle is energized in EV mode. Meanwhile, the metal catalysts are being heated before the engine can fire. The driver can select one of six drive modes: Race Safe, Race, EV, Race Plus, Strat 2, and Individual.

Race Safe is the standard operating program with on-demand hybrid driving and pure electric startup. The combustion engine kicks in when more power is needed. The Race mode provides hybrid operation with the engine running continuously to provide full electric power from the battery pack. The EV mode allows the vehicle to be driven as an electric; however, the range, as mentioned earlier, is only about 11 miles (18 km).

Race Plus, the first track-only mode, lowers the ride height by about 1.5 inches (4 cm) up front and an inch in the rear and engages the active aerodynamic devices while firming up the suspension. Within Race Plus, the Energy Flow Control System (EFC) allows the driver to select between 4 different strategies managing the energy consumption of the hybrid system over multiple laps. Strat 2, also for track use only, is designed for a qualifying lap using the full electric

ABOVE Technicians check tire pressures and temperatures as they ready the AMG ONE for its first record run at the Nürburgring.

OPPOSITE Engel smiles broadly after setting the production car record with a time of just over six minutes, thirty-five seconds in October 2022. He would return nearly two years later and smash that mark with a sub six-minute, thirty-second run.

energy during 1 fast lap (HV-battery charge status from 100% to 0%). The final mode, Individual, allows for specific chassis and performance management inputs.

In addition to these drive modes, the Mercedes-AMG ONE also provides specific settings for the active aero. The Highway setting in Race Safe, Race, EV, and Individual modes keeps the fender louvers closed and the rear wing retracted while extending the flaps on the front diffuser. In the Track mode in Race Plus and Strat 2, the front flaps are folded back into the diffuser, the rear wing fully deploys along with a rear wing flap, and the louvers open to provide more front axle downforce. This mode also drops the vehicle's ride height. Downforce increases fivefold. Race DRS allows the rear wing flap to retract along with the front louvers, decreasing downforce by as much as 20 percent. DRS disconnects either manually, when the brakes are applied or a certain amount of lateral force is detected.

Unlike the AMG SLS, which was built in Germany, the Mercedes-AMG ONE was assembled entirely in England. The drivetrains were built alongside the Mercedes-AMG Petronas F1 engines in Brixworth before being sent over to Multimatic in Coventry, where they were mated with the monocoque body and chassis. The body panels, which use 1.2-mil-gauge carbon fiber, were fitted together, then removed for individual hand painting. Meanwhile the interior was installed and the body panels reassembled. Finished models were checked for water leaks and noise, run on a dyno, and given a quick test drive on a proving ground. The models then were sent off to Affalterbach for additional inspection and handover to the client. Only 275 were built and sold for over $2.7 million each.

What's it like to drive? *Top Gear* was able to take a few laps on the grand prix circuit at the Nürburgring and said, "We're in street mode, no aero deployed, but full power is available. The steering weight is delicious, the brake pedal feels weird, the noise is painful. That's right, the car everyone thought too quiet at Goodwood is (from the inside) one of the loudest cars we've ever driven. The V-6 combines with all the other bits to produce something that burrows behind the eardrum into your skull. For the first half lap it makes us grin. Then it hurts.

"The car understeers, but maybe that's just tire temperature. We pile down the main straight and the Black Series [driven by AMG ace Bernd Schneider] is already holding up the hypercar. . . . Forget everything you've experienced from a normal super-hypercar powertrain. This may not be the fastest thing out there, but it's intense and plain wonderful and, crucially, unique. The engine is frantic above 9,000 rpm, but upchanges sound slovenly, albeit without any sense of acceleration being clipped. Turns out some electricity is deployed between changes to sustain momentum. The chassis is supple in the street mode, but firm as hell in Race."

Jastrow said one reason to build the AMG ONE was to demonstrate its ability by setting a record lap on the Nürburgring's Nordschleife. "There may be cars out there that are quicker from 0–100 kph [0–62 mph] or other cars that are faster than 352 kph [218 mph]. But on the track, the time is the time. And if you think you have a better car, then come to the Nordschleife and show us."

In October of 2022, Mercedes-AMG took the car to the legendary circuit. With Maro Engel at the helm, AMG ONE set a new lap record for a production car covering the nearly 13-mile (21-km) distance in just over six minutes and thirty-five seconds. It beat the previous record held by the AMG SLS Black Series in 2020 by more than thirteen seconds. This was despite the fact that rainstorm had wet part of the track and some oil had spilled on it by vehicles driving back and forth to dry the surface.

"We had the record, and we sort of sat back and waited to see if someone would break it. And then we were waiting over the last two years, but nobody came," Jastrow said, adding that on the earlier record attempt the track was damp in spots and Engel thought a faster lap could be set. In September 2024, the team returned to the 'Ring.

The record attempt was again scrapped due to rain, but two weeks later, the AMG ONE returned. Engel went out and lapped near the 6:30 mark. He pitted for a new set of preheated tires and posted a time of 6:29.09, more than five seconds faster than the car's previous record.

The Mercedes-AMG ONE stands alone for bringing Formula 1 technology directly into a roadgoing vehicle. As such, it is the perfect halo car for the brand, with its deep roots in motorsports. It's a remarkable accomplishment given the tenor of the times, with ever-tightening emission and fuel economy regulations. It may also prove to be the first and last car to apply F1-style internal combustion power to the street.

"We won't be able to do so facing all the regulations from EU7," Jastrow said. "So that's not possible anymore to fulfill that. I think for somebody, not just AMG or Mercedes, who wants to bring a Formula 1 engine to a production car, I think this is the one time it could be done. And that's why I say there won't be a second one. Maybe something different? You can probably do it with an electric car, but it's not the same thing. It's not Formula 1."

Mercedes-AMG ONE may be a one-off, but the bringing together of HPP, F1 technology, and the road car expertise of Affalterbach has changed the relationship among these seemingly disparate functions. In doing so, AMG will continue to break new ground in electric-assisted internal combustion performance engines.

AMG's English Connection

THE DEVELOPMENT AND ASSEMBLY OF THE AMG ONE'S hybrid engine at Mercedes-AMG High Performance Powertrains (HPP) in Brixworth, England, neatly closes the loop between the UK-based unit and its parent in Affalterbach, Germany.

While the F1 team and the entity that builds its engines both carry the AMG brand, it's been at best an arm's length relationship until the development of the AMG ONE hypercar. Most motorsports activities carried out by Affalterbach have been in support of sports or touring car competition either in-house or through its relationship with HWA AG, the race shop run by Hans Werner Aufrecht.

Formula 1, however, is a different beast. Other than Italy's Ferrari, virtually all the expertise that supports F1 is found in England. And while the roots of Mercedes-AMG HPP and Mercedes-AMG Petronas F1 are deep in England, the AMG branding only goes back to the 2011–2012 timeframe. Developing and building the engine and assembling the 275 examples of the AMG ONE at Multimatic in Coventry, England, is part of an ongoing process of bringing this operation further into the AMG fold.

In its own way, HPP's history has parallels to AMG's story. Just as AMG was founded by two enterprising engineers, Hans Werner Aufrecht and Erhard Melcher, HPP traces its roots to Ilmor Engineering Ltd., which was founded in 1984 by Paul Morgan and Mario Ilien, both of whom had been working at Cosworth.

Ilmor, which was backed by Roger Penske with funding from General Motors, initially built engines for IndyCar before branching out into Formula 1 in 1989, building 3.5-liter V-10 engines for Leyton House and Tyrrell. In 1993 it partnered with Mercedes-Benz to make engines for the newly formed Sauber team when the German company acquired GM's 25 percent stake in Ilmor.

In 1995 the partnership began building engines for McLaren. Their first win came at the Australian Grand Prix in 1997. The V-10 and later V-8 engines would power the McLaren-Mercedes team to victory in the driver's and manufacturer's titles in 1998 and 2009 as well as the driver's championships in 1999 and 2008.

The introduction of the Kinetic Energy Recovery System (KERS) earned the company the prestigious Dewar's Trophy for Technical Excellence in 2009. It was the first hybrid powertrain to win an F1 victory that year at the Hungarian Grand Prix.

After Paul Morgan's untimely death in 2001 in a plane crash, Mercedes increased its share to 55 percent and renamed the company Mercedes-Ilmor in 2002. Three years later, DaimlerChrysler bought the rest of the company, renaming it Mercedes-Benz HighPerformanceEngines (later changed to High Performance Powertrains *with* spaces between the words).

Also at that time, the special projects department was broken out into a separate entity called Ilmor Engineering, which went its own way under the guidance of Ilien and Penske.

In 2010 Mercedes-Benz acquired Brawn GP from Ross Brawn. Based in Brackley, not far from the Brixton engine facility, the new operation was called Mercedes GP Petronas F1, as part of its sponsorship deal with the Malaysian oil giant. Two years later, the team was rechristened Mercedes AMG Petronas F1. At the same time, AMG was added to HPP's official name.

The F1 team went on to win eight consecutive manufacturer titles from 2014 to 2021 and seven straight driver championships from 2014 to 2020. HPP currently supplies engines to the Mercedes F1 team as well as to McLaren, Aston Martin, and Williams.

Situated on 20 acres, the Brixworth complex now employs 1,000 in diverse roles that include designing, assembling, and testing F1 hybrid powertrains, plus working on projects to transfer that technology to other products such as the AMG ONE and the Mercedes Vision EQXX concept. The EQXX, which was shown at the Consumer Electronics Show (CES) in 2022, promised a range of 1,000 kilometers (621 miles) using battery technology similar to that employed in the F1 hybrid.

In addition to leveraging the resources at HPP in Brixton, the F1 operation in Brackley has been greatly expanded to create a large tech campus similar to those found in California's Silicon Valley. With over 1,200 employees, the operation includes a wind tunnel, dynamometers, and a driver-in-loop simulator to support the manufacture and maintenance of the team cars.

Brackley is also the home of Mercedes-AMG F1 Applied Science, which offers F1 levels of engineering and support to other automotive and nonautomotive applications. Among the projects currently in-house is its work on INEOS Britannia, which is working with Sir Ben Ainslie to build an America's Cup racing yacht.

ABOVE The AMG ONE, right, closes the loop between the road-going Mercedes-AMG models (left) and the company's Formula 1 efforts.

LEFT One of the key takeaways from adapting the Formula 1 power unit to road use was the use of electrically powered turbochargers to reduce turbo lag and increase overall engine efficiency.

Vision
AMG

15

AMG TODAY AND TOMORROW

IT'S MID-NOVEMBER IN THE SWABIAN countryside north of Stuttgart. The leaves are off the trees, but the fields are still green. Cloudy, cold, and rainy, the weather is typical for the time of year. This rural setting isn't what one would associate with a global performance powerhouse like Mercedes-AMG. Two of its main rivals, Porsche in Zuffenhausen and BMW in Munich, are not far away in more urban environments.

Still, there's something about Affalterbach, a village of about 4,000 residents, that echoes places such as Gaydon in England's Midlands or northern Italy's Sant'Agata Bolognese or Maranello, the respective homes of Aston Martin, Lamborghini, and Ferrari.

There's tremendous local pride in these hometown heroes and it manifests itself in the employees who also view it as more than just a place to work. Driving into Affalterbach from the south on L127, also known as Affalterbach Strasse, you'd miss AMG's complex in what appears to be a light industrial area in the southeast quadrant of the town's limits. Turn left at a tire store onto Robert Bosch Way and you see streets named for Mercedes, Carl Benz, and Gottlieb Daimler. Turning left on Daimler Strasse, there's a building on the left with a large sign that simply states, "Welcome to the World's Fastest Family." You've arrived at Mercedes-AMG.

The feelings of many who work here are best summed up by its CEO, Michael Schiebe. With over twenty years' experience at Mercedes-Benz, he has only been at the helm for about two years, having taken over from Philipp Schiemer. "If you had asked me what my dream job within Mercedes was, I would have pointed to this position. It is a dream come true. Every morning as I drive into this little town I still get this feeling of 'Oh my gosh, how cool is this?' Or when I see little kids standing by the road and they get all excited when they see our GT drive by. It's something very special, and it's a feeling that doesn't fade. When I get behind the steering wheel of an AMG, I still get goosebumps."

Schiebe is not alone; he sees it all around him. "What makes AMG so special is the passion of the people. There's great team spirit and a huge passion for our products. You need to be a product-loving person. You cannot run this company if you are not interested in high-performance cars."

Unlike its competitors, Mercedes-AMG lacks one thing: a factory assembling cars. It produces all its four- and eight-cylinder engines in Affalterbach, but the final build on its road cars is done elsewhere in the sprawling Mercedes-Benz production system. But, as AMG has grown from a tuner into its own car brand, it has built up its expertise in engineering, design, product development, and sales and marketing, all of which is centered in Affalterbach.

Vestiges of the early days can still be seen if you look closely. The original building where vehicles were modified sits across the court from the main showroom. It's attached to what had been the Aufrecht home on the corner, which now also serves as office space.

The showroom's motif has changed over time. Currently, it's highlighting motorsports; the floor resembles the tarmac on a racing circuit with a checkered finish line. On the wall is a huge

painting of the Red Pig. Out the door and upstairs, the private lounge and restaurant await customers coming to take delivery of their cars. Right now, except for clients taking delivery of the AMG ONE, headquarters delivery of cars is limited only to German customers. In the building opposite the courtyard is a vehicle prep center and private studios in which the cars are rolled into for the handover to owners.

Even though no cars are built here, other than the racing machines assembled by HWA, the campus bustles with camouflaged prototypes appearing from and disappearing into highly secure garages. With more than 3,500 employees on site, Mercedes-AMG is responsible for nearly doubling the population of Affalterbach on a regular workday.

There's a huge construction project going on in the center of the complex. The new facility will house software engineers, a sign of the change that's coming with greater electrification of the product lineup.

"Software has become hugely important," Schiebe explained. "We figured out that to work as efficiently and effectively as possible in the software environment, we need the right setup. So we will have workshops on the ground floor and all the coders on the second floor. If, for example, the team develops a steering component that affects driving dynamics, they can just go downstairs to test it on the real car. This speeds our processes and also helps to troubleshoot potential issues in real time. That's why we're investing into this new area to become even more efficient and work on next level technology."

Not far from the construction site is another nondescript building that houses an equally important piece of equipment in the vehicle development process: a dynamic vehicle simulator. Vehicle dynamic engineers Max Eberle and Rene Szczepek explain that the full motion simulator allows test drivers to evaluate a wide range of chassis setups over a variety of road surfaces.

A vehicle cockpit rides on the simulator mount that receives inputs from hexapod (six-legged) and tripod arms. The hexapod moves the cockpit through rotational movements including

PREVIOUS Mercedes-AMG lays out its past, present, and future in this artwork that depicts its start with the Red Pig on the right. This icon shares the idea of a high-performance sedan with the current Mercedes-AMG GT 4-Door Coupe. The AMG ONE project (center left) ties together the company's Formula 1 efforts, while the Vision AMG speaks to its coming electric products.

ABOVE AMG's sprawling operation in Affalterbach, which employs over 3,500, had a humble start in two small buildings with red roofs seen in the lower left side of the complex. The front two-story structure was the home of Hans Werner Aufrecht.

Handcrafted
by Racers.
AMG
DRIVING PERFORMANCE

AMG
DRIVING PERFORMANCE

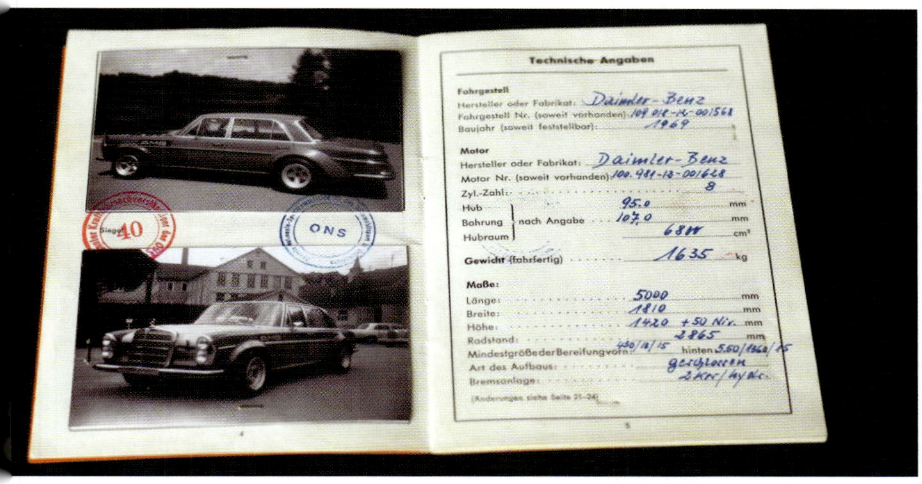

rolling, pitching, and sways, as well as translational movement, which includes longitudinal pitch, lateral, and vertical motions. "But, if we relied only on this hexapod, the acceleration the driver feels would be quite small," Eberle pointed out. "In order to increase the perceptible forces, we also use the tripod, which highlights the yaw movements and the movements in the x and y [axes] more clearly."

The screens in front of the driver extend 180 degrees and the simulations include all sorts of road surfaces, everything from test tracks within Mercedes' proving grounds to Nürburgring Nordschleife. Maro Engel spent time in the simulator to prep for his record runs in AMG ONE.

The simulator has two cockpits for different applications. "The cockpits often confuse our visitors," Eberle said. "In principle, we can drive any vehicle on the driving simulator. The X1 Cockpit was manufactured explicitly for the development for the AMG ONE; the AMG GT four-door cockpit is a good compromise between compact cars, sedans, and SUVs. If you want to take it to the extreme, you could also tune the chassis setup of a G-Wagen in the AMG ONE cockpit. Whether this is so easy for the driver [to experience] is another question."

While the simulator's movements are realistic, even some experienced drivers can suffer motion sickness from it. Still, the ability to narrow down the range and choices for spring, shock, and anti-roll bar settings—and even simulate the effects of different tire compound and tread pattern selections—greatly speeds up the development process.

OPPOSITE, TOP Visitors are greeted at AMG's modern showroom, which forms a courtyard next to the original facility that housed the company after its move from Burgstall.

OPPOSITE, BOTTOM The showroom's décor emphasizes the connection Mercedes-AMG maintains with motorsports. The vehicle display rotates with the season and will show a combination of both road-going and racing cars.

TOP LEFT The third side of the courtyard is bounded by the stairway leading up AMG's private lounge, which is used to host clients, VIPs, and special events.

TOP RIGHT Inside the private lounge, customers can browse through books, grab a coffee, or have a meal while finding some respite between tours and vehicle deliveries.

ABOVE, LEFT Mercedes-AMG's archives include a treasure trove of photos, artifacts, and documents, like the original registration papers for the Red Pig.

ABOVE, RIGHT Across the street from the showroom and private lounge is the vehicle-prep and delivery area where customers take possession of their vehicles. There are three separate private studios for vehicle handovers. Once a vehicle is prepped, it is loaded into the studio, which has its own private lounge where the owners are briefed before being led into a room to see their purchase for the first time. Additional time is spent going over the vehicle's features.

Steffen Jastrow, head of development for AMG derivatives, believes that "[w]ith the simulator, it gives us about 80 percent of what we need. You still have to do that last 20 percent on the road." It saves a lot of time and costs being able to narrow eight different setups down to two for prototype testing.

Design is another area where the latest in computer technology blends with traditional skills, including working from sketches and clay modeling. Like Schiebe, Bastian Baudy has just over two years into his job as head of design. But he is more than familiar with AMG. Early in his twelve-year career with Mercedes-Benz, he led the advanced design team that created the Mercedes AMG Vision Gran Turismo that was used in the video game of the same name.

Baudy said that design has three teams. One sketches and comes up with themes for interiors and wheels. A second team does exterior design and is responsible for translating their drawings into full-size clay models. Baudy said the use of clay results in better surfacing in the purity of the form in its finished product. He said he can tell by the way a car looks and reflects light off its surface on whether it was rendered in clay or came directly from a computer model.

Finally there's a third team of software designers who specialize in the user interface and graphics used in the vehicle's instrument and infotainment displays, which are specific to AMG models.

Their work is not just confined to the Mercedes-AMG GT family. "We do all the design on the production cars, the front and rear end differentiation for the AMG cars," Baudy said. "We have wider tracks, and way more aggressive front styling." It's in the smallest details that designers are able to draw out the AMG difference in something like the wide rear track on the GT Pro model. Standing by the right rear quarter panel, Baudy points out that the flared fender is accentuated by a dished rear wheel. "From here, you can't see the little three-pointed star in the hub, that gives the rear a greater 3D effect," which helps to call out the wider stance, he added.

Beyond these small details, the designers tap into the rich traditions of both Mercedes and AMG. "We draw our inspiration from the past. Mercedes has a great heritage, while AMG cultivated its own styles," he said. "We see the strong, iconic DNA and bring it into the future. We always try to be bold, innovative, and sometimes even provocative. That is where our heritage comes in. This is what makes our cars so extraordinary."

To have access to that history means that it must be preserved. To that end, AMG has the benefit of an in-house team tasked with finding and cataloging all sorts of memorabilia dating back to the company's earliest days. Ever-smiling archivist Daniela Sigl works in a small second-floor office on the edge of the AMG complex along with her boss and another archivist. The collection of material is impressive and ranges from significant finds such as the original registration documentation for the Red Pig to a photo album from a 1987 party marking the twentieth anniversary of AMG's founding. In addition to photographs, design drawings, and catalogs, there are engine components, body panels, and racing trophies, each with their own story to tell.

Nearly every day holds new discoveries, and many from unlikely sources. Sigl said the original patent for the AMG crest was found in a filing box that was produced from an office of a retiring employee. Part of the files had been exposed to water and were being thrown away, but in riffling through the folders, Sigl found the patent in its bound

cover. The family-oriented nature of AMG is another source, with second- and third-generation employees contributing personal photos and other memorabilia handed down to them.

In a nearby town not far from Affalterbach, Mercedes-AMG has a building where it houses a growing collection of recent and historic models. The centerpiece is the 2005 replica of the Red Pig. Other cars housed there include at least a half-dozen DTM racers, two Hammers, a CLK DTM coupe, the full range of Black Series models, the E-Cell SLS, as well as several other SLS models. Many of the recent models were culled from the press fleet, while older collectibles were purchased on the secondhand market, some from owners who wanted their vehicles to go to AMG. This building and growing fleet of vehicles may someday evolve into a proper museum open to the public.

"It's all about passion at AMG. And that starts in our history," said Schiebe, who quickly acknowledged, "but is especially important for the future. There is this inner unrest that our engineers have. If they have developed a component for the predecessor GT, they want to improve it for the next GT. When I come to the office, I want to be better that day than the day before. This is what I see in our team. It's like in sports, you try to improve every day and it's all about competition."

He also recognizes that AMG has a built-in advantage in being able to leverage the larger Mercedes-Benz organization. "Our mothership is hugely important. All the qualities you expect from a Mercedes, you can expect from an AMG, like reliability, the quality, the safety, everything that you know is part of that DNA."

As AMG has grown its engineering and development teams, the working relationship with Mercedes-Benz has grown tighter. "We are deeply integrated into the development process," Schiebe said. "So, when we take a Mercedes and turn it into an AMG, we are involved at a very early stage. Certain factors must be incorporated from the start, things like certain tire dimensions for example. That's why our early collaboration is essential–to lay foundation of what ultimately makes an AMG."

The growth in the number of employees from the hundreds to the thousands is one of the reasons why the Mercedes-AMG lineup has been able to expand to thirty-six models that include gas engines, hybrids, and pure electrics in coupes, sedans, convertibles, roadsters, and SUVs.

OPPOSITE, TOP Michael Schiebe, CEO of Mercedes-AMG, worked for Mercedes for two decades before taking over the AMG reins in 2023. He describes his job as a dream come true. He believes AMG's mission is to imbue all its branded products, gas, electric, or hybrid, with race-bred performance. No matter the technology, he believes models must be an AMG first and foremost.

OPPOSITE, MIDDLE The dynamic simulator at Mercedes-AMG can re-create just about any driving experience. Here it displays the Nürburgring's Nordschliefe. The feedback generated from the simulator greatly speeds vehicle development.

OPPOSITE, BOTTOM Mercedes-AMG's approach to blending traditional internal-combustion technology with the instant response of electric motors is its high-tech solution to maintaining a leadership position in building performance vehicles.

ABOVE While it is building its own EV, Mercedes-AMG has lent its expertise in handling to create its own version of the parent company's EQ line of electrics. Both the EQE Sedan, above, and EQE SUV incorporate the division's Panamericana theme on their front fascias.

AMG

Sales have likewise grown exponentially from 2008, when 24,200 AMG vehicles were sold to a total of 143,200 in 2023.

As the industry increases its reliance on electrified vehicles, Schiebe is confident that for the near term, at least, there will be robust demand for more traditional powerplants. "Even at the end of the decade, maybe the beginning of the next decade, many customers will still want to have combustion-engine cars," Schiebe said. "And our one man, one engine principle is part of our brand and our product. So, we will continue this."

He also is eagerly anticipating the addition of new electric models to the Mercedes-AMG lineup, following the announcement of an SUV and a sedan replacement for the four-door GT Coupe based on AMG's own electric architecture.

"We are using that platform to develop high-performance electric car," Schiebe said, adding, "What do I mean by that? Our future EVs need to be as emotional as a combustion-engine AMG today and it needs to have the same performance. So, it's an AMG first and an EV second."

In developing this product, AMG faces a daunting task in distinguishing these new models from its competition in the EV space. "There are a lot of electric cars coming to the market," he said. "They all accelerate very fast. This is not a differentiator anymore. One very differentiating criterion, however, will be continuous performance."

Repeated hard acceleration runs and extended high-speed usage adversely affect range and the ability for the battery to recoup enough energy for sustained track sessions. To be able to do that requires new battery technology with the same kind of characteristics for quick cycling as demonstrated in the AMG ONE. The car's battery pack, adapted from the F1 racer, has a unique approach to thermal management by keeping the lithium-ion cells bathed in coolant.

"We are talking about the next level of battery cells," Schiebe said. "We are working intensively together with our Formula 1 team to do this. With our AMG.EA platform, we will launch cutting-edge technology to deliver next level performance from AMG. That's what people expect from us."

"Electric vehicles provide new opportunities that we don't have in combustion-engine cars," Schiebe said in referring to AMG's ability to tailor the experience to fit drivers' needs and, more importantly, expectations. "So, this is something that we will use in our electric portfolio in the future, and this is why I'm really excited."

To share that enthusiasm with top management, Schiebe invited Dr. Martin Brudermüller, a former BASF executive who was elected supervisory board chairman of Mercedes-Benz Group, for a prototype drive at the Immendingen test track south of Stuttgart.

"We discussed our electric architecture in our supervisory board. And I told him [Brudermüller], 'you need to drive this car.' After the drive, [Brudermüller] jumped out of the car and gave high fives to my entire team. He was clearly excited about the product. This is what I mean when I say it needs to be an AMG first and an EV second. It needs to provide this emotion and that's what we are working on."

Schiebe believes this program at AMG opens the door to a wider range of technological possibilities. "I see there are a lot of opportunities that electric motors and high-performance batteries provide that combustion-engine cars may not have. So, our customers will have the chance to choose from both." The all-of-the-above approach to offering products that span the range from pure electric through plug-in and standard hybrids to conventional internal combustion engines will position Mercedes-AMG to follow the market wherever it goes.

In the end, the ability to give customers what they want is precisely what Hans Werner Aufrecht and Erhard Melcher intended from the beginning.

OPPOSITE, TOP The AMG Vision concept introduced in 2022 laid the groundwork for the upcoming all-electric GT 4-Door Coupe replacement based on Mercedes' EA architecture for EVs.

OPPOSITE, BOTTOM Well into development, a camouflaged prototype of the EA-based 4-Door Coupe undergoes winter testing in Sweden. Beyond the 4-Door Coupe, Mercedes-AMG will also have its own electric SUV.

The AMG Experience

NOT EVERYONE CAN JUMP ON A PLANE, fly to Stuttgart, rent a car, and drive to Affalterbach, though you'd be surprised just how many have done it. But to get a taste of what the company has to offer, Mercedes-AMG has set up over 600 Performance Centers around the world. Some in larger markets are free standing; the rest are associated with Mercedes-Benz dealerships.

These Mercedes-AMG Performance Centers are staffed by specialists who can assist with test drives and demonstrate the car's features. The centers also provide direct contact with the headquarters in Germany to answer questions or fulfill specific needs. The Performance Centers are a touchpoint for customers to work directly with Mercedes' Manufaktur program to customize their purchase.

Designed and furnished to reflect the AMG brand, these centers are also used to host specific activities and partner events for prospective clients and owners alike. In the past, traveling AMG Performance Roadshows that feature specific new models or historical vehicles have included stops at these centers.

For a more dynamic interaction with the brand, there's the AMG Experience that offers a wide range of activities that include track time, on- and off-road tours, and even an ice driving experience. In the United States, the track programs range from for a one-day performance driving session up through two-day advanced and pro sessions. One-day courses in drifting and a Pro+ program that prepares drivers for their SCCA (Sports Car Club of America) licenses also are offered. All track activities take place at Road Atlanta in Georgia, the Circuit of the Americas (COTA) in Austin, or in California at Sonoma Raceway. Starting in 2025, the program returns to California's Laguna Seca since its last stop in 2022 and travels to the Indianapolis Motor Speedway for the first time.

Another experience with AMG features a four-day tour of the Napa Valley in California, which includes driving the local roads in coupes and roadsters, some off-roading in a G 63, and a day of track time at Sonoma Raceway.

The Ice Driving Experience takes participants to Crested Butte in Colorado. Two programs, a 1.5-day advanced class and a 2.5-day performance session, are offered. The activities allow drivers to experience drifting on a circular ice track, to learn slalom and performance driving techniques in a low friction dynamic area, and then to apply these skills on the track.

For the more adventurous, AMG in Germany offers longer ice- driving programs near the Artic Circle in Sweden. There are also European road tours, an advanced driving school at the Immendingen Proving Grounds, and motorsport programs that combine touring with attendance at DTM and twenty-four-hour races at the Nürburgring and where it all started, the 24 Hours of Spa.

AMG in Germany also offers the opportunity to let clients to customize their experience just as they would their car. According to AMG, the location can be a "City tour, coastal road, mountain panorama—no matter on which continent, no matter in which country—you put your finger on the map, and we bring you to your destination."

In addition to the vehicles, customers can specify an on- or off-road, track, or ice experiences plus the duration of the trip. AMG encourages creative thinking: "An AMG Experience Customized thrives on your individual ideas. Think big. We do everything we can to make sure you have a great time."

OPPOSITE, TOP LEFT Since 2011 Mercedes-AMG has been building up a worldwide network of Performance Centers, which are essentially showrooms dedicated solely to the brand. Here, specialists guide prospects through the ordering process, including meeting specific needs through Mercedes' custom Manufaktur program.

OPPOSITE, TOP RIGHT Previously known as the AMG Driving Academy, these customer-oriented driving programs have been expanded to include a wide range of activities, including ice driving training. Other programs include track days, tours, and outings to motorsports events.

OPPOSITE, MIDDLE The ice- driving programs are not limited to cars. Mercedes-AMG has a G-Class program that can take you as far afield as the Arctic Circle.

OPPOSITE, BOTTOM LEFT Track instruction and lapping sessions are now part of the wide range of experiences available to the brand's clients at the Mercedes-AMG driving academy.

OPPOSITE, BOTTOM RIGHT Touring in Europe is another experience AMG offers, which also serves a secondary purpose in exposing its newest products to its loyal customer base.

AMG

LB MA 6319

LB MA 6449

ABOUT THE AUTHOR

Matt DeLorenzo is a veteran auto journalist who has worked in top editorial positions at *Automotive News*, *Autoweek*, *Road & Track*, and *Kelley Blue Book*. A founding member of the North American Car, Truck, and Utility of the Year Awards, he has authored automotive books across a wide range of topics, including *Volkswagen New Beetle*, *Modern Chrysler Concept Cars*, *Legendary American Cars*, *2005 Mustang*, *Corvette Dynasty*, *Dodge 100*, and most recently, *How to Buy an Affordable Electric Car: A Tightwad's Guide to EV Ownership*.

ACKNOWLEDGMENTS

This book would not have been possible without the help of Mercedes-AMG and its public relations staff. Many thanks go to Jochen Uebler, Felix Siggemann, and especially Catrin Dutz-Ludwig, who was my go-to contact on my many email requests and made my visit to Affalterbach informative and rewarding. Additional appreciation is extended to the Mercedes-AMG Classic archive staff, in particular Daniele Sigl. Thanks also go to Dirk Sinn for the in-depth tour of the AMG engine-assembly facility. At HWA, marketing director Jens Birkelbach arranged and gave a tour that provided an inside look into its relationship with Mercedes-AMG. On the American side, thanks go to the former PR director at Mercedes-Benz USA, Rob Moran.

In doing research for the book, the Mercedes-Benz Classic M@RS (Multimedia Archive and Research System) and Mercedes-AMG Classic and the US and Global Mercedes press sites were invaluable for their access to photos, press releases, and specifications as well as video interviews with Hans Werner Aufrecht and Erhard Melcher. Two books commissioned by Mercedes-AMG provided key information about the company's history: *AMG 45: The Story, The Cars* and *AMG: Reaching for the Stars*, by Frank Mühling and Markus Bolsinger. I was delighted to see that a key interview involving Aufrecht and Melcher with Ola Källenius and Mario Spitzer in *AMG 45* was conducted by an old friend and colleague, Jürgen Zöllter.

Two other works, *Mercedes-Benz Quicksilver Century* by Karl Ludvigsen and *The Star and The Laurel* by Beverly Rae Kimes, were helpful in setting the corporate scene at Mercedes-Benz and how it related to AMG. Other key resources include Grant Viljoen's *Rote Sau* website, *touringcarracing.net*, and *Mercedes-fans.de*.

My colleague and former *Road & Track* managing editor Andy Bornhop did much appreciated work in offering suggestions and reading the manuscript. While John Lamm is greatly missed, his photos live on in this work through the access to his archives courtesy of Scheri Lamm. Thanks also to the team at Quarto/Motorbooks: Zack Miller, Brooke Pelletier, Anne Re, and Leah Noel. Supporting friends and colleagues include Jack Nerad, Art Garner, Jim Finn, Mike O'Brien, Eric Prichett, and Alex Varela.

The love and support of my spouse, Jane, is, as always, a constant inspiration and comfort. Thank you for enduring the many months of my AMG immersion. Finally, all thanks to the Lord, who provides the grace and blessings to do this work.

INDEX

24 Hours of Spa, 10, 11, 12, 14–15, 18, 42–43, 218
24 Hours of the Nürburgring, 176
"50 Years Legend of Spa" series, 18
53 GT, 170
190 2.5–16 Evolution, 78
190 D, 22
190 E, 74, 75, 77, 80
190 SL, 40
200 SE Fintail, 22
220, 28
220 SE, 26, 32
230 S, 32
230 SL, 28, 40
240 D, 63
280 SE, 53
280 SL, 50
280 SLC, 50
300 CE, 69
300 E, 97, 99
300 SD, 65
300 SE, 22, 26, 28, 31, 32, 40
300 SE Cabriolet, 44
300 SE Coupe, 44
300 SE Fintail, 42
300 SEL ("Red Pig"), 10–12, 14–16, 17–18, 43, 44, 48, 50, 53, 70, 74, 101, 211, 214, 215
300 SEL 6.3, 42, 43, 44, 90
300 SEL 6.9, 42
300 SL, 22, 23, 37, 111, 150, 157, 167, 179
300 SL Gullwing, 40
300 SLR, 23, 137, 144
300 SLR Coupe, 134
300 SL Roadster, 40
300 TD, 100
350 SE, 53
350 SL, 50
350 SLC, 50
450 SL/SLC, 50, 74
450 SL/SLC 5.0, 50
500 GE V-8, 183
500 SEC, 65–66, 102
500 SL/SLC, 50
502, 78
560 SEC 6.0, 69
560 SEC AMG Widebody, 70
560 SEL, 69, 99

A

A32K AMG city car, 115
Aaltonen, Rauno, 12, 42
ADAC Bavaria race (Salzburgring), 11
ADAC Solitude Race, 12
Affalterbach, Germany, 36, 48, 60, 61, 86, 90, 93, 99, 100, 102, 106, 115, 116, 134, 143, 151, 158, 162, 166, 169, 170, 176, 179, 183, 196, 204, 205, 206, 210–211, 215, 218
Ahrens, Kurt, 42
Ainslie, Ben, 206
Allsopp, Adam, 197–198, 201
Alpina, 10, 12, 60
America's Cup yacht race, 206
AMG.EA platform, 217
AMG Hammer, 90, 93–94, 97, 99–101, 102
AMG ONE, 43, 144, 193, 196–198, 201, 202, 203–205, 206, 211, 213, 215, 217
AMG Performance Tour, 18
AMG Private Lounge, 190
AMG SLS Black Series, 205
Argentine Gran Premio Standard rally race, 22
Asch, Roland, 78, 83
Aston Martin DB11, 143
Aston Martin DBX SUV, 143
Aufrecht, Friedrich, 37
Aufrecht, Hans Werner, 10, 12, 15, 18, 22, 25, 26, 31, 32, 36, 37, 39, 48, 60, 61, 74, 85, 112, 116, 120, 122, 130, 141, 206, 217
Australian Grand Prix, 206
Avus, 77, 78, 83

B

"Baby Benz." *See* C 36 AMG
badging, 18, 44, 48, 55, 57, 115, 116, 138, 141, 166, 172, 183, 184
Barényi, Béla, 23, 32
Baudy, Bastian, 70, 214
Behrmann, Klaus, 15, 43
Benz, Carl, 210
Betzler, Thomas, 15
Blackbird, 154
Black Falcon racing team, 176
Black Series, 57, 120–124, 155, 157, 190, 193, 205
BMW E28 5 Series M5, 90
Böhringer, Eugen, 22, 26
Bracq, Paul, 32, 44, 49
Braungart, Martin, 28
Brawn, Ross, 206
Breitschwerdt, Walter, 75
Brudermüller, Martin, 217
Bruhnke, Ulrich, 148
Brysch, Daniel, 55
Bryzmann, Friedrich, 28
Buchmann, Rainer, 141
Bussell, Jan, 42
Buxbaum, Richard, 97, 100

C

C 36, 106, 107, 110
C 36 AMG ("Baby Benz"), 74, 106–108
C 43, 110
C 63, 124
C 63 AMG Coupe Black Series, 123–124
C 63 Black Series, 190
C 63 DTM, 85
C-111 Wankel prototype, 11, 70
C 126, 63, 102
C 209, 121
C 280, 107
C 280 Sport, 106, 107
C-Class, 70, 84, 85, 106
Cecotto, Johnny, 78
Christodoulou, Adam, 176
Chrysler Crossfire SRT-6, 143
Cigarette AMG Electric Drive Concept, 190
Cigarette Marauder, 190
Cigarette Nighthawk AMG Black Series, 193
Cigarette Racing, 190
Cigarette Racing 50 Marauder AMG Monaco Concept, 190, 193
Cigarette Rider, 190
Circuit of the Americas (COTA), 218
CLK 63 AMG Black Series, 121–122
CLK coupe, 85
CLK DTM AMG Cabriolet, 130
CLS 55 AMG IWC Ingenieur, 130
CLS 63 AMG Shooting Brake, 130
"Cocaine Hammer," 102
Cohen, Andy, 97, 99, 102
Concept Mercedes-AMG PureSpeed, 144
Costin, Mike, 74
Cosworth Engineering, 60, 74
CW 311 concept, 141

D

Daimler, Gottlieb, 210
Danner, Christian, 80
Deer, Rob, 102
Denzel, Jörg, 74
Der Große Mercedes, 39–40
Desert Gold SLS, 153–154
Deutsche Toureinwagen Masters (DTM), 85
Deutsche Toureinwagen Meisterschaft (DTM), 74, 75
Dodge Viper, 151
Dolhem, Jose, 15
Duckworth, Kevin, 74

E

E 36, 110
E 50, 110
E 55, 111
E 420, 106
Eberle, Max, 211, 213
E-Cell prototype, 158
E-Cell SLS, 196, 215
E-Class, 70
Editions models, 126, 130
Electric Drive Coupe, 158
Elford, Vic, 28
Engel, Maro, 176, 205, 213
Eppler, Richard, 80
European Rally Championship, 22
European Touring Car Championship, 15
EVO II, 80, 83, 86, 87

F

Facetti, Carlo, 15
Fangio, Juan Manuel, 25, 143, 179

Fetherston, Mark, 148, 162
Feyhl, Hartmut, 48, 93, 94, 97, 99, 100, 102
FIA GT Championship, 112
Fingold, Malka, 100
Fingold, Paul, 100
Franchitti, Dario, 84
French Production Car Championship, 77
Frère, Paul, 113

G

G 43 AMG, 184
G 55 AMG, 184
G 63, 187, 189, 193
G 63 4×4², 189
G 63 6×6, 184, 187, 189
G 63 Cigarette Edition, 193
G 65, 184
G 65 AMG, 184
Galant AMG, 141
Gallina, Leopold, 77
G-Class, 182, 182–184, 187
Geiger, Friedrich, 32, 53
German Touring Car (DTM) series, 26, 112, 176
GLC, 70
GLE, 70
Glemser, Dieter, 12, 14, 15, 42
Götz, Maximillian, 176
Grand Prix W196 300 SLR, 23
Gran Turismo video game, 214
Grauls, Ivo, 12
Großaspach, Germany, 10, 36, 116
Große Mercedes, 39–40
GT, 162–165, 172, 175
GT2 Pro, 176, 179
GT3, 85, 176
GT3 Edition 130Y Motorsport, 179
GT 4-Door Coupe, 166, 169
GT 43, 175
GT 43 Coupe, 175
GT 55, 175
GT 63, 175
GT 63 4-Door Coupe, 170
GT 63 Pro 4Matic+, 175
GT 63 S, 170
GT 63 S E Performance, 175
GT Black Series, 127, 129
GT C Coupe, 165
GT Concept, 166–167, 196
GT Coupe, 169–170
GT R, 165, 166
GT race cars, 86
GT Roadster, 165–166
GT R Pro, 166
GT S, 164–165
GT. *See* Mercedes-AMG GT
Günzler, Ranier, 22
G-Wagen, 182–183
G-Wagen 500 GE, 183

H

Hahne, Huber, 26
Hamilton, Lewis, 193, 201
Hammer. *See* AMG Hammer
Hartmann Motorsport, 77
Hart, Nick, 130
Hart, Spencer, 130
Hermann, Hans, 42
Hermann, Jochen, 201
Heyer, Hans, 12, 14, 15
Heyer, Kenneth, 18
Hezemans, Toine, 15
Hitzinger, Walter, 22
Hodgman, Jonathan, 100, 102
Hoffmann, Peter, 12
Hubbert, Jürgen, 77
Hungaroring, 78
Huntress, 190
HWA AG, 85–87, 115

I

Ice Driving Experience, 218
Ickx, Jackie, 42
Ilien, Mario, 206
Immendingen Proving Grounds, 217, 218
Imola, 54
International Touring Car (ITC) series, 81, 84, 112
Isdera Imperator 108i, 141

J

Jabouille, Jean-Pierre, 15
Jäger, Thomas, 18
Jastrow, Steffen, 196, 205, 214
Jenkinson, Denis, 137
Jones, Parnelli, 80
Jung, Christoph, 150

K

Källenius, Ola, 158, 196
Keimola Motor Stadium, 43
Kelleners, Helmut, 12
Kimes, Beverly Rae, 23
Kinetic Energy Recovery System (KERS), 158, 175, 206
Klenk, Hans, 167
Kling, Karl, 22, 25, 32, 167
Korff, Baron Alexander von, 42
Kübler, Michael, 55

L

Lafitte, Jaques, 80
Lahtinen, Urpo, 43
Larini, Nicola, 83
Larrousse, Gerard, 12
Lauda, Niki, 12, 15
Legate, Trevor, 69
Le Mans, 15, 22, 23, 85, 112, 144, 167, 178, 202
Léméret, Stéphane, 18
Liebeton, Christian, 87
Lotus, 26, 141, 143
Ludvigsen, Karl, 43, 75
Ludwig, Klaus, 78, 84, 112

M

M100 engine, 10, 42, 43, 44, 53, 74, 141
M102 engine, 62, 74, 75, 78
M104 engine, 183
M106 engine, 83
M110 engine, 50, 53, 55, 62, 65, 182
M112 engine, 143
M113 engine, 108, 111, 121, 184
M113 K engine, 134, 136
M116 engine, 50, 53, 62, 65
M117, 182–183
M117 E 50 engine, 183
M117 engine, 53, 65, 66, 90, 100, 102, 183
M119 engine, 83, 102, 111, 141
M120 engine, 143
M123 engine, 62
M127 engine, 32
M139 engine, 57, 143
M155 engine, 136, 152–153
M156 engine, 121–122, 123, 124, 126, 152
M158 engine, 143
M159 engine, 152, 155
M177/176 engine, 55
M178 engine, 179
M178 LS2 engine, 127, 143
M180 engine, 32
M189 engine, 32, 40, 43
M256 engine, 55, 170
M275 engine, 123
M279 engine, 184
M297 engine, 115
Manufaktur program, 130, 218
Mathay, Raymond, 15
Matra aerospace firm, 16
Maybach, 55, 144, 162
Melcher, Erhard, 10, 22, 26, 31, 32, 36–37, 39, 48, 50, 54, 55, 63, 94, 116, 120, 206, 217
Melcher, Hans-Jürgen, 31, 37
Mercedes AMG Vision Gran Turismo, 214
Mercedes SLR McLaren roadster, 138
Metzger, Manuel, 176
MGU-H (Motor Generator Unit-Heat), 197, 201
MGU-K (Motor Generating Unit-Kinetic), 197, 201
Mille Miglia, 23, 137, 140, 167
Mitsubishi Debonair V300 Royal AMG, 141
ML 55 AMG, 148
Mobilia Museum (Finland), 43
Moers, Tobias, 163, 196
Moll, Rolf, 22
Monoblock Aero I/II, 70
Monte Carlo Rally, 22
Moorat, Ted, 42
Morgan, Paul, 206
Mornhinweg, Volker, 130, 148–149, 157, 158
Moss, Stirling, 137, 144
Murray, Gordon, 134
Mythos Series, 144

N

Nallinger, Fritz, 44
Nannini, Alessandro, 80, 84
Napa Valley experience, 218
Nardo Test Track, 75, 77
Neerpasch, Jochen, 26
Neubauer, Alfred, 22
Niefer, Werner, 77, 84
Night Edition package, 70
Norisring, 16, 28
Nürburgring, 15–16, 22, 23, 26, 28, 54, 74, 77, 165, 205, 218

O

OM115 engine, 63
OM116 engine, 63
Ommen, Jörg van, 77

P

Paffett, Gary, 85
Pagani, Horacio, 143
Pahlavi, Mohammad Reza, 182
Passenger Car Testing department, 40
Penske, Roger, 206
"Penta" wheel design, 70
Performance Centers, 218
Pfuhl, Albert, 31, 54
Phillips, John, 100
Piedade, Domingos, 83
Pierpont, Roy, 26
Poon, Albert, 42
Porsche 928 S, 94
Porsche, Ferdinand, 144
Project ONE. *See* AMG ONE
PU106B engine, 197
Pullman limousines, 16, 40, 115
PureSpeed. *See* Concept Mercedes-AMG PureSpeed

R

R 63, 115
R 232, 172
Ravaglia, Roberto, 78
R/C107, 50, 53, 70
Red Pig, 10–12, 14–16, 17–18, 43, 44, 48, 50, 53, 70, 74, 101, 211, 214, 215
Reitzle, Wolfgang, 80
RENNtech, 48
di Resta, Paul, 85
Reuter, Edzard, 77
Reuter, Manuel, 84
Road Atlanta, 218
Rosberg, Keke, 80, 84
Rosberg, Nico, 193
Rosqvist, Ewy, 22
"Rote Sau," 10–11
Rote Sau website, 18

S

S 63 AMG, 18
S 600 Pullman AMG limousine, 115
Sacco, Bruno, 65
Salzburgring, 11
Scheider, Bernd, 84
Schickentanz, Clemens, 12, 15, 74
Schiebe, Michael, 144, 210, 211, 215, 217
Schiek, Manfred, 22, 28
Schiemer, Günter, 28
Schiemer, Philipp, 210
Schneider, Bernd, 81, 83, 84, 85, 112, 176, 205
Schnitzer, Josef, 28, 60
Schock, Walter, 22
Schöning, Gordian von, 86
Schulz, Eberhard, 141
S-Class, 53, 55, 63, 65, 74
Sears, Jack, 26
SE Fintails, 22, 37, 42
Shock, Walter, 26
Sigl, Daniela, 214
Signature Series, 130
Silverstone, 54
simulator, 211, 213–214
Sindelfingen factory, 40, 151, 162, 170, 172
SL, 172
SL 6 AMG Coupe Black Series, 123
SLK 55 AMG Black Series, 130
SLK 55 AMG Ultimate Experience Asia (Tracksport), 120–121
SLR, 134
SLR McLaren, 134, 136–137, 149
SLR McLaren 722 Crown Edition, 138
SLR McLaren 722 Edition, 137, 138
SLR McLaren 722 GT Coupe, 138
SL Roadster, 172
SLR Stirling Moss Edition, 140
SLS AMG, 157
SLS AMG Black Series Coupe, 126–127
SLS AMG Coupe Electric Drive, 158
SLS AMG E-Cell prototype, 158
SLS AMG Electric Drive Coupe, 158
SLS AMG GT, 158
SLS AMG GT3, 18
SLS E-Cell concept, 196, 215
SLS Final Edition, 155, 157
SLS GT3, 157
SLS GT Black Series, 155, 157
SLS Roadster, 155
SLS (Super Leicht Sport), 148–155
Snobeck Racing Service, 77
Soler-Roig, Alex, 12, 15
Sonoma Raceway, 218
Spa, 10, 11, 12, 14, 15, 17, 18, 22, 31, 42, 50, 74, 157, 196, 218
Sporr, Ralf, 120
Steinmetz, 10, 60
Strassenversion CLK GTR, 115
Stroke-8, 49
Stroll, Lawrence, 143
Stuck, Hans, 80
Szczepek, Rene, 211

T

Targa Florio, 144
Thiim, Kurt, 78, 84
Thirty-Five concept, 18
Tirranna AMG Edition, 193
Tour d'Europe rally, 28
Trace program, 57
Tracksport (SLK 55 AMG Ultimate Experience Asia), 120–121
Trans African Rally, 22
Troska, Hubertus, 148
Tyrell, Ken, 37

U

Uhlenhaut, Rudolf (Rudi), 23, 25, 26, 31, 40, 42, 134

V

Valmet company, 172
Viljoen, Grant, 18
Vision EQXX concept, 206
Vision SLR concept, 134

W

W100 limousine (Der Große Mercedes), 39–40
W108, 49
W108/109, 32, 53
W108/109 SE, 44
W108/109 SEL, 44
W109 300 SEL, 10, 44, 74
W109 SEL, 40
W111/112 Fintail, 32, 49
W112 300 SE, 32
W114, 48, 49
W114/115, 49
W115, 48, 49
W116, 53, 70
W116 S-Class, 61, 63
W123, 61–62, 90
W124, 69, 74, 90, 102
W124 E 500/500 E, 110
W124. *See* AMG Hammer
W126, 61, 63, 69, 97, 99
W126 S-Class, 90
W154, 167
W201, 70, 74
W201 190, 106
W201 190 E, 86
W202 C-Class, 83, 106
W210 E-Class, 110
W460 utility vehicle, 182
W463, 182, 184
Wagener, Gorden, 162, 167, 169, 190
Waxenberger, Erich, 11, 39, 40, 42, 43, 44, 50, 90
W/C126, 70
W/C/S123, 70
Weber, Thomas, 163
Wehrlein, Pascal, 85
Weidler, Volker, 77
Werner, Christian, 144
Werner, Friedrich, 55
Werner, Hans, 36, 55
wheel design, 70
Whitmore, John, 26
Wieselmann, Heinz-Ulrich, 37, 44
Wiley, John, 102
Wilfert, Karl, 23
Wirth, Ursula, 22
Wunstorf Airfield, 28

X

X290, 170

Y

Yoon Il-hun, 140

Z

Zahn, Joachim, 22–23, 43
Zetsche, Dieter, 148
Zolder, 77, 80